Educational Trends and Development Among Muslims of India

Educational Trends and Development Among Muslims of India

(With Special Reference to Bihar and Jharkhand)

Dr. Mukhtar Ahmad Makki

SHIPRA

ISBN: 978-81-7541-554-6

First Published in India in 2010

Educational Trends and Development Among Muslims of India (With Special Reference to Bihar and Jharkhand)

Published by:
SHIPRA PUBLICATIONS
H.O.: LG 18-19, Pankaj Central Market, Patparganj,
I.P. Ext., Delhi-110092, Tel: 91-11-2223 5152, 2223 6152
Br.Off.: 4617/18, Ansari Road, Darya Ganj,
New Delhi-110002, Tel: 6594 6453, 9810522367
E-mail: info@shiprapublications.com
www.shiprapublications.com

Foreword

I am glad that Mukhtar Ahmad Makki chose to research an area, which is of considerable topical interest.

Respecting chronology the scholar has gone back to the advent of Muslims in India. He has given the reader a bird's eye view of the five and a half centuries of Muslim rule and about two centuries of the British Period. Having done this he proceeds to discuss in some detail the post-independence education status of Bihari Muslims and the causes of the educational backwardness of Muslims of Bihar.

The work throws up the significant fact that in 1836 Shah Kabiruddin of Sahsaram, Khankah applied to the Governor General of India to appoint persons to teach the English Language in the local Madarsa. Let us remind ourselves that this request for modernization of education preceded Sir Syed's massive endeavour by four decades. Shah Kabiruddin's request is in contrast to the dogged resistance in our time to introduction of modern subjects in religious madarsas.

The Chapter on education among Muslims of Bihar (1757-1947) reveals a situation that is difficult for us to imagine in the post-independence period. The senior posts in Bihar towards the turn of the last century had been pre-empted by Bengalis. As regards the officers of Bihar origin, Muslims outnumbered non-Muslim by 13:7. This shows that advance in modern education achieved by Hindus of Bengal did not take Bihar in its sweep. It would be an interesting exercise to dig out corresponding figures for the North Western Provinces (approximating to modern UP) and see whether Muslims in UP during the same period kept pace with their counterparts in Bihar or in Bengal. A deeper probe would in any case be required to determine the causes of the drastic slide back in the representation of Muslims in the Civil Services in Bihar.

The book does not confine itself to Bihari Muslims, it goes in depth into the causes for the educational backwardness of Indian Muslims. One could have wished that in order to counter balance the narrative that focuses primarily on North India, the scholar should have digressed into an account of the strides made/over the last about thirty years in the southern states and in Maharashtra. This however, is not to take away from the sweep of the author's total assessment.

One cannot but be impressed by the diligence which Mukhtar Ahmad Makki has brought to bear on the very significant study.

I feel that the recommendations in this work flow from a proper grasp of the situation as it has developed over about a century. Muslims in Bihar as well as in UP underwent during the years preceding the years preceding the partition of the country and the years immediately following, a traumatic experience, which had a devastating effect on their morale. They were deprived of the sense of security; their confidence was eroded. The communal riots that occurred in an unending chain continued to sap their vitality. Such a situation is seldom conducive to the emergence of leadership. This factor too has not escaped the perceptive scholar. It is a tragic circumstance indeed that those who were capable of leading Indian Muslims sought refuge in Pakistan and left the Muslim masses leaderless and rudderless. It is a pity indeed that the government failed over the last half a century to pay any real heed to he predicament to which the Muslims had been reduced. The situation became confounded when having been totally demoralized disheartened and disenchanted, Muslims became insensitive to their collective interest. This spelt stagnation; I have personally been associated with organizations involved in the resurgence of Indian Muslims. We took the innovative step of taking out what we called caravans of education throughout the length and breadth of the country. We discovered a very reassuring streak, in fact a silver lining in the dark cloud of apathy and insensitivity. We discovered that Muslims have started waking up; we came across a craving for education and a desire laming them to lift themselves by their bootstraps. If this desire is channelised into comprehensive educational efforts, a transformation in a matter of two decades will be quite on the cards. I thought I owed it to the learned research scholar and to the vast array of the readers of this work when it is published to add this realistically optimistic post-script to the assessment contained in the valuable work. I have no doubt that the perceptive diligence of the author will be recognized in all quarters that matter. The work can spur the Muslim community to some hard thinking. What is equally importance the sharp decline in the condition of Muslims; particularly those inhabiting Bihar, could perhaps jolt the national conscience. With the new alignments that are in the offing in the political arena, the book may serve to provide food for thought and action to those who matter. Even if this kind of fall-out does not occur the book will be valued as a piece of significant research that meticulously profiles a large segment of the Indian population.

It is not difficult for a Bihar watcher to perceive the tremors of a cataclysmic change that is currently occurring. Despite its acute poverty, young men and women from Bihar have moved out in large groups in search of education and employment. They have done exceedingly well in the civil services Examination. More often than not Bihari Muslim students have registered remarkable successes at this examination. Moreover, taking a clue from the southern states, Bihari Muslims have started establishing Professional colleges. The rumblings of an educational resurgence are audible.

To a layman the reasons for the decline of Bihari Muslims after independence fall into two broad groups: (1) discrimination against Muslims in admissions and recruitment; (2) the failure on the part of Muslims to lift themselves by their bootstraps. The discrimination in its broader sense of adversity would include the holocaust of partition, the communal riots and the reluctance of government to allow Muslims access to echelons of power. The lack of effort could be traced back to the large-scale demoralization caused by the all-pervasive hostility and the exodus of the influential sections of the community consequent on the partition. It is time the community finally shed the hangover of those calamitous events and moved forward valiantly to surmount the hurdles that obstruct its progress.

Saiyid Hamid
Former V.C., A.M.U Aligarh
Chancellor Jamia Hamdard, New Delhi

Acknowledgements

At the outset I would like to express my deep gratitude to Dr. Lal Mani Prasad (M.A, B.L., D.Litt) Professor of Political Science, Ranchi University, Ranchi. He encouraged me to take up this difficult subject and allowed me his able and inspiring guidance.

It would be invidious of me not to mention the encouragement, moral and material support provided to me by Dr. Manzoor Alam, Institute of Objective Studies, New Delhi, Prof. B.N. Singh, Department of Poltical Science, Ranchi University, Dr. Imtiaz Ahmad, Professor in the Centre for Political Studies, Jawaharlal Nehru University, New Delhi and Prof. Hassan Ahmad, Department of Poltical Science, Aligarh Muslim University, Aligarh.

I shall be failing in my duty if I do not record here what I owe to those who helped me in great measure from behind the curtain. I am grateful to all those dead or alive scholars and writers whose works I have consulted. But except versions attributed to them, opinious expressed are of course mine and I take the responsibility for the same. Some of my senior collegues deserves my special thanks for very minutely checking the language of the manuscript and providing sustained help in revision of my study. Indeed, they were both friend and guide in this arduous task. My other friends and colleagues also deserve my thanks who offered valuable suggestions and gave helping hands whenever I most needed.

I owe a great deal to number of my younger relatives—especially Fauzia, Saadia, Rehan, Monazzah, and Safia. They tolerated and cooperated an engrossed father and gracefully allowed my negligence in sharing love, affection and time to which they were entitled and what is more, always manifested pride in my academic endeavours.

In all the important enterprises undertaken by me, my wife Barida has been a source of strength to me. She has been playing a pivotal role in our family who not only gave me moral support, patience, perseverance and continued encouragement in writing the present work but also spared me ungrudgingly from all my domestic duties and responsibilities.

I have no words to express my gratitude—the contribution of my Nana (late) Alhaj Md. Yasin Haider, who endevoured a lot in shaping the personality of mine and my sibling, my Ammi Mrs. Sabira Khatoon who loved, cared and always prayed for my well being and my Abbu M. Najmul Huda Nadvi, who always kept enquiring about my academic achievements.

Finally conscious of my shortcomings and limitations, I alone take the full responsibility for all errors of fact or opinions expressed or conclusion drawn in this work.

Dr. M.A. Makki

Contents

Foreword	v
Acknowledgements	ix
List of Tables	xiii
Introduction	1
1. Education among Muslims of Bihar and Jharkhand: A Brief Historical Development (Turk-Afghan, Mughal and British Period: 1206-1947)	13
2. The State of Education among Muslims of Bihar and Jharkhand	28
3. Socio-Economic Status Scale of Muslims	48
4. The Concept of Minorities and Situation of Indian Muslims	65
5. Educational Backwardness of Muslims: Explanation and Causes	93
6. Action Programme for Educational Development among Muslims: Conclusions and Suggestions	139

Appendices

I	Prime Minister's 15 Point Programme on Welfare of Minorities (1984)	155
II	Extract from New Education Policy and Programme of Actions (1986)	158
III	Educational Rights of Minorities: Supreme Court Judgement (2002)	165
IV	The National Commission for Minority Educational Institutions Act, 2004	167
V	Prime Minister's New 15-point Programme for the Welfare of Minorities (2006)	169

VI Sachar Committee on Social Economic and Educational Status of Indian Muslim 2005-06 171

VII Status of Implementation of the Follow-up Action on the Recommendations (Sachar Committee) 176

VIII Plan of Action on Sachar Committee's Recommendations, 2008 179

Glossary 185

Bibliography 188

Index 204

List of Tables

1.1:	Employment Position of Bihari	23
2.1:	Educational Qualification of Muslims and Non-muslims Respondent	35
2.2:	Statement showing Muslim population in different districts of United Bihar, percentage of Muslim population, per cent of urban population, literacy rate, electricity, (house hold) toilet facilities (1981)	36
2.3:	Classes of District according to the Percentage of Muslim Population in the Various districts of United Bihar (1981)	40
2.4:	Distribution of Person by General Education Sex and Religion (Rural India) 1987-88	41
2.5:	Distribution of Persons by General Education, Sex and Religion (Urban India) 1987-88	41
2.6:	Participation at Elementary level of Education	42
2.7:	Muslim Performance at Secondary School level	42
2.8:	Participation and Performance of Muslims at Graduation, Post-Graduation, M.B.B.S. & B.E. Level Universal Examination 1981	43
2.9:	Muslim Educational Backwardness (Kishan Gunj Town)	45
2.10:	Employment of Muslims in Government Offices/Public and Private Sectors in Bihar	46
3.1:	Socio Economic Status	49
3.2:	Parental Occupation and Percentage in Different Sample groups	49
3.3:	Father/Guardians and Mother's Education	51
3.4:	Parents or Guardians Monthly Income	52
3.5:	Possession of House	52

3.6: House Type 53
3.7: Numbers of Rooms in Houses 53
3.8: Expenditures on Magazine and Books 54
3.9: Purchase of Daily Newspapers 55
3.10: Number of Brothers and Sisters 55
3.11: Education of Brothers and Sisters 56
3.12: Level of Aspiration—Academic 57
3.13: Level of Aspiration-Professional 58

4.1: Casualties in Communal Riots in India 73
4.2: Riot Prone Area 75
4.3: Employment of Muslims under Central Government Class-wise 79
4.4: Muslim representation in Lok Sabha 80
4.5: Percentage of Muslims in Central Government Services 80
4.6: Number of Speakers of Major Languages as Mother Tongue in India (2001) 83
4.7: Urdu Speaking Population (1991) State wise Break up and Status of Urdu Education 84
4.7: Trends in Fertility Level 87

5.1: Economic Factors Resulting in Increasing Number of Drop Outs at School Level (out of 14 Reasons) 106
5.2: Reason for Dropout of Students in Muslim Managed Schools 108
5.3: Occupational Classes 111
5.4: Per Capita Income 111
5.5: Religious and Historical Personalities 126

Introduction

Muslims in India have always been the subject of great political and academic controversies. They are a major minority in India consisting of 13.4 per cent of India's population. All other minorities put together (Christians, Sikhs, Buddhists, Jains and others) come to not more than 5.8 per cent as the following table shows:

Community	*Number*	*% of the Total population*
INDIA	1,02,70,15,247	
Hindus	82,75,75,868	80.5
Muslims	13,81,88,240	13.4
Christians	240,80,016	2.3
Sikhs	19215730	1.9
Buddhists	7955207	0.8
Jains	4225053	0.4
Others	6.6 lakh	0.6

Sources: The Registrar General & Census Commissioner of India Series I Paper I, 2001-Religion.

Muslims in India are not merely the single largest and significant minority, as one out of every eight Indian is a Muslims and are spread through out the country', but at the same time they are the world's third largest Muslim concentration after Indonesia and Pakistan and so an international community too. In India only the Scheduled Castes and Scheduled Tribes collectively (21.5%) outnumber Muslims. Muslims have been recognized as cultural minority as they follow a distinct religion i.e. Islam and most of them speak Urdu as their mother tongue. They are not ethnic minority and racially, with the exception of a very microscopic minority they belong to the same ethnic stock as the rest of the population.[1] They are minority not only in numerical sense but also in terms of their position in the power structure as somewhat differentiated for discriminatory treatment in the socio-political system of the country legally and constitutionally but in actual behavioural pattern they suffer from some sort of discriminatory treatment.[2] Due to their numerical strength they have the potentiality of influencing the course of events and no one should undermine the growth potential of such a major segment of India's population.

By virtue of their numerical strength and changed world scenario, they cannot be annihilated or absorbed in the majority community. It is practically impossible as the enormity of cost both materials and moral will be beyond the imagination. The investment on such an endeavour will far outweigh its benefits and will be counter productive. In the present day world examples are numerous as the Nazis of Germany in spite of all its atrocities were unable to exterminate a small Jewish settlement (population), or Israelites with all its might and active help and support of the super power *and nod of another* and the western European nations were unable to wipe out the Palestinians. The case of *Chechaniya* and other republics of the mighty former Soviet Russia are in sight. *Despite the despotic communist rule and the iron curtain for more than seven decades was unable to hold them up*. What was possible then in medieval Spain or only partially in the colonized North America is now not possible. If the dominant chooses the path of repressing the minority surely it has to go into isolation from the rest of the world.

National integration is practically the problem of every nation. Even a despotic and totalitarian regime strives to achieve it by all means. It is because that no nation has a perfectly homogenous group of people and there is no device to eliminate such differences in order to have a uniform pattern. National integration is thus, an experiment in peaceful coexistence, which is only possible when its different segments are satisfied. In a democratic setup its importance increases further as it can only prevail in peace and harmony after taking fully in confidence and solving the problems confronting the various groups. The democratic norms recognize and demand equal rights and duties for all irrespective of any consideration what so ever. The essence of democracy lies in giving a fair treatment to its minority. The wrong treatment has always been a serious issue as wrong methods or policy adopted and pursued to deal with them have resulted into a number of civil wars or open clashes between the two or more nations. Numbers of national and international treaties have been concluded for their protection and fair dealing at various intervals of history. Further if the redresses of minorities' grievances are not done, ignored or delayed it ultimately leaves the community alienated, fatalist or they reacting violently by losing faith in constitutional means. A backward and segregated minority either rationalizes its present status as per ordained or unscrupulous leadership may exploit its injured feeling. Moreover as the minority loses faith in all government machinery it also loses aspiration to progress or prosperity.

Scholars and social scientists are working since second world war to solve the problems associated with poverty and backwardness. In the United States on the observation of Negro-White situation, these social scientists provided three distinct views.

Nathan Glazer (1966) and Daniel P. Moynihan (1963-65) observed that unless the defects in the life style of the poor or backward are removed amelioration of the condition that for a solution of the social problems associated with poverty and backwardness, it is the poor who must be changed and not the society as a whole.[4]

Another school of thought represented by Oscar Lewis (1959-1961 & 1966) claims that his work is an indictment of the society and not of the poor, but at the same time his proposals indicate that it is the life style of the poor that must primarily be reformed. He assigned first priority to the removal of such life ways which he terms culture of poverty.

Charles Valentine (1968) located the chief sources of deprivation suffered by the poor in the discriminatory behaviour and in actions and attitudes of the non-poor, which assigns a structural position to the former in the wider social system i.e. marginal and privileged. According to this school of thought it is the wider system under the control of the privileged section, which is responding for the exploitation and plight of people and their backwardness. Valentine suggests that granting real power in a democracy to the under privileged in order to enforce compulsory positive discrimination is essential.[5]

Viewed in absolute secular terms, it has been observed that in our present state of economy backwardness is perpetuated on the poor by the advanced section in the latter's interest such as ensuring a steady supply of cheap labour to keep lower cost of production and higher margin of profit. This phenomenon has been termed as "strategic deprivation". It is a source of exploitation of the under dog by the forward in many walks of socio-economic life.

Most of the problems, which Indian Muslims are facing, are due to socio-economic backwardness or more accurately its recession into the state of backwardness particularity since Independence. This socio-economic backwardness has led to educational backwardness though it is not an isolated or unconnected one and cannot therefore be dealt with separately or in isolation without reference to others. The low performance in socio-economic and educational fields require a thorough and detail investigation, patient debates, deliberation & planning of proper strategy for lifting them up and allowing coming out of their backwardness. Education is closely linked with the development as numerous studies have demonstrated positive correlation between education and modernity, belief to be the pre requisite for development.[6] Indian Planning Commission while formulating the Third Five Year Plan in 1961-62 regarded education to be most important single factor for economic development. *Educational Commission Report* (1964-66) commonly known as Kothari Commission displays in its belief that education is the key to development, it asserts that for social change and development there is only one instrument i.e. education.

For minorities it is of special significance as they are facing new challenges in the developmental process to adjust properly with the majority. It is an input not only for their economic development but also promoting self-confidence and inner strength to confront with new situation and challenges. So on the one hand community should make efforts and take lead to revitalize and mobilize its own resources constructively in a planned & systematic manner as God Commands in the **Holy Qura'n**—*"ALLAH does not change the condition of the community unless it strives to bring about changes itself"*. On the other hand it is also important, rather a foremost duty of a democratic and welfare state to look after and deal them fairly and adopt a suitable strategy, which is known in the United State as the "affirmative action of the state".

A proper understanding of these problems by the community and the nation as a whole is an important pre-requisite for devising measures for their solution. In the Indian context Muslims are important segments of a larger whole or an equal partner so their problems, are like the problems of the majority community i.e. Hindus, are the Indian problems—a national problem (and not a communal or sectarian problem). Because both of them are the only two pan India communities which are fragmented, on the basis of region, language, culture and race, and whose problems have relevance at each level and in all sectors of national life.[7] To a great extent socio-economic, cultural and educational problem of Indian Muslims is a horizontal rather than a vertical phenomenon. As such they should not seek their solution in isolation but in active cooperation with the rest of the countrymen. Only the will ensure an effective and lasting solution.

But to the ruling elite's, comprising the members of the dominant community (Hindus) it appears that the country's unity and integrity is at stake or under serious threat due to the separate or distinct minority. On the other hand, minorities especially Muslims feel that their right to be different with their distinct faith and identity is under attack from the centralizing, homogenizing roller of the state. Thus they are hurt and have a growing sense of betrayal, which they want to articulate but cannot. Any assertion of their legitimate rights and manifestation of their authentic, constitutional and legitimate identity—cultural, religious or linguistic, raises alarm from various quarters around them.[8]

Accurate and authentic data regarding the socio-economic and educational conditions of Indian Muslims is not available as the government agencies though collect, but due to their own expediency never analyze and publish the data. However a number of macro or micro studies, conducted since the publication of K. L. Gauba's *Passive Voice* (1973) through various agencies or private bodies, clearly and unmistakably indicate that Muslims as such, suffer from a number of disadvantages. They are educationally handicapped and a deprived lot and are not responding positively. Gopal Krishna, in his report to the Home Ministry admitted that Muslims as a group in India are poorer than the national average; their educational levels are lower and drop out rates higher. The two final documents on the Government of India's New Educational Policy and Programs of Action (1986) with the approval of the Parliament also subscribes this theory as it incorporated a separate section on minority education. This will be more clear when we see that in comparison to the national male literacy rate of 54 per cent Muslims male literacy rate is 18 per cent while the female literacy rates is even less than 5 per cent as compared to the national rate of 38 per cent[9]. The survey conducted by the ministry of Health and Family Welfare, Govt. of India revealed in its report, that proportionally Muslim women are more illiterate (87.7%) than Hindu women. In undivided Bihar Muslims women at the High School level are five times backward (i.e. 1.3%) while at the post High School level they are more than five times backward (0.5%) in comparison to their sisters professing Hindu religion (6.3% and 2.7%). This means that illiteracy levels among Muslims women are very high and the levels of higher education is very low.[10]

Since it is not possible for the writer to analyze the various aspects of educational problems of Indian Muslims as a whole so in this study an endeavour has only been made to deal specifically with the "Trends and Development in Education

Among Muslims of Bihar and Jharkhand Since Independence—A Socio-political study". The reference to other problem has been made only to the extent it is necessary to elucidate or substantiate a point that has a direct bearing on the education of Bihari Muslims. An attempt has also been made to suggest some remedial measures. In addition, the word "Muslim Education" should not be confused with the philosophical proposition of "Islamising Education". Education of Muslims simply means endeavour on the part of Muslim within a particular time and space to over come their socio-economic backwardness within the existing systems or "Communication of Knowledge and Skill" in a particular physical and social environment. While Islamising education involves a global concept—a conscious effort Islam evolves a system of education that is in consonance with Islam, its tenets and culture throughout the world cutting across time and space.

In contemporary India the educational backwardness of Muslims is commonly attributed to the two prevalent explanations. First, Muslims have been slow to take advantage of the vast educational opportunities because of their particular attitude or cultural ethos. It is argued by some that problem arises from the close linkage between the religious and secular spheres of life in Islam and the emphasis upon religious education by Muslim parents than to achieve secular education as they prefer to send their children to traditional Islamic Educational Institutions i.e. Maktab or Madarsa rather than to a modern secular institution and they reflect secular learning for religious education. This argument had a long history of having been forwarded first during the early phase of the establishment of British Raj by W.W. Hunter—*The Indian Musalman* (London 1871). This thesis has been picked up later on by a host of historians and writers of the British period and was reiterated time and again even after the independence of the country, till the works of Anil Seal, *The Emergence of Indian Nationalism* (London 1968) & Paul Brass, *Language, Religion and Political in North India* (Delhi 1975) appeared on the scene.

Others subscribing to the same mode of explanation argue that Muslims are reluctant to take up secular education because of an acute psychological complex. As a religious minority they coiled themselves into their cultural shell and are suffering from an acute minority complex. This act is a serious barrier to their integration into the mainstream of national opportunities in contemporary India. Authors like A.B. Shah, *Challenges to Secularism* (Bombay) M.R.A. Baig, *The Muslim Dilemma in India* (Delhi, 1974) Shibani Roy, *Changing Status of Muslim Women in North India* (Delhi, 1979) & *Times of India*, Delhi editorial—*"Living in the Past"* (dated 4th September 1983) etc. support this thesis.

Another view which is now a days gaining momentum and is advocated by most of the national and regional English and Hindi dailies and supported by a particular brand of social scientist is that in the contemporary India the disadvantageous condition of Indian Muslims is due to the fact that intellectually most of Muslims are below average as they belonged to the backward caste in their pre Islamic phase and after all among Hindu too, all castes did not take equally to English Education (Editorial, Some Soul Searching—*The Hindustan Times*, Patna 9th August 1993). Further it is also due to the creation of Pakistan when those who were educationally, socially and economically bankrupt, socially uprooted, economically deprived and morally depressed lot.

The second explanation for educational backwardness of Muslins blames society at large, and its discriminatory attitudes. According to this explanation they are neither reluctant to take up secular education due to preoccupation with religion or religious education nor because of their acute minority complex. Moreover psychologists, educationist and sociologists admit that the distribution of potential talent among the same ethnic group or other social group too of a fairly large number of people is more or less the same. So far the partition of the country is concerned, a period of more than half century is enough in the life of a community to heal wounds (if any) and a completely new generation has emerged since then which is not aware of those conflicts which disturbed the previous generation.

The present generation argues that a constant lack of opportunities and of motivation for the use of talent over a long period of time is the reason for their backwardness. They ask that, since independence, has the government ever provided educational environment for them sincerely? So far the Indian Muslims are concerned their performance only at the formal educational level both qualitatively and quantitatively is negligible while their creativity in the fields of arts, music, poetry, drama, films, games and sports, handicrafts, decorative arts etc. is laudable. They insist that their educational backwardness is explicable in terms of an invidious discrimination practiced against them since independence, which has reduced them to this deplorable state, so that the community has reached to such dismal levels. It is a recurrent theme in much of the Urdu dailies and periodicals published from Kashmir to Kanya Kumari and number of Muslims scholars and social scientists share this view; authors like K.L. Gauba, *Passive Voice* (Bombay, 1973) S. Harman, *Plight of Muslims in India* (New Delhi, 1976), Irfan Habib, *Problems of Muslims minority in India, Social scientists* (1974-1976), Rasheeduddin Khan, *Minorities Segments in Indian Polity, Economic &Political Weekly* (1913-1978) pp. 1509-15. A.R. Shirwani, *Educational Backwardness, The Seminar* 240-1979 pp. 32-34 & *Assessing Educational Backwardness—A right approach, The Radiance* vol. XX no. 32, 16/12/1984. Iqbal A. Ansari (editor) *Muslim Situation in India* (New Delhi, 1989), Abdus Salam, *Socio-Economic Problems of Muslims of India, The Radiance,* (New Delhi, vol. X no. 1 13/5/1984) O.P. Gupta, *Why Muslim Community Shuns Government Schools in UP*—The Educational Review (Madras, April 1983) K. Rangchander Rao, *Indian Muslims are feeling insecure,* The Manjuwani (Hyderabad, July 1983) Hasan Ahmad, *Starling Revelation,* The Nation and the World (New Delhi, 1/11/93) Syed Hamid, *Educational Status of Indian Muslims,* The Muslim India (New Delhi, December 1985), Syed Shahabuddin, *Educating Muslim Community,* The Muslim India (New Delhi, January 1995), A.M. Khusro, *Economic and Cultural Problems of Muslims,* Reports of intellectuals Meet on the Problems of Muslims (New Delhi, January 5, 1983) and justice sacher committee report (2006) etc. and a host of other social workers and scientists share the same view.

In this study, a combination of research methods has been followed i.e. historical, analytical and empirical, and the development of Education among Muslims of Bihar was traced from Primary and Secondary Sources as well as contemporary writings. An analytical description and interpretation of the available literature was made. To know the socio-economic conditions and the academic and professional aspirations of Muslims and Non-Muslims boys and girls studying at various schools and colleges spread in different corners of the state a socio-economic status scale questionnaire was administered. A survey of the Muslims managed educational institutions of Bihar and Jharkhand was conducted to know the infrastructure and their specific problems and working condition of these institutions.

As the Secondary and contemporary sources various reports of the surveys and projects compiled by the Governments agencies such as High Power Panel Committee, Ministry of Home affairs, Ministry of Education, Minority Commission, census data of India & combined Bihar, occasional papers of Registrar General of India etc. as well as private agencies like Hamdard Education Society, Institute of Objective Studies etc. were considered and analyzed. Besides available literature on various aspects of the problems of Indian Muslims was also consulted.

NOTES AND REFERENCES

1. *The Registrar General & Census commissioner of India* series I, paper I, 2001 (Religion) Government of India, (New Delhi 2005).
2. Publication Division—*Muslims in India,* Govt. of India (New Delhi 1964) p. 1, and also K.L. Gauba, *Passive Voice—A penetrating study of Muslims in India* (Bombay, Thacker & Co. 1973) p. 13.
3. M.K.A. Siddiqui—*Educating a backward Minority,* (Calcutta, Abadi 1984).

   Race is a biologically inherited physical characteristic with manifests itself in the form of the body, stature, head shape, form and shape of hair, physical measurement etc. while culture, language and religion are acquired characteristics and are not transmitted from one generation to the other like habits, through contact association and environmental influence. Racial features are relatively unchangeable accepting marginal modifications through an extremely lengthy process of mutation over a period of million of years. The cultural features of language, social customs, beliefs and practices as also the language are subject to changes. Eminent anthropologists like Sir Herbert Risley (1891) and B.S. Guha (1944) maintained that racial groups in India do not coincide with linguistic, cultural and religious divisions. They are of the opinion that term such as Aryan, Dravidian, Semitic, Latin etc. are merely linguistic and it is wrong to use then in racial connotations. Similarly Hindu, Muslim, Christian, Jew etc are religious categories and it will be in correct to identify them with races.

Negroid, Proto, Australoid Mongoloid, Mediterranean, Alpinoid, Dinarie, Armanoid & Nomadic etc. are among the races or subtypes which have entered into the Indian subcontinent at various times in the remote past and many of these races and their subtypes are common to both Hindus and Muslims. The last great race movement in India was Vedic or popularly known as Aryan invaders. They swept into India during the second millennium B.C. these Vedic invaders spread far and wide in the country and mixed with either oriental or dinaric elements or with older longheaded races with broad headed types, which had earlier arrived and settled in the country. The Pathan of N.W.F.P. and tribes of swat, Panjkora, Kunar & Chitral belongs to this pure race of Vedic invaders through they are Muslims. The same race is also found mixed with older longheaded racial types of Mediterranean stock in Pan jab Rajputana upper classes of Northern, Western & Eastern India. In this way the vast bulk of the Indian population both Hindus and Muslims have their origin in the Middle East Countries where their distant cousins are now Muslim.

M.K.A. Siddiqui—*Hindu Muslims Relation,* (Calcutta Abadi 1994) p. 13-15.

4. Glazer, Nathan & Moynihan: *Beyond the Melting pot* (Cambridge M.I.T. press 1963).
5. Charles, Valentine—*The Culture of Poverty and Counter Proposals* (Chicago University 1968)
6. Amar Kumar Singh—Education and Development in India—The God that failed, *Social Change,* Journal of the Council for Social Development, vol. 15 No. (September, 1985) p. 3.
7. Rasheeduddin, Khan—Introduction, *K.D. Sharma's book, Education of National Minority* (New Delhi, Kalamakar, 1978) p. 14.

8. Iqbal, A. Ansari (editor)—*Muslim Situation in India,* (New Delhi, Institute of Objective Studies 1987) p. 7.
9. Ahmad, A. Hai: Welcome Address—3rd International Annual Educational Conference, hosted by American Federation of Muslims form India (AFMI) & All India Muslims Educational Conference (AIMEC), Patna 21-23 December 1996.
10. Malika, B. Mistry—*Women's Education and Exposure to Mass media—A Comparison of Muslim and Hindu Situation—Religion and Law Review,* vol. VI, No. Summer 1997, Institute of Objective Studies, New Delhi p. 113.

1

Education among Muslims of Bihar and Jharkhand: A Brief Historical Development (Turk-Afghan, Mughal and British Period: 1206-1947)

The ancient name of Bihar was Magadh Desh as it has been named in the ancient Hindu Scriptures. The word Bihar has been used for this part of the land since Raja Gopal (740-785 AD) of the Pal-dynasty due to the presence of many Boudh Vihar. Muslim historians also used Bihar for this region as *Qila-e-Bihar, Wilayat-e-Bihar* or *Sarkar-e-Biha*r etc. Before the advent of Muslim rulers, the region was governed by Kings of the Pal dynasty (730-1197 AD). In 1179 AD, during the reign of Raja Inderman Deo Pal the last king, Akhtiyaruddin Mohd. Bakhtiyar Khilijee conquered Bihar and Bengal and till 1758 it remained the part of Turk and Mughal Empire.

The Muslim immigrants who settled down and become the part of the population of Bihar had certain distinctive features. Their cardinal doctrine was the absolute monotheism (Unity of Allah) emphasizing upon eternal distinction between transcendental god and man, the creator being separate from the creature. It was directly opposed to absolute Monism of Shankaracharya's Vedantic thought, *'I am a Brahma'* and stressing the identity and unity of God, the phenomenal world. Islam admitted no compromise even for illustrative or artistic purposes. They believed in congregation prayers (Namaz) thus showing solidarity and were impressive in their unity, discipline and simplicity. There social outlook was democratic and equalitarian which was in contrast to the tendencies of the social system prevalent then in India. They had different ideals and concept of social life and could be distinguished by their names, dress, religious rites, ways of addressing, ceremonies, festivals, marriages, culture and personal laws etc. Thus they formed an entirely separate identity and a firmly wedded community distinct from the local inhabitants.

Muslims after gaining a strong foothold in the country constructed Mosques in different part of the country, almost all of which had Maktabs & Madarsas (Schools and Colleges) attached to them providing instructions in three R's i.e. reading, writing and simple arithmetic as well as higher education through their mother tongue i.e. Arabic, Persian or Turkish. Besides the houses of Scholars, Sufis and Saints were also the seats of learning. In these institutions young Muslims received elementary and higher education as well as military training. According to *Tabqat-e-Nasri*, Bakhtiyar Khilhjee had established Mosque, Maktabs, Madarsas and Khanqah (Schools, Colleges and Monastery) in different parts of Bihar particularly at Maner his chief centre of military operation. His Amirs and other officials also imitated this example, and through these institutions learning and languages had propagated amongst the people.[1] In the latter period we found that educational institutions were of several grades ranging from elaborate colleges known as Madarsas or Jamia to maktabs representing higher secondary and primary stages of education. As religion formed backbone of education so most of the Maktabs and Madarsas were attached to Masajid, Khanqah and Dargahs. Some Madarsas were equipped with libraries of hand written books named as Kutub Khana and boarding houses. In the course of time we find that many educational institutions grew up at Maner, BiharSharif, Barh, Rajgir, Amjhar, PhulwariSharif and Hajipur etc. Hazart Mukhdumul Mulk Sharafuddin Bin Yahya Maneri (1263-1381AD) and Ahmad Charamposh (1373AD.) were noted for their erudition in poetry and theology and commanded respect not only of scholars of neighbouring states but also of Sultan Mohammad Tughlaq and Firoz Shah Tughlaq of Delhi. Firoz Shah himself a scholar, lover and patron of learning gave them a land grant for the maintenance and ordered a centre to be constructed for them.[2] During those days about one thousand Madarsas were in Delhi itself.[3] The *Maktubat* (Letters), *Mulfuzaat* (Conversation) and other contemporary writing of those days tell us that education was considered as a panacea for all evils and means of improving the moral and physical condition of fairly considerable section of population who formed the basis of the social pyramid.[4] The elementary course for the beginners consisted of acquisition of the knowledge of alphabets, continuance or combination of letters, division into syllables, recitation of a few hemistiches or distiches, repetition of the which had been read before and writing with reed pens on a piece of paper or on a *Takhti* (wooden tables). They were also to memorise the texts of some prescribed treaties including short lexicons and books of synonyms so as to enable them to store up a copious vocabulary in mind. Students were provided education free of cost, free board and zealous patrons of learning also provided lodging and clothing to them and every man of some means supported at least one student as a *Kafeel*. Sirat-e-Firozshahi contains among other things a catalogue of worldly advises supposed to have been given by Sultan Firoz Shah Tughlak to his officials concerning the line of action, which the official should pursue in private life. It maintains that all should secure knowledge and learning for themselves and should not neglect to educate their fellow Muslims. The knowledge that is acquired must not be forgotten but brushed up by constant discussions.[5] The education consisted of self-study, lecture by teachers, *Amokhta* (repetition of previous lessons), discussion among students with *Moin-e-Muawin* (senior students) as well as with teachers, recapitulation by teaching the classmates or the students of lower classes and conferring the *Sanad* (degree) at the *Fraghat* (completion).

Education among Muslims of Bihar (Mughal Period—1526-1756 A.D.)

The advent of Mughals in India and establishment of Mughal dynasty heralded a new chapter in the history of Bihar. *With its restoration* Bihar was organized for the first time into a separate province of Akbar's Empire *(1575)*. The reigns of the three successors of Akbar (1555-1605 A.D.), Jehangir (1505-1626 A.D.) Shahjahan (1627-1658 A.D.) and Aurangzeb (1658-1707 A.D.) were comparatively peaceful and prosperous for Bihar and its further consolidated the Mughals hold on some of the inaccessible parts of the province such as Chhotanagpur etc. it was only after the death of Aurangzeb (1707 A.D.) when separatist tendencies once again raised their heads that towards the middle of the 18th century Bihar was tagged with Bengal as force.

During the reign of Sher Shah Suri Maner, BiharSharif, PhulwariSharif, Rajgir, Sherghati, Sahsaram and Hajipur etc. were the chief centres of learning and culture in Bihar. The most celebrated teacher and scholar of Bihar at that time were Maulana Shamsul Haque alias Budh Haqqani, Mulla Budh Danishmand & Mulla Abdur Rahim Suri Al Bihari etc. In the later period several scholars of Bihar served as teacher (Preceptors) to Timurid princes and princesses. Emperor Shahjahan had appointed Maulana Mohiuddin alias Mulla Mohan Al Bihari of Bihar Shrief as Aurangzeb's tutor. Maulana Mohiuddin completed his Hifz at the age of 9 and got fraghat at 17 years and after teaching in his fathers Madarsa left for Delhi to teach prince Auranzeb and remained there for twelve years.[6] Qazi Mujibullah taught Jahandarshah, Mulla Abdul Hassan alias Mulla Jiwan of Darbhanga taught Zaibun Nisa, the accomplished daughter of Aurangazeb and a poetess and scholar of repute. Five eminent jurists and scholars of Bihar like Qazi Syed Anayatullah Suraj Garhi (Munger), Maulana Fasihuddin of Phulwari Sharif, Mulla Mohammad Shafi and his brother-in-law Mohammad. Afaq of Amthua (Gaya) and Syed Mohammad Raziuddin of Bhaghalpur were members of the syndicate that compiled *Fatwa-e-Alamgiri* the famous book on Sunni Islamic Jurisprudence[7] Maulana Amanullah, Ziauddin Mohaddis and Sirajuddin Ahmad of Faridpur were Prince Muazzam's (Shah Alam) *ataliq* (teacher).

The details regarding the curriculum prescribed during the under review period are not available. However Abul Fazal, the celebrated author of *Ain-e-Akbari* had given us some ideas that every student ought to read books in *Akhlaqiat,* (ethics) (morality), *Hindsa* (arithmetic), *Siyaq* (notation), peculiar arithmetic, *Ziraat* (agriculture), *Paimaish & Naqsha* (survey), Masahat (mensuration), Longimetry, Tahrir aqlidus (geometry), Najum (astronomy), Ramal (geomancy), Tibb (medicine), Mashiyat (economics), Mantiq (logic), Nahav (grammar), Siyasat madan (art of administration), the Tabiyati (physical), Reyazi (mathematical) and*IllahiUloom* (divine knowledge) *Fiqah* (jurisprudence), *Vedanta,* as Hindi grammar *Vayakran* and history etc. all of which might gradually be acquired.[8]

The elementary education started with the *Tasmiya Khwani* or Bismillah Khwani ceremony. The child at the age of 4years 4months and 4 days (though the average age was 5 to 6 years) was made to utter *Bismillah Hir Rahman Nir Rahim* (in the name of Allah, the most gracious and the most merciful) followed by the versus of Sura Iqra, the first Ayat (verse) revealed to Prophet Muhammad (PBUH). The child was then taught the Arabic Alphabets and the Holy Qura'n as the chief textbook.[9] The non-Muslim students were first taught the alphabets and began with what was called *Tashrihul Harrof* (Explanation of words). Though both Persian and Arabic were the medium of instructions but for them emphasis was more on Persian as it was the language of the court and administration.

Education among Muslims of Bihar (British Period—1757-1947)

The defeat of Nawab Seraj-ud-Daula (1719-1757) of Bengal in the Battle of Plassey (23.06.1757) was a decisive step in the history of British expansion in India and Bihar was affected fully as the Deputy Governor of Bihar, Raja Ram Narayan though loyal to Nawab of Murshidabad could not resist much and in a few months he accepted the new regime. Emperor Shah Alam II invaded Bihar three times in 1759, 60 and 61 but in vain. Nawab Mir Qasim tried his best to be a de-facto ruler but luck did not favour him. His efforts to fight against the English in collaboration with emperor Shah Alam II and Nawab Shujaud Daula of Awadh at Buxer (23rd October 1764) resulted in a crushing defeat. Buxer supplemented the works of Plassey in reverting the shackles of the company's rule upon Bengal and Bihar. It was in 1858 that British Parliament had taken over the charges of administration from East India Company, which had brought some relief to the people of the country.

With the establishment of British rule an era of neglect, apartheid and obstacles in the way of progress started in socio-economic, educational and cultural fields. The upper middle classes were reduced to beggary. The English aimed to destroy the economy of the Muslim aristocracy and sophisticated skilled workers by its fiscal policy. "Those who lost heavily" observed B.B. Mishra, "with the establishment of British rule in Bengal and Bihar were mostly Muslims".[10] Regarding the strategy of the British during its early days of rule Hafiz Mallick remarks "it was to oust the Muslims from the professions and positions of economic and administrative control and ultimately this policy pauperized".[11]

Till the 19th century i.e. prior to the modern pattern of education, Muslims were well advanced in education as William Adams in his report on the state of education in Bengal and Bihar (1835-38) admits that "there were 1,00,000 indigenous schools in Bengal and Bihar i.e. roughly two schools for every three villages.[12] So far the course of study for higher education is concerned; it constituted grammar, rhetoric, logic, theology, metaphysics, literature, jurisprudence, and science etc. But as it was a period of decline for Muslim rules in India, the curriculum were bound to be affected, and a declining trend was visible with greater emphasis on logic and less on language & literature, history, geography & Quranic aesthetics etc. The system was a perverted from of *Darse-e-Nizamia*. Despite of that its contents reveal that in 18th &19th centuries the subjects whom English boys learnt in their colleges through Latin & Greek, the students of Bihar learnt through Arabic & Persian. They talk fluently about Socrates and Aristotle, Plato, Hippocrates and Avicenna.[13] Selman observes, "the Muslims who held offices with twenty rupees a month, commonly gives his son an education equal to that of a Prime Minister" in England.[14]

The East India Company in its early days of administration followed a policy of laissez faire i.e. not to interfere in education of native because it did not regard the promotion of education among the natives its proper concern. As a commercial and trading company its main objects was to earn more and more profits. It used its political gains exclusively to sub serve its economic interests. It exploited much in the field of trade, industry and agriculture for their selfish end and the result was, with the tightening grip of the company, we find a rapid decay in Muslim education.[15] Howell had commented, "education in India under the British Government was first ignored, then violently and successfully opposed, then conducted on a system now universally admitted to be erroneous".[16]

Till the arrival of William Bentinck and T.B. Macaulay the officials of the company were divided on the proposal to introduce the new learning in India. Charles Grant appears to have been one of the exponents of English education as he maintained in 1792 A.D. "it would be odious and immoral to keep India ignorant owing to apprehended risks to British rule". But the introduction of education was not for their intellectual growth rather to propagate Christianity as M. Elphenstein & F. Warden in their memories wrote, "though they agree with the Governor not to interfere in the religious affairs of the natives, but secretly they would encourage the Christian preachers so that they might renounce their own religion and adopt Christianity".[17] When William Bentinck declared the policy of religious neutrality, the missionaries and certain overzealous Europeans protested arguing that "Christianity should not be sacrificed to worldly expediency"[18] and at last Macaulay system of education aimed at creating class of citizens who would be Indians in blood and colour but English in taste, opinion and intellect had been approved.

In this way due to rapid changes on the political scene and in the socio-economic condition of the people, the deceitful nature of the British rule, Muslims realized that material progress was essential but not at the cost of their religion and culture. British policy of discrimination and divide *et. empera* encouraged the Hindus for the western education and job at the cost of the Muslims. Arrogance of race and power, which British officials manifested at every step made the people of India in general and the Muslims, in particular look at the western education with serious misgivings and at times with hostility. The attitude of the British bureaucracy can well be gauged from the following quotations of Henry Harrington Thomas of Bengal Civil Service, "I have stated that the Hindus were not the contrivers of the 1857 rebellion and I now shall attempt to show that it was the result of Mohammedan conspiracy".[19] The British were satisfied with the Hindus as Charles Grant, the then director of the company, maintained, "vegetable diets and absence of maritime taste among the Hindus will check ardent designs of independence".[20] While British considered imparting of education to Muslim as highly dangerous. The friends of India maintained, that Government of India confesses it to be injurious and absurd "we are suppressing Mohammedanism (sic) in Constantinople longing for its down fall in London and sharpening it weapons in Calcutta".[21]

So far the progress of western education among the Muslims of undivided Bihar is concerned as an individual attempt, Lord Minto in his minutes dated March 6, 1811 recommended for the opening of the Muslim college at Bhagalpur for advancement of Muslim language and literature.[22] In 1836 Shah Kabiruddin of Sahsaram Khankah applied to the Governor General of India to appoint persons to teach English language in the Madarsa of Sahsaram.[23] W. Taylor an enthusiastic Commissioner of Patna tried to create an interest among the people of Bihar for English education as he observed, that there is a strong and inveterate dislike and general apathy for it both among Hindus and Muslims. To remove it he suggested exerting the strongest available influence and for this cooperation of local Zamindars was sought.[24] The first English school was opened in 1835 at Purnea and Patna, while in 1859 Zila schools in Patna, Arah, Chapra and Bhagalpur were established. Subsequently in 1863 school at Deaghar, Motihari, Hazaribagh and Chaibasa were also opened.[25] In the same year Patna College was founded with five students. The first donation of Rs. 5,000 to college fund was contributed by Wilayat Ali Khan (1818-1869), followed by the Darbhanga Raj and the Bettiah estate.[26] Later an amount of rupees 30,000 was granted from the Wahabi fund for the repair and renovation of the Patna College building.[27]

The revolt of 1857 had been devastating in its nature particularly for the Indian Muslims. After the revolt thousands of Muslims elites were hanged till death as they revolted against the British imperialism. Gradually Muslims realized that they had to adjust with the British Raj and the English education. The publication of Sir William Hunter's book—*The Indian Musalmans* (1871) also heralded a change in British policy towards the Muslims. Mohammad Hasan son of Wilayat Ali was awarded the title of Shamsul Ulema and Amjad Ali son of Maulana Yahya Ali studied English and become a professor at Muir Central College. These symbolize the process of adoption to English education which spread steadily among the Muslim elite's but that does not appear to have extinguished their passionate concern for there self respect and freedom.[28]

Under the direct influence of Sir Syed Ahmad Khan (1817-97) for the social and educational regeneration of Indian Muslims *Anjuman-i-Islamia*—a literary and educational society was established at Arrah in August 1866. Its chief patrons were Waris Ali Khan, Khawja Fakhruddin, Munshi Ahmad Hussain, Babu Suraj Mal and Khuda Bakhsh (1842-1908) etc. It played a very active role in education and in literary fields of Bihar and its door was open for both Muslims and non-muslims.[29] Syed Imdad Ali started the Bihar Scientific Society at Muzafferpur in May 1868 with an identical object of Sir Syed's Scientific Society of Ghazipur in 1863. It had about 500 members and a bi-monthly journal in Urdu named—*Akhbaraul Akhiar* was published. It also managed many schools in the province and invited the Lieutenant Governor Cambell at Muzaffarpur in 1871 to lay down the foundation of Collegiate Schools that was later handed over to Langat Singh in 1899 to start a College there. The society had its branches in Gaya, Patna, Bhagalpur and Mongyr etc.[30]

In 1869 a new society *Anjuman-i-Tehzeb* (Cultural society) was formed at Muzafferpur to organize seminars and discussions on subjects of philosophical interests and to promote liberal education.[31] The other associations established during those days for social and cultural reforms among Muslims of Bihar were *Anjuman Hayat-e-Islam*, Mongyr (1888) *Anjuman Momenin*, Patna (1875) *Amjuman Islah*, Desna (1899) etc. Wahabis or Ahle Hadis started a number or Madarsas and Orphanages with the missionary zeal like Madarsa Islahul Muslimin in Patna, Muzakira Ilmiya of Arrah and Darul Uloom Ahmadia Salfia of Darbhanga.[32]

The first three Bihari Muslims namely Syed Sharfuddin (1856-1921), S.N. Huda (1855-1939) and Ahsanuddin Ahmad who had gone to England for study, returned by 1880. These three along with Samshul Ulema Md. Hasan son of prominent Wahabi leader Wilayat Ali (1794-1852), Qazi Riza Hussain, Nawab Imdad Hussain Khan and Khuda Bakhsh Khan *(1824-1908)* etc. were pioneers of modern education among Muslims of Bihar and extended full cooperation and support to Sir Syed's mission.[33] Mohammadan Education Committee, a branch of AIMEC was founded in March 1884 with the personal interest of Wilfred Scawan & Blunt to induce and encourage modern education and science among the Muslim youth of Bihar. Its constitution was drafted under the guidance of Syed Mahmood (1850-1903) and its first secretary was Maulvi (later Shamsul Ulema) Mohammad Hassan (1889). Among its other prominent members were Khuda Bakhsh Khan, Ahmad Hussain, Nawab Wilayat Ali Khan, Syed Sharfuddin, Syed Noorul Huda, Amjad Ali, Nawab Sarfraz Hussain Khan and Sir Ali Imam (1869-1932) etc.

The Mohammadan Anglo Arabic School was established on first march 1884 under the guidance of Mohammadan Education Committee. With the strength 97 Sunni, 29 Shia, 26 Mohammadis (Wahabis) and 48 Hindus. The school imparted instruction up to standard of University entrance examination. A petition was submitted to the lieutenant governor of Bengal in 1886 for financial assistance from Wahabi fund created out of the sale proceeds of the movable and immovable properties confiscated of the members of the Sadiqpur family, the so called Wahabis or rebels against the government after their arrest and imprisonment during 1863-65 which was about Rs. 1,21,948 only and the interest accruing to the unused fund. The government agreed to provide an endowment of Rs. 15,000 from this fund and monthly grant of Rs. 100 and another grant of Rs. 5,000 for acquisition of a site for the building were also sanctioned.[34]

Due to these several efforts made by these institutions and organizations educational condition of the Muslims of Bihar improved to the signification extent. Consequently for four decades of the present century the educated families of the Muslims occupied and secured a decent place in the cultural, educational, economic and political life of Bihar and felt neither discouragement nor inhibition. So far fellowship in the university and employment in Government administration are concerned. The Bihar Times, Patna reports, we find that while the name of Bengalis and Europeans may be counted by scored in the list of fellows there are only five Biharis all Mohammadans.[35] The employment position of the Bihari Muslims and Hindus on the key post can be understood from the table 1.1.

Table 1.1: Employment Position of Bihari.

	Total Employment			*Muslim*			*Non Muslims*		
Year	*D.C*	*Sub D.C*	*Total*	*D.C*	*Sub D.C*	*Total*	*D.C*	*Sub D.C*	*Total*
1895	7	17	24	1	3	4	1	1	2
1896	7	17	24	1	3	4	1	2	3
1897	7	7	14	1	3	4	0	1	1
1898	5	5	10	1	0	1	0	1	1
Total	26	46	72	4	9	13	2	5	7

Source: V.C.P. Chaudhry, *The Creation of modern Bihar* p. 26.[36]

In this way out of total 72 appointments made in four years in Bihar Civil Cadre only twenty were Bihari and out of twenty 13 were Muslims and the rest 7 were Hindus. Thus it is clear that Bihari Hindus got much less jobs than their percentage of population. Further in 1901 out of 17 Barristers practicing at Patna 12 were Muslims. Prominent among them were Syed Ali Imam, Hasan Imam and Maulana Mazharul Haque.[37] In 1921 there were 155 permanent subs assistant Surgeons employed in Bihar and Orrisa out of that 9 were Bihari Hindu and 24were Muslims while the rest were Bengalis and Oriyas.[38]

Dr K.K. Dutta writes, "The Mohammedans got English education and before that advent of Bengalis such offices in Bihar were held by Mohammedans. (Sic) It is the Mohammadan (Sic.) therefore, who first raised the slogan of Bihar for Biharis—a slogan which was picked up by Bihari Hindu particularly the Kayastha when after making some progress in education they had found prospect of their employment blocked".[39]

First Conference of students for the separate province was held in 1906 under President ship of justice Syed Sharfuddin (1856-1921). The first session of Bihar provincial conference was held in Patna in April 1908, under the chairmanship of (Sir) Ali Imam. And (Sir) Fakhruddin moved a resolution for the separation of Bihar from Bengal. The proposal for separation of Bihar from Bengal and shifting of India's capital from Calcutta to Delhi was approved in 1911 by the government of India. Sir Ali Imam was then the member of Viceroys Executive Council. Bihar state was formed as a separate province in 1912.[40]

With the formation of a separate state of Bihar demands for a new University in Bihar had started. In a large and representative gathering of the citizen of Patna in February 1912 Maulana Mazharul Haque proposed that province of Bihar and Orissa should have a separate University of its own at the earliest and that in the mean time there should be adequate representation of the people of Bihar in Calcutta University senate and syndicate. Purnendu Narayan Sinha seconded the move.[41] It was advocated on the ground that there were 84 High schools and six colleges in Bihar and an approximately 2,000 candidate appeared for Matriculation, 98 for Intermediate and 68 for B.A. in 1912.

As Islam has attached so much importance to education or acquisition of knowledge so the Muslims of Bihar in Turko, Afghan and Mughal periods considered it as the Divine commands Education during above mentioned period was imparted by three fold agencies i.e. (a) Muktab at private houses (b) Mosque and Khanqah and (c) Madarsas or Jamia representing primary, secondary and higher stages of education respectively. Religions formed the backbone of education so most of the Maktabs and Madarsas were attached to Masjid, Khanqah or Dargah. Rulers and noble of the period under review took keen interest in the spread of Knowledge and education. It was considered as the panacea for all evils and means improving physicals moral and spiritual condition of the people.

After the advent of the British education was ignored as the new ruler adopted a policy of neglect indifference and obstacle. The antagonistic attitude of the British towards the Muslims halted the progress of education among Muslims but due to the sincere effort of Sir Syed Ahmad Khan Muslims gradually realized the importance of western education in Bihar and in a short span, as all the available record indicates, Muslims once again picked up the momentum and in the beginning of present century, they were once again well advanced in comparison to Bihari Hindus. This situation more or less prevailed till the Independence of the country.

REFERENCE

1. Minhajuddin, Siraj—*Tabqat-e-Nasri*, Elliots translation (Calcutta), p. 309.
2. Paul, Jackson—*Letters from Maneri* (New Delhi, Horizon India 1990).
3. Syed, Tufail Ahmad—*Musalmano Ka Raushan Mustaqbil* (Delhi, Azizia 1945), p. 128.
4. S. Hasan, Askari—*Islam and Muslims in Medieval Bihar* (Patna, Khuda Bakhsh 1889), p. 125.
5. R.R. Diwaker(ed)—*Bihar through the Ages* (Calcutta 1959), pp. 30-33.
6. Syed Manazir Ahsan Geelani—*Hindustan Mein Musalmano Ka Nizam Talim wa Tarbiyat* (Delhi Nadwa 1966), pp. 30-33.
7. R.R. Diwaker *Op cit.*, p. 524.

8. Abul Fazul—*Ain-e-Akbari*, vol. I, Chap II, Ain Amozish, p. 46, quoted by M.A. Hasnat Nadvi—*Hindustan mein Qadeem Islami Daragahein* (Azam Garh, Maarif 1971), p. 119.
9. S.M. Jaffar—*Education in Muslim in Bihar* (100-1800 AD) (Delhi, 1973), pp. 151-153.
10. B.B. Mishra—*The Indian Middle Class* (London Oxford, 1962), p. 61.
11. Azizur Rahman Mallick—*British policy and Muslims in Bengal* (1757-1856) (Dacca, Asiatic, 1961), p. 15.
12. J.P. Naik & Syed Nurullah—*A Student History of Education in India* (1800-1973) Delhi Macmilan, 1947), p. 15.
13. Mujeeb Ashraf—*Muslim Attitude Towards British Rule and Western Culture in India* (New Delhi, Adbiyat 1982), p. 52; R.R. Diwaker, *Op cit.*, p. 751.
14. Mujeeb Ashraf—*Op cit.*, p. 252.
15. Syed Mahmood—*A History of English Education in India (1781-1873)*(Aligarh 1895), p. 20 Maulana Tufail Ahmad, *Op cit.*, p. 128.
16. H. Sharp(ed)—*Selection from Educational Records (1781-1893)*(New Delhi 1965), p. 35; Mujeeb Ashraf, *Op cit.*, p. 141.
17. Syed Mahmood—*Op cit.*, p. 40; Tufail Ahmad, *Op cit.*, p. 95.
18. Syed Mahmood—*Op cit.*, p. 64.
19. Henry Herrigton Thomas—*Rebellion in India and our Future Policy* (Calcutta1858), p. 41; S. Tufail Ahmad—*Hukumat Khud Akhtiare* (Aligarh), p. 35.
20. Syed Mohd. Mian—*Ulmal Haq* (Moradabad, 1955), p. 32.
21. Mujeeb Ashraf—*Op cit.*, p. 289.
22. M. Singh—*History and Culture of India People*, Vol. X, Part II, pp. 31-32.
23. S. Abdur Rahim—*Alpanch* (Patna, 28/2/1903).
24. *Letter of Mr. Taylor to W. Gordon*—Young D.P.I, January, 1856.
25. *Educational Proceeding* (Govt of Bengal) August 1893 No. 79-80, pp. 4345.
26. *Ibid.* April & Now 1863, No.19.
27. Qeyamuddin Ahmad—*Mohammadan Education Committee and M.A.A. School* (Patna, 1884-1984) Souvenir, p. 31.
28. Ali Ashraf—*Muslim Elite* (New Delhi, Atlantic 1982), p. 55.
29. J.S. Jha—*Origin and Development of Cultural Institution in Bihar* Journal of Historical Research Society, Vol. III (Ranchi, 1963), p. 55.
30. Shamin Ahmad—*Muzaffarpur Scientific Society*, Souvenir, 4th A.I.M.E Confrence, (Patna, 1973), pp. 69-73.
31. Qeyamuddin Ahmad & J.S. Jha—*Mazaharul Haque* (Delhi P.D. 1976), p. 3.
32. K.K. Dutta & J.S. Jha—*Comprehensive History of Bihar* Vol. III, Part I (Patna 1976), pp. 310-311.
33. Shad Azimabadi—*Shad Ki Kahani Shad Ki Zubani* (Patna), p. 70.
34. Qeyamuddin & J.S. Jha—*Mazaharul Haque. Op cit.*, p. 3.

35. *The Bihar Times*, Patna—Dated 15th January, 1899.
36. V.C.P. Chawdhry—*The Creation of Modern Bihar* (Patna Motilal, 1965), p. 26.
37. B.B. Mishra—*Op cit.*, p. 145.
38. G.E. Owen.
39. K.K. Dutta—*Op cit.*, p. 218; Ali Ashraf, *Op cit.*, p. 32.
40. Ali Ashraf—*Op cit.*, p. 32.
41. The Biharee—(Patna, 9th February 1912) and S.N. Pandey, *Op cit.*, pp. 106-107.

2

The State of Education among Muslims of Bihar and Jharkhand

(Since Independence)

The independence of India (1947) was accompanied by the partition of the country which cost in terms of human sufferings terribly." It was nothing short of a traumatic experience for millions of People on either side of the border".[1] According to one such estimation more than 60 lakh Muslims migrated to Pakistan while more than 40 lakh Hindus crossed the border. For quite some time after the partition, Muslims remained in a state of shock and bafflement Recrudescence of communal violence on both sides of the border added not only to human suffering but also to mutual hatred and acrimony. Instead of solving, it has created many more problems. The amount of distrust between the two communities was really immense—"any Indian was" according to Hudson, "Muslim or non-Muslim".[2] The unity between these two communities which was forged during the freedom struggle particularly Khilafat Movement was adversely shattered. Asghar Ali Engineer; remarks "Indian Muslims paid a very heavy price for the creation of Pakistan".[3] The first few years of the independence were indeed very difficult years for the Muslims as they were confused and made to feel guilty for the creation of Pakistan by their Hindu neighbour.

On the other front a substantial portion of urban educated Muslim elite—the backbone of any society or community, migrated to Pakistan for security and in search of employment and better opportunities, which existed there at that time. Many Muslims approximately 3.5 lakhs,[4] specially from central and north Bihar migrated to East and West Pakistan and those who remained in their home land were faced with a traumatic experience, bewildered and demoralized. There was a sense of insecurity and uncertainty about their future in the land of their birth. Amidst these adverse circumstances, the most important task was to wash away the stains of the recent past and promote the rehabilitation of Muslims in their homeland. Syed Mahmood (1889-1971) Shah Omair, Ahad Md. Noor (1894-1975) and Abdul Qayum Ansari (1905-1963) tried and helped to boost up the shattered morale of Muslims of Bihar. The socialist Muslims like Ahad Fatimi (1915-1980), Abul Hayat Chand (1914-1958), and Razi Azimabadi worked and through the help and intervention of the socialist leader Jay Prakash Narayan (1902-1976) stopped the raid and search of Muslim houses and thus helped to remove fear from Muslim mind. Imarat Sharia, Jamiatul Ulema and Momin Conference etc. also helped to promote a spirit of confidence to prevent the demoralization of Muslims.[5]

On the national front, India declared that it would be a Democratic and Republic state based on the principles of socialism, secularism, equality, justice and fraternity. These ideals were duly incorporated in the preambles of the Indian Constitution. Besides the constitution guarantees various rights and privileges through both the Fundamental Rights and Directive Principles of state Policy to all citizens irrespective of caste, creed, race, religion and place of birth. But as it is a secular, democratic nation and democracy means the rule of majority our Constitution makers tried to erase any doubt from the mind of the minorities by providing safeguards under fundamental Rights. The articles 28, 29 and 30 deals exclusively with the religious, cultural and educational rights of the minorities with the marginal note to the last two articles as protection of interest of minorities. It would therefore be obvious that these articles intended to protect the special position of religious, linguistic and cultural minorities.

The report of the Education Commission published in 1966 embodies the principles of the constitution and applies them specifically to educational opportunity..."a society that values social justice and is anxious to improve the lot of the common man and cultivate all available talent, must ensure progressive equality of opportunity to all sections of the population. This is the only guarantee for building up of an egalitarian and human society in which the exploitation of the weak will be minimized".[6]

In the pre-independence period there were 13 Muslim managed schools in Bihar. The oldest one established in 1884 while the remaining 12 established between 1901 and 1946,[7] but gradually their number increased and now they are only 71.[8] though the total number of recognized, aided religious and linguistic minority secondary schools are 216[9] and out of that only 45 schools i.e. 20.8 per cent are *Muslims managed*. A large number of Muslim managed schools are unrecognized and unaided and their students appear in the Board examination from other recognized schools as private candidates. The survey further reveals that the large numbers of Muslim managed institutions were established after 1971 i.e. after the down fall of Dacca when the exodus of Muslims to Pakistan came to a complete halt. Besides a large number of Muslim students also attend the classes in other private or government run schools. According to the fourth All India Educational survey report (N C E R T) total number of primary, middle and secondary schools in Bihar in 1981 was 64,618 in which 3,041 were secondary schools while the remaining were primary and middle schools.[10] So far the management of the schools are concerned according to the management 60,603 schools were Government schools while 3,867 were private aided and 152 were private unaided. Among the private aided and unaided 2,944 were secondary schools which were usually managed by the religious and linguistic minorities like Christians, Muslims and Sikhs as well as private bodies, public and private companies. As per the survey report the total students in these schools from class I to V were 11,90,551 while from VI to VIII were 17,32,395 and class IX & X were 7,78,880. In this way the total number of students from class I to X were 1,45,15.686. The said Survey further reveals that in class X the total number of students were 3,14,951.[11] While according to one notification of the Bihar School Examination Board, Patna in 1985 Annual Board Examination 4.91 lakh students appeared and 3.56 lakh passed (Total pass percentage 72.43 per cent).[12] While from 71 Muslim managed Urdu medium High school a total number of 6,183 Muslim students appeared in 1985, out of which 5,337 students passed the Board Examination (Total pass percentage from Urdu medium schools was 86%).[13]

So far as the Madarsa education in post independence era is concerned there are approximately 6,500 Madarsas spread through out the state. Every village and mohalla with Muslim population has such Madarsas. They are of following types.

1. Madarsa affiliated to Madarsa Education Board, Patna:

   (a) Aided and affiliated.
   (b) Unaided but affiliated.
   (c) Unaided and Unaffiliated.

2. Independent Madrasas:

   (a) Darse—Nizamia.
   (b) Madarsa managed by private bodies.
   (c) Darul Qura'n specific for Quranic Education.

At present there are about 1,315 recognized Madarsas affiliated to Madarsa Education Board, Patna. Out of that state government provides financial assistance to 1, 253 Madarsa with a sanction strength of 7,325 teachers for salary fund as 1,027 Madrasas are financed through the board while 226 directly by the government. Beside the salary of the teachers, these institutions exploit their own resources for other purpose.193 Madarsas are at the advance stage of non-financial affiliation while 2,793 more Madarasas applied for affiliation and financial assistance.[14]

Among these affiliated Madarsas, 29 Madarsas provide the teaching of *Fazil, 43 Alim, 104 Maulvi, 142 Fauqania* & 987 Wastania degrees. The strength of Students (Both boys and girls) in these Madarasas are about 5 lakhs and approximately 55 thousands candidates appear every year in the Board

Examination in various classes from Wastania to Fazils.[15] Duration of courses in these Madarsas are of 17 years and it has been considered at par with that of schools and colleges. They are as follows:

I. Elementary and Secondary Education:

1.	Tahtania	equivalent to	Primary	4 years
2.	Wastania	-do-	Middle	4 years
3.	Fauqania	-do-	Secondary	2 years
				= 10 years

II. Higher Education:

4.	Maulvi	-do-	Intermediate	2 years
5.	Alim	-do-	B.A. (graduation)	2 years
6.	Alim (Hons.)	-do-	B.A. (Hons.)	1 years
7.	Fazil	-do-	M.A.	2 years
8.	Kamil	-do-	Research (Ph.D)	2 years[16]
				= 19 years

Curriculam in these Madarsas, besides *Tafseer, Hadith, Fiqah, Ilmul Kalam* etc, include Mathematics, General Science, Civics, History, Geography, etc. in accordance with the various levels of courses. In language and literature, in addition, to Arabic, Persian and Urdu, Hindi and English as compulsory and optional subjects have also been included. Up to *Wastania* stage crafts education is also a compulsory subject with carpentry and calligraphy etc. If the result of the *Fazil* examination 1990 is any indication of the trend it clearly maintains that most of the students shifted from theology to language studies as the special subjects opted by 564 students were as follows:

Tafsir:	02	Arabic:	12
Hadith:	03	Persian:	256
Fiqah:	02	Urdu:	286
		Total:	**564**[17]

Madarsa Education Board which was constituted in March 1977 under the Bihar State Madarsa Education Act 1977 for looking after the affairs and administration of new Madarsas, holding examinations, distribution of degrees and formulation of Madarsas curriculum etc. It consists of—

1. The Chairman, to be nominated by the state Government.
2. The Chairman, Bihar states Sunni Waqf Board, Patna.
3. The Chairman, Bihar states Shia Waqf Board, Patna.
4. Director of the Institute of Arabic &Persian Research, Patna.
5. Principal, Madarsa Islamia ShamshulHuda, Patna.
6. Special Director, (Secondary Education) Government of Bihar, Patna.
7. Two M.L.A's.
8. One M.L.C.
9. Three Education experts, to be nominated by the Government of Bihar, Patna.
10. Two Senior Madarsa teachers, to be nominated by the state Government.[18]

The Board conducts the examination from *Wastania* to *Fazil* degree. Candidates after passing from the Madarsa Board are eligible for admission in Degree colleges, Teacher's Training schools or colleges etc. under Bhagalpur, Bihar, Magadh, Mithla, Patna, Osmania, Jamia Millia Islamia, and J.N.U. New Delhi etc. They can appear even in various competitive examinations conducted by the Bihar Public Service Commission Patna.[19]

Besides the Madarsas affiliated to Bihar State Madrasa Education Board, Patna there are about 350 Madarsas known as *Darse Nizamia.* These institutions are the centres of Islamic learning and as there Syllabi are mostly comprised of theology, Arabic language and literature, logic & philosophy etc. These Madarsas usually have allegiance with Deoband school of thought and are mostly based on public endowment, charity (*Zakat, Atiya & Fitra* etc.) to meet all recurring & non-recurring expenses. They also provide boarding and lodging free of cost to the needy and meritorious students. Those who want to pay either fully or partially for their boarding and lodging can also do so. These institutions do have their own *Matbakh* (Kitchen) to supply meal two times a day with break fast or refreshment in accordance with their standard and financial position to both teachers as well as students. Their discipline is very strict but they lack facilities of sports, games and other recreational activities. After successful completion of the prescribed courses, these institutions issue their own certificate or degrees and as these institutions are not interlinked or affiliated to any central body so they vary in courses of studies, methods of teaching and examination system etc.

Jamat-e-Islami, AhleHadith, evaluation Ahle Sunnat wal Jamaat (Barailwi) etc. have also established a chain of Madarsas in different part: of the state. These Madarsas have their own syllabi in accordance with their own school of thought and jurisprudence. But unlike the *Darse Nizamia* or Madarsa affiliated to Madarsa education board these Madarsa include some new disciplines such as oratory, comparative religion etc besides the traditional and other secular subjects which even we do not find in our modern schools and colleges. Standard of teaching and discipline in these institutions are comparatively better than above-mentioned Madarsas. Most of these institutions also provide technical education like calligraphy, carpentry, Urdu, Hindi and English typing or computer education etc.

The post independence India discarded the policy of compiling and publishing the educational statistics on community basis, neither census reports provide any data on this subject nor empirical or large scale survey or studies have been conducted to understand the situational status and problems of Muslims community. Therefore no objective statements can be made as to the position of Muslims in the educational field. However, whatever the information is available both from macro and micro studies on Indian Muslims it clearly indicate that the community as such suffers from a number of disadvantages. They are educationally handicapped deprived and are not responding adequately to contemporary educational development and expansion. Enrolment of girls and enrollment for higher education among

Muslims in general lag considerably behind than the non-Muslims taken together.

Gopal Krishna (1972) studied the socio-economic conditions of Indian Muslims in 35 districts covering 15 state. A sample of 2,995 Muslim males and 997 non-Muslims males were randomly selected from enumeration list for the purpose of research. It was interesting to note that on the basis of random sampling the educational qualification of Muslims and non-Muslim respondents was strikingly different as the table 2.1 shows the findings.

Table 2.1: Educational Qualification of Muslims and Non-muslims Respondent.

	Illiterate to Primary education	*Up to High Schools*	*Colleges, University*	
			Technical	*Higher Technical*
Muslims	55.4	40.8	2.8	1.1
Non Muslims	29.8	55.0	11.0	4.2

Source: Gopal Krishna—Socio-Economic Status scale of Indian Muslim 1972. (New Delhi Govt. of India 1973).

According to 1981 census the total population of Muslim in Bihar was about 98.74 lakh i.e. 14.1 per cent of the total population of the state. Then Bihar was divided into 31 districts but during 1991 census, the state was having 42 districts. Since then the number has further increased to 50. The increase during 1981-91 was consequence of splitting 7 old districts (i.e. Gaya, Saharsa, Munger, SanthalPargana, Purnea, Ranchi and Singhbhum) into 18 new districts. For example old Purnea district was sub-divided into 3 new districts Purnea, Araria and Kishanganj etc.

As the table 2.1 and 2.2 show Purnea and Katihar are the only district which have more than 25 per cent Muslim of their total population. These two districts together contain 20-23lakhs or about 20 per cent of total Muslim population of Bihar. These are 9 districts, which have between 15 and 25 percentage of Muslim population, Darbhanga topping the list in this group.

Table 2.2: Statement showing Muslim population in different districts of United Bihar, percentage of Muslim population, per cent of urban population, literacy rate, electricity, (house hold) toilet facilities (1981).

Districts	*Muslim Populatio in lakh*	*% of Muslim to total population*	*% of Muslims. population of the dist. Living in urban areas*	*% of total population Living in urban areas*	*% of literate person in the dist.*	*% of literate female in the dist.*	*% of electricity with household*	*% of No. literate members in family*	*Toilet facility*
1. Purnea	14.96	41.6	5.5	8.0	19.3	9.4	3.4	56.8	34.2
2. Santhal*	6.11	16.5	6.9	6.9	22.3	10.5	4.3	50.8	51.7
3. Katihar	5.27	36.9	4.9	9.4	21.0	11.3	5.5	54.4	51.9
4. Darbhanga	4.33	21.6	10.6	8.8	23.9	12.6	3.8	51.7	60.2
5. E. Champaran	4.27	17.6	5.8	4.6	23.8	10.8	3.1	56.0	46.1
6. W. Champaran	3.87	19.6	9.8	7.3	15.3	7.2	3.8	57.1	45.5
7. Saharsa	3.71	12.6	8.6	5.7	20.3	9.2	3.1	53.0	32.4
8. Madhubani	3.68	15.8	4.6	3.1	21.7	9.5	2.9	51.3	41.2
9. Bhagalpur	3.65	13.9	21.6	11.7	27.5	15.8	7.8	45.2	52.7
10. Sitamarhi	3.56	18.4	4.5	4.5	19.6	9.7	2.0	57.1	35.1
11. Muzafferpur	3.36	14.3	1.6	8.1	34.3	13.2	8.1	50.8	76.8
12. Gaya	3.28	10.5	22.2	10.9	13.8	15.3	9.0	39.7	62.5
13. Siwan	2.95	16.6	7.8	4.4	23.7	10.7	5.0	40.5	54.6
14. Munger	2.83	8.5	20.5	14.1	26.7	14.3	11.0	45.2	47.8
15. Hazaribagh*	2.70	12.3	17.8	15.1	23.5	10.9	14.0	47.6	52.1
16. Giridih*	2.61	15.1	14.6	14.3	23.9	10.0	12.8	44.0	51.4

(*Contd.*)

(Contd.)

Districts	*Muslim Populatio in lakh*	*% of Muslim to total population*	*% of Muslims. population of the.dist. Living in urban areas*	*% of total population Living in urban areas*	*% of literate person in the dist.*	*% of literate female in the dist.*	*% of electricity with household*	*% of No. literate members in family*	*Toilet facility*
17. Dhanbad*	2.57	12.2	56.0	50.6	39.2	23.2	43.0	30.3	47.0
18. Ranchi*	2.39	7.8	42.7	22.9	31.4	19.6	11.7	38.7	54.7
19. Patna	2.25	7.4	65.8	37.1	39.7	25.5	25.7	27.3	69.4
20. Rohtas	2.18	9.2	24.0	9.7	30.5	15.6	12.5	31.8	51.4
21. Palumu*	2.18	11.1	8.9	5.6	20.4	9.1	4.6	51.4	46.0
22. Gopalgunj	2.07	15.2	6.3	5.0	21.4	8.5	4.5	45.3	39.6
23. Samstipur	2.06	9.7	4.8	4.2	24.9	12.8	5.9	48.0	58.1
24. Saran	2.01	9.8	13.4	8.1	27.3	12.0	3.8	36.9	45.9
25. Begusarai	1.76	12.1	14.2	10.6	26.1	15.1	7.2	47.1	40.4
26. Bhoj Purr	1.56	6.5	30.8	10.7	31.4	15.1	8.8	30.0	51.4
27. Vaishali	1.51	9.1	9.4	6.5	25.6	12.7	4.0	42.9	37.9
28. Nalanda	1.37	8.3	52.5	13.6	32.9	18.2	8.1	33.5	56.2
29. Singhbum*	1.30	4.6	981.5	32.1	34.6	21.5	18.9	38.2	57.4
30. Nawada	1.25	11.4	14.4	6.6	26.5	12.8	7.4	40.7	50.8
31. Aurangabad	1.19	9.6	16.8	6.9	28.5	13.8	5.2	34.7	45.9
BIHAR	**98.74**	**14.1**	**15.2**	**12.5**	**31.6**	**13.6**	**9.2**	**44.9**	**52.9**

Note: 1. The district are arranged in descending order according to absolute Muslim population.
2. Data on toilet facilities are for urban areas only.

Sources: Census of India 1981 Occasional paper no. I of 1989 R.G.I office New Delhi 1989)

This group of districts contains about 33 per cent Muslim population of the state. There are 19 districts each of which contain between 5 and 15 per cent of the districts population as Muslim. This group contains around 44 per cent of total Muslim population of the state. The district of Singhbhum is the only district containing less than 5 per cent of its population as Muslims though according to the percentage of Muslims Singhbhum is at the bottom (with 4.6%) Aurangabad is the district with the least Muslim population (i.e. 1.19 lakh) ranking 23rd according to the percentage (9.6%).

Usually Bihar is divided into three main regions viz North Bihar, South Bihar and Chotanagpur plateau (Present Jharkhand). About 60 per cent of total Muslims population of Bihar resides in North Bihar where as south Bihar and Chotanagpur each contain about 20 per cent of Muslim population. It is a well-known fact that north Bihar is the most back ward region of the state with low literacy, extremely low female education and virtually no industrialization. The region is highly ruralized and the regional economy revolves around agricultural out puts still being dominated by traditional equipments and obsolete techniques. As religion wise data is not available it is extremely difficult to have any precise idea about the socio-economic development of Muslims. But on correlating Muslim population with certain general indices of development some ideas can be obtained about the development of the Muslims in these districts.

As the table 2.2 shows that the degree of urbanization in Muslim population is more than the general population with the exception of Purnea and Katihar in all districts, the proportion of Muslims living in urban is more than that of the total population. But among first eleven important districts having percentage of Muslim above 15 per cent (nearly 58% of total Muslim population) the urbanization is less than the average and Purnea and Katihar perhaps are the least urbanized districts of the state so far the Muslim population is concerned. The table further tells us that eleven important districts having more than 15 per cent Muslim population have values of these indicators well below the state average. From the bottom Purnea ranks second and third according to total literacy and the female literacy levels respectively.

Registrar General of India (R.G.I) published occasional papers in 1989, which contains general information, percentage of households having electricity and toilet facility etc. This provides us the tentative idea regarding the development of Muslim concentrated area *vis-à-vis* the state as a whole and according to it about 9.2 per cent of house holds in Bihar have electricity while in Purnea, Katihar Darbhanga and both Champaran though the Muslims are 23.58 per cent of the total Muslim population of the state i.e. is 3.4, 4.3, 5.5 and 3.1 per cent respectively. It can also be observed from the said table that according to this indicator Purnea ranks 4th, Darbhanga and west Champaran (bracketed) rank 3rd etc. from the bottom of the ladder.

The table further shows that the percentage of the household with not a single literate in Bihar is 44.9 while the six Muslim concentrated districts like Purnea, Katihar, Darbhanga, West Champaran, Sitamarhi and East Champaran have more than 50 per cent of household with not a single literate member in the family. As the indicator of illiteracy shows in the entire state of united Bihar, Sitamarhi, Champaran (W), Purnea, and Champaran (E) are ranked first, second, third and fourth. The R.G.I Occasional Paper No. I has further documented the list of 397 districts of India in descending order as the indicator of illiteracy among these Champaran (W), Sitamarhi, Purnea, Katihar, Champaran (E), etc. find places among first 34 districts as the most illiterate districts of the country. All the 5 districts of Bihar happen to be among the first 6-important Muslim concentrated districts of Bihar as the following table indicates.

The R.G.I. documents further reveal that five out of six, most significant district (With regard to percentage of Muslim population) have less toilet facilities in the urban area than to the state average. Toilet facility is an indicator of development and Saharsa, Purnea & Sitamarhi occupy first second and third place from the bottom with only 32,4, 34.2 and 35.1 per cent respectively, as against the 52.9 per cent for Bihar as a whole.

Table 2.3: Classes of District according to the Percentage of Muslim Population in the Various districts of United Bihar (1981).

Percentage of Muslims population in districts	*No. of districts*	*Name of Districts*	*Muslim Population in lakhs*
1. More than 25%	2	Purnea (2497) Katihar (1232)	20.23 (20.5%)
2. More than 20% but less than 25%	1	Darbhanga (1058)	4.33 (4.4%)
3. More than 15% but less than 20%	8	W. Champaran (1363) Sitamarihi (987) E. Champaran (1283) Siwan (1437) S. Pargana (10,015) Madhubani (1032) Gopalgunj (1286) Giridih (2885)	29.12 (29.5%)
4. More than 10% but less than 15%	9	Muzaffarpur (1729) Bhagalpur (2524) Saharsa (1319) Hazaribagh (3314) Dhanbad (1364) Begusarai (692) Nawada (967) Palamu (3266) Gaya (3513)	24.41 (24.7%)
5. More than 5% but less than 10%	10	Saran (1570) Samastipur (1111) Aurangabad (1749) Rohtas (3003) Vaishali (1399) Mungar (2636) Nalanda (1004) Ranchi (3783) Patna (1294) Bhojpur (1799)	19.35 (19.6%)
6. Less than 5%	1	Singhbhum (4365)	1.30 (1.3%)
Total	31	67,546 villages	98.74 (100.0%)

Notes: The Brackets following the name of the districts contain total number of villages.

Source: Census of India 1981 paper 3 of 1984.

The data available through the National Sample Survey (N.S.S.) organization a reliable source of a formation on social economic information on relative level of education is revealing.

Table 2.4: Distribution of Person by General Education Sex and Religion (Rural India) 1987-88.

Educational Level	*Hindu*		*Muslim*		*Christian*		*Other*	
	Male	*Female*	*Male*	*Female*	*Male*	*Female*	*Male*	*Female*
Not Literate	55.3	75.0	58.2	76.1	33.7	431	45.3	61.4
Primary	19.0	11.8	18.6	13.1	20.5	17.8	17.9	15.7
Middle	22.7	11.2	19.6	9.9	35.4	292	25.5	19.4
Secondary	5.7	1.7	3.4	0.8	9.3	8.1	9.0	3.9
Graduation &Above	1.2	0.2	0.6	—	8.1	1.5	2.3	0.3

Sources: N.S.S. 43rd Round 1987-88 Table 31.4 p. 582-83.

Table 2.5: Distribution of Persons by General Education, Sex and Religion (Urban India) 1987-88.

Educational Level	*Hindu*		*Muslim*		*Christian*		*Other*	
	Male	*Female*	*Male*	*Female*	*Male*	*Female*	*Male*	*Female*
Not Literate	25.3	42.2	42.4	59.5	18.8	22.7	18.0	31.2
Primary	18.8	17.2	20.9	18.5	16.0	17.5	15.6	14.7
Middle	30.5	25.3	26.3	16.8	36.7	33.4	30.0	8.5
Secondary	17.2	10.7	8.0	4.3	20.1	20.8	23.6	17.5
Graduation &Above	7.9	4.2	2.3	0.8	8.1	5.5	11.7	7.9

Sources: N.S.S. 43rd Round 1987-88 Table 31.4 p. 585-86.

Level of Literacy and percentage of younger generation in educational institutions are considered good indicators of social development Table 2.4 and 2.5 shows that in rural and urban areas Christians are by far the most educated groups. Similarly among all religious groups males are more educated than the female while illiteracy among urban and rural Muslim man is 50.6 per cent, it is 40.6 per cent among Hindus and only 26.3 per cent among Christians. For females, respective percentage of illiteracy is 68, 58.6 and 33 per cent respectively.

Table 2.6: Participation at Elementary level of Education.

	Participation at Elementary level of education				*Drop out rate at Primary Level*	
	Class I to VIII (1980-81)				*Class I to V (1980-81)*	
Districts	*% Of Muslim Population Average drop Muslim drop*	*Total Enrollment*	*Enrollment of Muslim*	*% Of Muslim Enrollment*	*Average drop Out rate %*	*Muslim drop Out rate %*
Patna	7.31	116421	16137	14.03	N.A	N:A
Nalanda	7.02	208249	2990	1.44	45.63	41.99
Gaya	10.07	325353	15670	4.82	66.42	6.51
Madhuban	15.19	260566	26348	10.11	58.75	48.09
Purnea	39.62	321990	32601	10.12	76.54	74.75
Bhagalpur	—	—	—	—	53.18	65.74
Total	18.56	1232579	93946	7.62	63.61	61.41

Table 2.7: Muslim Performance at Secondary School level.

Percentage of Population	*Participation & Performance of Appeared candidates*	*Pass total*	*Percentage Muslim*
Bihar 13.48	6.33	61.54	73.63

Source: Report Minorities of High power panel on Minorities S.C, S.T & other weaker section Govt. of India New Delhi 14th. June 1983.

Table 2.8: Participation and performance of Muslims at Graduation, Post-Graduation Uni. M.B.B.S & B.E. Level Universal Examination 1981

	Graduation						*Post-Graduation*					
	Appeared		%	*Passed*		%	*Appeared*		%	*Passed*		%
	Total	*Muslim*		*Total*	*Muslim*		*Total*	*Muslim*		*Total*	*Muslim*	
Bhagal	9517	1113	11.69	4578	700	15.29	1069	109	10.20	955	98	10.26
Patna	2609	367	14.07	2243	275	12.26	999	100	10.01	841	80	9.51
Ranchi	15094	1973	13.07	5188	622	11.99	1348	44	3.26	405	16	3.95
Total	27220	3453	12.69	12009	1597	13.20	3416	253	7.41	2201	194	8.81
	M.B.B.S. Examination 1981						*Bachelor of Engineering Examination 1981*					
	Appeared		%	*Passed*		%	*Appeared*		%	*Passed*		%
	Total	*Muslim*		*Total*	*Muslim*		*Total*	*Muslim*		*Total*	*Muslim*	
Bhagal	61	10	16.39	49	5	10.20	114	10	8.77	90	06	6.67
Patna	181	20	11.05	132	12	9.09	128	12	9.38	87	09	10.34
Ranchi	525	22	4.19	108	4	3.70	965	48	4.97	290	12	4.14
Total	767	52	6.18	289	21	7.27	1207	70	5.80	467	27	5.78

Note: % of Muslim population in the State 13.48

Sources: Gopal Singh Panel Report on minorities Vol. II Government of India, New Delhi, 16-06-83; Muslim India, New Delhi, January 86, p. 33.

Christians retain their lead in higher education i.e. 14 per cent of Christian males and 14.4 per cent of females have obtained secondary education, whereas the figures of Hindus and Muslim are 11.8, 6.2 and 5.65, 2.55 per cent. Further a negligible proportion of Muslim female and only 1.45 per cent of Muslim males is found in graduate and above category, these proportions are 22 and 4.55 per cent for Hindus and 3.5 and 4.95 per cent for Christian's. In this way Muslim are worse than the Hindus and Christians in education.

In 1983 Ministry of Home Affairs, Government of India, New Delhi, collected some data on percentage of Muslim students enrolled in different levels of education in selected districts. The following table 2.6 shows that though the Muslim population in selected 6 districts of Bihar was 18.56 but Muslim enrollment at primary level in these districts was not more than 7.62, as the following table shows.

Gopal Singh panel report, while evaluating the participation and performance of Muslim at Graduation, post Graduation, Medical and Engineering level, suggests that though the Muslim students appeared in less number than their population percentage but their pass percentage and achievement was much higher in comparison to the average as table 2.8 shows.

A sample survey conducted in Kishan Gunj Town regarding the extent of educational backwardness of Muslim shows that Muslim constitute 65.91 per cent i.e. 648, 624 (1991 Census) of the total population (984,107) of the district. It was assumed that in town they will be nearly 60 per cent but in educational institutions their percentage was only 31.41. The survey further reveals that out of the total number of students 11,384 in 36 Schools of the town only 3,606 (31.41%) were Muslim and among the Muslim students 2,230 (19.33%) were Muslims boys while remaining 1,376 (12.09%) were Muslim girls (Table 2.9).

Table 2.9: Muslim Educational Backwardness (Kishan Gunj Town).

Total Population of District (1991) 9,84,107
Muslim Population and Percentage 648.624 and 65.91 per cent
Percentage of Muslims in KishanGunj Town nearly 60 per cent.

	Private School		*Government School*	*Total*	*Percentage of Muslim*
	Muslim	*Non-Muslim*			
No. of Schools	6	14	16	36	—
No. of Students	593	3222	7569	11384	—
Muslim Boys	383	466	1351	2230	19.33
Muslim Girls	184	268	924	1376	12.09
Total M Students	***567***	***734***	***2275***	***3606***	***31.41***
Non-Muslim Boys	16	1416	2975	4407	38.71
Non-Muslim Girls	10	1072	2319	3401	29.87
Total non-Muslim Students	26	2488	5294	7808	68.51
Total Muslim Students in non-Muslim Schools				734	22.78%
Total Non-Muslim Students in Muslim Schools				26	4.38%

Sources: Muslim India New Delhi Vol. XXI No. 187, July 1998.

So far the Muslim employees in Bihar are concerned, they are also not in a comfortable position as the following table no. 2.10 indicates that they are 5.43 per cent out of which a majority of the employees are in class III and IV cadre. Further their percentage in class I state services are higher than those employed in class II, III and IV services.

On the basis of above mentioned finding it can easily be concluded that Muslim in Bihar are educationally backward and they are not responding adequately to the expansion of educational facilities in this state. Government of India's New

Table 2.10: Employment of Muslims in Government Offices/Public and Private Sectors in Bihar.

	Central Govt.	*State Govt.*	*Public Sector*	*Private Sector*
Class I Executive	—	8.14	2.95	4.00
Class II Supervisory	2.11	7.51	4.56	5.00
Class III Clerical	6.50	5055	21.30	6.64
Class IV Menial	5.78	6.74	12.45	3.44
Total	5.43	5.92	16.45	5.13

Source: Selective survey based on Gopal Panel Report 1983 on Minorities Vol. II, Government of India New Delhi, 16-06-83 and *Muslim India*, New Delhi, Vol. IV No. 37, January 86, p. 34.

Education Policy and Programme of Action (1986) with the approval of Parliament and Home Ministry declaration of educational backwardness confirmed it. It was further been confirmed by the Sachar Committee findings and its report.

The constant denial of opportunities and lack of motivation for the use of talent over a long period of time have rendered them backward. One of the very important reasons of their backwardness is weak economic foundation. This has resulted into a vicious cycle of poverty, unemployment, illiteracy, conservative attitude and lack of interest in education. High Power panel on minorities in its report submitted to the ministries of Home Affairs, Government of India (1983) has supported this idea when it remarked that ... particularly Muslim could not avail the opportunities in the fields of education, employment and economic activity...because they developed certain complex and aloofness... feeling of separatism and group isolation... due to communal conflicts and tensions... (Thus) depressed and dejected they have developed certain fatalistic outlook and feel that nothing can be done to improve their lot.[20]

This is true in the case of Bihar than to any other State. The community is caught in the vicious circle of social-economic backwardness leading to psychological alienation, their past exaggeration of religion, discrimination, lack of motivation, ambition & deprivation leading again to social-economic backwardness. And no panacea can serve if the circle is not broken.

NOTES AND REFERENCES

1. The estimated figure of death toll because of partition differs from writer to writer, but the exact figure will never be known. Moon an I.C.S officer stationed in West Punjab gives the number of killed 1,20,000 while Ian Stephen in his book *"Pakistan"* and Michael Edwards in his book *"Last Days of the British Raj"* gives their estimate of casualties as 5,00,000 and 6,00,000 respectively. Leonard Mosley wrote that in Punjab itself 6 lakh people were murdered 1crore 40lakh (1.40crore) people became refugee and about 1lakh women were kidnapped and converted to another faith, Leonard Mosley—*The last days of British Raj* (London 1961), p. 1.
2. H.V. Hudson—*The Great Divide* (London, Hutchin 1969), p. 87.
3. Asghar Ali Engineer—*Indian Muslim—A Study of the Minority Problems in India* (Delhi Ajanta 1985), p. 117.
4. Shams Alam Khan—*Demography and Development*—A Study in Bihar (Patna, 1992), p. 4.
5. Ali Ashraf—*The Muslim Elite* (Delhi Atlantic 1982), p. 22.
6. N.C.E.R.T.—*Report of Education Commission* (1964-66) (New Delhi N.C.E.R.T. 1986) p. 198.
7. Shamim Shah—*Educational Survey Report of Muslim managed school and colleges in India* (Delhi, Hamderd Education Society 1982) p. 14.
8. A.R. Shirwani—*Result of Muslim schools of Bihar,* Cyclostyle stencil No. 449 dated 15.5.1986 (Delhi, Bharat seva trust).
9. N.M.P. Shriwani—*Minorities teachers sore at Government apathy,* The Hindustan Times (Patna 19.9.1989).
10. N.C.E.R.T. *Fourth All India Educational Survey Report*—(Delhi N.C.E.R.T. 1982), pp. 380-81.
11. *Ibid.* p. 836.
12. News item. *The Indian Nation* (Patna 16.7.1985)
13. A.R. Shirwani—*Op cit.*
14. S.M. Jamshedpuri—*Bihar Madarsa Education Board,* The Afkar (New Delhi 15.4.1988).
15. *Ibid.* p. 35.
16. Ali Ashraf op, cit. p. 79.
17. Reference Handbook—*The Bihar Madarsa Education Board Patna.* The Muslim India (Cultural Trust 1992) p. 35.
18. *Ibid.* p. 34.
19. Ali Ashraf—*Op. cit.,* p. 79.
20. Gopal Singh Panel Report on Minorities' vol. II (New Delhi, Government of India Publication 1983), p. 165.

3

Socio-Economic Status Scale of Muslims

The questionnaire applied was a modification of *socio* economic status scale questionnaire (S.E.S.S.Q urban revised 1979) prepared by Dr. S.D. Kapoor of Psycho Centre, New Delhi. It aims at seeking information about the following component variables.

1. Parental occupation and their income.
2. Parental education and education of sibling.
3. Economic index—Possession of house, house type rooms in the house, size of families.
4. Cultural level of the family as judged by expenditure on newspaper and magazine etc.
5. Psychological indicator as level of aspirations both academic and professionals.

It was administered on 600 students of different classes studying in various schools and colleges of United Bihar. Among the students 500 were Muslims and remaining Non-Muslims (2 Sikhs, 5, Christians Scheduled tribe and the rest Hindus). Both of them were classified in two groups the raw scales of both are given in table 3.1.

The table 3.1 shows that none of the students studying and surveyed belongs to the lower & lower strata. Respondents belonging to the upper lower strata among the Muslims are 17.4 per cent i.e. 1.4 per cent more than the other groups in the lower middle strata 53 per cent were Muslims 17 per cent more then the other groups while in upper middle strata Muslims were 29.2 and other groups 45 per cent i.e. 15.8 per cent less.

Table 3.1: Socio Economic Status.

Sl. No.	*Categories*	*Raw Score*	*Muslim*	*Non Muslim*	*Difference*
1.	Lower & Lower Strata	16 & below	Zero	Zero	Zero
2.	Upper Lower Strata	17 to 32	17.4	16	+ 1.4
3.	Lower Middle Strata	33 to 49	53.0	36	+ 17.0
4.	Upper Middle Strata	50 to 72	29.2	45	–15.8
5.	Upper Strata	73 & above	0.4	3	–2.6
			100.0	100.0	

Source: The table is based on the responses of the questionnaire administered by the researchers.

The same tendency exist with the upper strata were non-Muslims are 3 per cent while Muslims are 0.4 per cent i.e. less than 2.6 per cent. Thus the analysis reveals that in the social economy status most of the Non-Muslims belong to high status group while Muslims in the lower status group. Even among the students studying in the same institution we find that non-Muslims are of higher group compared to Muslim.

Table 3.2: Parental Occupation and Percentage in Different Sample Groups.

Sl No.	*Parental occupation*	*Muslims*		*Non Muslims*		*Differe-nces*
		No.	*%*	*No.*	*%*	
1.	Higher profession group	21	4.2	15	15	–10.8
2.	Average Adm. Group	97	19.4	22	22	–2.6
3.	Clerical/trade/skilled	244	48.8	32	32	+ 16.2
4.	Semi skilled workers	95	19.0	19	19	—
5.	Unskilled workers	35	7.0	12	12	–5.0
6.	Not mentioned	18	1.6	—	—	—
	Total	500	100	100	100	

Source: *Ibid.*

The tables 3.2 shows that in the parental occupation groups which consist of the occupation of the parents or guardians of the respondents, the high profession groups comprising of high administrative job, Gazetted officers, big Doctors, Pleaders, Judges, Engineers, University and college Professors, big factory or farm owners, managerial job and big businessmen etc. the Muslims percentage is 4.2 while non-Muslims is 15 per cent i.e. is Muslims are 10.8 per cent less. In the average administrative groups such as non-Gazetted officers average professionals, average lawyers, doctors, traders, wholesale dealers, high schools or Inter college teacher's, technical job etc. Muslims percentage is 19.4, i.e. 2.6 per cent less than the non-Muslim. In the clerical job or traders such as skilled workers, ordinary businessman, technical workers, farmers, primary or middle school teachers etc. 48.8 per cent are Muslims while 32 per cent are non-Muslims which means that the Muslims are much inclined to these jobs as in the urban area they are mostly associated with certain petty business. In the group of semi skilled workers agriculturists, artisan's, peons or class IV employers both are 19 per cent but with a difference that Muslims are related with the semi skilled jobs while non-Muslims are either government servants like peon or grade IV employees. So far the unskilled labourers, menial and manual workers are concerned Muslims are 7 per cent while non-Muslims are 12 per cent.

Which means that Muslims are 5 per cent less than the non-Muslims working in the urban or rural areas. This 5 per cent is basically Christian students belonging to scheduled tribe picked up and adopted by a catholic society from the poor rural family. 18 per cent Muslim respondents i.e. 1.6 had not mentioned their parental occupation.

It aims at knowing the paternal and maternal educational background of the respondents. There are eight categories; highest among them is the Doctorate degree. Both Muslims and non-Muslims respondents belong to the same category as only 1 per cent of them have Ph.D. degree and so far as the post graduation degrees including professionals like Engineers, Doctors, Lawyers etc. are concerned 6 per cent are Muslims and 15 per cent are non-Muslims i.e. 9 per cent ahead of Muslims. 16.2 per cent Father/Guardians of the Muslim students are graduate while in the case of non-Muslims guardians is 19 per cent i.e. 36 more than Muslims 13.2 per cent. Muslim guardians are merely literates while the ratio is

Table 3.3: Father/Guardians and Mother's Education.

Sl No.	*Variable*	*Muslims*		*Non-Muslims*		*Muslims*		*Non-Muslims*	
		No.	*%*	*No.*	*%*	*No.*	*%*	*No.*	*%*
1.	Doctorate Degree	5	1	1	1	—	—	—	—
2.	Postgraduate including professional	30	6			15	15	—	—
3.	Graduate	81	16.2	19	19	9	1.8	5	5
4.	Intermediate	65	13	8	8	14	2.8	4	4
5.	High School	141	28.2	20	20	82	16.4	22	22
6.	Middle School	72	14.4	21	21	144	28.8	27	27
7.	Elementary/Literate	66	13.2	10	10	103	10.6	17	17
8.	Illiterate	19	3.8	4	4	141	8.2	20	20
9.	Not mentioned	21	4.2	2	2	17	3.4	5	5

Source: *Ibid.*

less in the case of non-Muslims i.e. 10 per cent. If we include those who had not mentioned in the illiterate category 8 per cent Muslim guardians are illiterate, while 6 per cent Non-Muslims including 5 S.T. guardians are illiterates.

So far the educational back ground of the mother is concerned it is divided into six categories 1.8 per cent of the Muslim respondents mothers are graduates or above while among non-Muslim they are 5 per cent so far the illiterate mother are concerned in the class of Muslim it is 28.2 per cent so 20 per cent non-Muslim mother are illiterate i.e. in an average 8.2 per cent more Muslims mother of the Muslim are illiterate then the other. The table further shows that 21 per cent mother of the Muslims respondents have education ranging from high school to graduation and above while in the case of non-Muslim respondents it is 31 per cent i.e. 10 per cent more than Muslims.

The table 3.4 shows that 8.2 Muslims respondents' guardians earn more than Rs. 4500 per month while in the same category the percentage of non-Muslim guardian are 11 per cent. The earning of Muslim guardians between Rs. 3000 to 4500 is 25.4 per cent while 33 per cent non-Muslim guardians earn the same.

Table 3.4: Parents or Guardians Monthly Income.

Sl. No.	Variable	Muslim No.	Muslim %	Non-Muslim No.	Non-Muslim %
1.	More than Rs. 4,500 p.m.	42	8.2	11	11
2.	From Rs. 3,000 to 4,500	127	25.4	33	33
3.	From Rs. 1,500 to 3,000	181	36.2	25	25
4.	From Rs. 800 to 1,500	75	15.2	23	23
5.	From Rs. 250 to 800	40	8	6	6
6.	Not Mentioned	35	7	2	2
	Total	**100**		**100**	

Source: *Ibid.*

If we put the first two categories in one the earning is ranging from Rs. 3000 to 4500 and above, In the case of Muslim it is 33.6 per cent while in the case of non-Muslim it is 44 per cent i.e. 10.4 per cent non-Muslim earn more. The income ranging from Rs. 1500 to 3000 of Muslim guardians is 36.2 per cent while in the same category that of non-Muslim is only 25 per cent This means that on an average the income of Muslim guardians is less than that of non-Muslim, The non-Muslims are in higher income group while lower the Muslim families are.

Table 3.5: Possession of House.

Sl. No.	Variable	Muslims No.	Muslims %	Non-Muslims No.	Non-Muslims %
1.	Own house	302	60.4	38	38
2.	Rented house	195	39.0	62	62
3.	Not mentioned	3	0.6	—	—
	Total	**100**		**100**	

Source: *Ibid.*

It is an economic index and as the table shows 60.4 per cent Muslim respondents live in their own houses while 39 per cent live in the rented houses. On the vice versa 38 per cent non-Muslim testees live in their own houses and 62 per cent in the rented houses which may include the government quarters. It shows that a tendency exits among Muslim to build their own small houses and they prefer to live in their own.

Table 3.6: House Type.

Sl. No.	*Variable*	*Muslims*		*Non-Muslims*	
		No.	*%*	*No.*	*%*
1.	Big Bungalow with lawn telephone etc.	1	0.2	3	3
2.	Pucca House with lawn, electricity	35	7.0	14	14
3.	Pucca House with electricity	225	45.0	60	60
4.	Big Kachcha/Kachcha Pucca mixed	144	28.8	17	17
5.	Small Kachcha house	75	15.0	4	4
6.	Not mentioned	20	4.0	2	2
	Total	**100**		**100**	

Source: *Ibid.*

The table no. 3.6 shows that the percentage of Muslim respondents living in the big Bungalows with lawn and telephone etc. is only 0.2 per cent, while in the case of non-Muslims their percentage is much higher i.e. 3 per cent. Non-Muslim living in Pucca houses with electricity etc.74 per cent while 52 per cent Muslim respondents avail this opportunity 43.8 per cent Muslim students live in Kuchcha Pucca mixed and small mud houses while in the case of Muslims it is 2 per cent only.

Table 3.7: Numbers of Rooms in Houses

Sl. No.	*Variables*	*Muslims*		*Non-Muslims*	
		No.	*%*	*No.*	*%*
1.	6 and more rooms	24	4.8	9	9
2.	5 rooms	27	5.4	8	8
3.	4 rooms	40	8.0	20	20
4.	3 rooms	114	22.8	23	23
5.	2 rooms	237	47.4	30	30
6.	1 room	58	11.6	8	8
7.	Not mentioned	—	—	2	2
	Total	**100**		**100**	

Source: *Ibid.*

Number of rooms occupied by the family members of respondents show the social economic condition of the occupants the table reveals that 37 per cent of the non-Muslim occupied minimum 4 rooms quarter in a house or big bungalows in and the case of Muslims respondents their percentage was 38, 2 per cent the non-Muslim respondents did non mentioned their position.

Table 3.8: Expenditures on Magazine and Books.

Sl. No.	*Variable*	*Muslims*		*Non-Muslims*	
		No.	%	*No.*	%
1.	Spending more than Rs. 100	55	11.0	20	20
2.	Spending Rs. 50 to 100	143	28.6	44	44
3.	Spending Rs. 10 to 50	108	21.6	24	24
4.	Spending nothing	163	32.6	10	10
5.	Not mentioned	31	6.2	2	2
	Total		**100**		**100**

Source: The table is based on the responses of the questionnaire administered by the researchers.

It aims to know the cultural level of the family as judged by the expenditure on newspapers, magazine and books etc. the table shows that only 39.6 per cent Muslim families spend between Rs. 50 and more than Rs. 100 on an average on magazine and books etc. while 64 per cent of the non-Muslim families spend the same amount on magazine, periodicals and books per month 32.6 per cent Muslims spend nothing on Magazine while only 10 per cent non-Muslim are in this category. This shows that a large number of non-Muslims families have a tendency to read magazine and periodicals etc. while Muslims in less number study the same. It may be due to the economic factors or tendency to neglect.

As the table 3.9 shows 32 per cent Muslims families purchase newspapers daily while 46 per cent non-Muslim families are in this category. This means that 14 per cent of the families of Muslims respondents are not in habit of reading newspaper in comparison to non-muslims.

Table 3.9: Purchase of Daily Newspapers.

Sl. No.	*Variable*	*Muslims*		*Non-Muslims*	
		No.	*%*	*No.*	*%*
1.	Purchase daily	160	32	46	46
2.	Purchase occasionally	191	38.2	44	44
3.	Purchase never	145	29	10	10
4.	Not mentioned	4	8	—	
	Total		100		100

Source: Ibid.

The choice of newspaper may vary due to socio economic conditions, knowledge of particular language or taste, as most of the Muslim families prefer Urdu newspapers. 29 per cent of the Muslims families never purchase a single paper while 38.2% occasionally Purchase the paper, in the case of non-Muslims families only 10 per cent never buy while 44 per cent occasionally buy the same.

Table 3.10: Number of Brothers and Sisters.

Sl. No.	*Variable*	*No. of Brother*				*No. of Sisters*			
		Muslims		*Non-Muslims*		*Muslims*		*Non-Muslims*	
		No	*%*	*No*	*%*	*No*	*%*	*No*	*%*
1.	1	57	11.4	14	14	66	13.2	30	30
2.	2	172	34.4	36	36	140	28.0	23	23
3.	3	114	22.8	24	24	115	23.0	14	14
4.	4	78	5.6	19	19	70	14.0	11	11
5.	5	44	8.8	4	4	47	9.4	2	2
6.	6 & more	35	7.0	1	1	29	5.8	4	4
7.	Not mentioned	—	—	2	2	34	6.8	16	16
			100						**100**

Source: Ibid.

In this case an attempt has been made to know the size of the families, as a family having more children has greater liability to fulfil. The table shows that number of members in Muslims families is a bit higher than non-Muslims. The respondents with one to three brothers among Muslims are 68.6 per cent while in the case of non-Muslims it is 74 per cent. The students having one to three sister among Muslims are 64.2 per cent while among non-muslims it is 67 per cent the families with only one child among non-muslims are 22 per cent while among Muslim it is 12.3 per cent with regard to the number of sister 16 per cent non-Muslims respondents preferred not to mention the number while in the case of Muslim respondents only 6.8 per cent did not mention the exact number of sister.

Table 3.11: Education of Brothers and Sisters.

Sl. No.	*Variable*	*Brother*				*Sisters*			
		Muslims		*Non-Muslims*		*Muslims*		*Non-Muslims*	
		No	*%*	*No*	*%*	*No*	*%*	*No*	*%*
1.	Post graduate & above	50	10	43	43	—	—	—	—
2.	Graduation	69	13.9	18	18	30	6.8	50	50
3.	Intermediate	101	20.2	10	10	42	8.4	20	20
4.	High school	206	41.2	10	10	288	57.6	9	9
5.	Not mentioned	74	14.8	19	19	140	28.0	21	21
					100		**100**		**100**

Source: Ibid.

It was to know the educational level of siblings of the respondents. The table shows that 23.9 per cent Muslims respondents have brothers who are graduates, postgraduates and above while in the case of non-Muslims their number is comparatively higher than the Muslims i.e. 61 per cent of the lead of 37.2 per cent while only 20 per cent non-Muslims respondents have brothers with high level or intermediate level of education. In the case of Muslims it is 61.4 per cent i.e. 41.4 per cent more than the non-Muslims. So far the sister's education is concerned 70 per cent non-Muslims respondents have sister with intermediate or graduation or higher level of education. In the case of Muslims it is only 15.2 per cent. It means that among non-Muslims there is 54.8 per cent higher female education that is far ahead of Muslims. Only 9 per cent non-Muslims respondents mentioned that their sisters have education up to high school standards while in the case of Muslims it is 57.6.

Table 3.12: Level of Aspiration—Academic.

Sl. No.	*Variable*	*Muslim*		*Non Muslims*	
		No.	*%*	*No.*	*%*
1.	Post Graduate & Professional	200	40	50	50
2.	Up to Graduate	150	30	32	32
3.	Intermediate	50	10	10	10
4.	High School	20	4	5	5
	Not mentioned	80	16	3	3
	Total	**500**	**100**	**100**	**100**

Source: *Ibid*.

It is a psychological indicator and an attempt has been made to seek an information about the future academic aspiration of the tastes which they want to achieve. 70 per cent Muslim respondents want to achieve Graduation or Professional degrees while 82 per cent non-muslims respondents preferred for the same. 40 per cent Muslims respondents have opted for the highest degrees in the case of non-muslims it is 50 per cent and 16 per cent Muslims respondents did not mentioned their academic choice. This may be due to the fact that they have not yet planned their future academic target or do not know what they want to achieve or should try to achieve. In the case of non-Muslims it is only 3 per cent meaning that most of them have planned their academic life. Academic aspiration to achieve High School/Intermediate degree in both the groups is more or less the same i.e. 14 and 15 per cent respectively.

The table 3.12 shows that 50.6 per cent Muslims respondent opted for Doctor, Engineer, Professors Executives and Managerial jobs while 23.8 per cent preferred to became social worker, 'artist' and traders etc. In the case of non-muslims it is

61 per cent and 16 per cent respectively. This shows that ambition for higher position among non-Muslim respondents is 10 per cent more than Muslims. For middle class jobs Muslims are much inclined in comparison to non-muslims. For the profession of mechanic salesmen, School teachers, clerks and accountants etc. 20.4 per cent Muslims and 22 per cent non-muslim respondents opted.

Table 3.13: Level of Aspiration-Professional.

Sl. No.	*Variable*	*Muslim*		*Non Muslims*	
		No.	*%*	*No.*	*%*
1.	Engineer, Dr., Professional	253	50.6	61	61
2.	Social worker, Artist	119	23.8	16	16
3.	Mechanic, Clerk, Salesman	102	20.4	22	22
4.	Not mentioned	26	52	1	1
	Total	**500**	**100**	**100**	**100**

Source: *Ibid*.

The result of the socio-economic status scale of the Muslims of Bihar shows that the students studying at various schools and colleges belonging to the lower middle strata among Muslims were higher i.e. 70.4 per cent while among non-muslims it was 52 per cent, a difference of 18.4 per cent. So far the upper middle and upper strata is concerned, their percentages were 29.6 and 48 respectively maintaining a difference of 18.2 per cent. This means that those Muslims families which can afford to teach their wards at school and in colleges, were still poor in comparison to those non-Muslim students who are either their class mates or are studying in more or less same types of educational institutions in the surroundings. Further the parents of Muslim students are less qualified, their monthly income is less. Living in bad condition houses with less amenities and spending less money on magazines and Newspapers in comparison to non-Muslim respondents. Also the number of family members (brothers and sisters) among the Muslim family is more in comparison to those of non-Muslims. So far as the education of these siblings is concerned non-Muslims are in a very better position i.e. 44 per cent and 15.2 per cent brother and sister of Muslim respondents are at Intermediate and above, while 71 per cent and 70 per cent of the non-Muslims respondents respectively are Intermediate and above, even the academic and professional aspiration among the Muslim respondents are less than the non-muslims.

The Bihar state Minorities Commission in its report submitted to the government of Bihar in January 2005 highlighted that Muslims have sunk to the bottom from a relatively mid income position. Though the report is related exclusively to the condition of Muslims of Bihar but the situation in the newly created Jharkhand is not better but even worst as the new regime of the Jharkhand *too is being governed during this period by the party whose very existence is anti minorities.* The said report is the study of socio-economic status of the Muslims of Bihar based on the comprehensive survey covering 8,159 households both rural and urban areas of the 20 out of 37 districts of Bihar covering 169 villages and 14 town's altogether.

According to the 1991 census 87 per cent of the Muslims in Bihar live in rural areas while remaining 13 per cent in urban areas. The report says that though the Islamic ethos is basically egalitarian and in religious text no division of society ordained by birth is indicated but due to long interaction with Hindus, the Indian Muslims also got divided among castes. The survey identified 43 castes amongst the Muslim of Bihar in which 40.9 per cent both in rural as well as urban areas are upper castes. The economic condition of the Muslims in Bihar is very low endowed with lesser amount of land related and non land resources and mostly engaged in low paid jobs in the unorganized sector or in self employment activities where returns are very poor on account of the very limited access to resources. Their low-income levels affect their position in all other sectors. The over all literacy rate among the Muslims in Bihar is lower than the general population and to the extent of educational exclusion is substantial among young Muslims, death rates among the Muslims are also higher than that for the general population indicating the inferior health conditions prevailing among them and life expectancy is lower. There is thus a large and widening economic and social distance between the Muslims in Bihar and other communities.

The said Bihar state minorities commission report shows that 49.5 per cent of rural Muslim households and 44.8 per cent of those in the urban areas live below the poverty line as defined by the national sample survey organization (NSSO) and the planning commission of India. The NSSO data reveals that 44.3 per cent of the general population of Bihar in the rural areas and 32.9 per cent in the urban areas fall below the poverty line. As per the said report 87 per cent of the Muslim population lives in the rural areas and they derive their income mainly from the low wage occupation of agricultural labours (39.6 percent) remittances from out migrant members of the house holds (24.5 per cent) and other self employment categories (19.1 percent) while in the urban areas 48 per cent comes from wages or salary 33 per cent from other self employment categories and 9.3 per cent from remittances.

Very few Muslim houses hold both in urban and rural areas have access to decent employment sources like jobs in government and semi government organizations and in the organized sector. For the entire working population, the share of the organized sector employment will be about four per cent in the rural areas and six per cent in the urban areas. Only 10 per cent of the wage and salary earners have employment in government jobs, and the remaining vast majority of the salaried workers or wage earners are employed either in the unorganized private sector or in other organization like trusts NGOs etc. This pattern is by and large similar in both rural and urban areas. It is therefore not surprising that the percentage of Muslim workers not enjoying the benefits of a regular employment of provident fund facilities is as high as 92.5 per cent in the rural and 85.6 per cent in the urban areas. No doubt the proportion of workers employed in the organized service is low even for the general population but for the Muslim population it is so low that it cannot be explained except in terms of the segmentation of the labour market to the disadvantages of the Muslim workers.

The average Muslim worker employed in the organized private sector earns about Rs. 1770 and Rs. 3520 per month in rural and urban areas respectively. This is because that most of the Muslim workers are in lower order jobs in the organized private sector. The earning levels in the unorganized private sector where the large majority of the Muslim workers are employed are even lower—the average monthly income being just over Rs. 1000 and Rs. 1200 in the rural and urban areas respectively. 28.4 per cent of the rural Muslims workers are landless labours, and as the prevailing wage rates are so low (Rs. 23.73 in off season and Rs. 28.15 in peak season) the average earning of these labourers is less than Rs. 600 per month.

Due to poverty and lack of employment opportunities in their place of residence, out migration of workers of the Muslim household in Bihar is a common phenomenon. According to the present survey 12.7 per cent of the urban Muslim households had migrated to their present residence after 1971. For every 100 Muslim household, in rural Bihar there are about 63 Male out migrants. In other words two out of every three Muslims households in the rural areas send at least one each of their working members away to earn income and most of the Muslim migrants are males with an average age of 28.5 years. The low level of income lead not only to the low consumption levels but also to consumption loans for their biological existence. An about 45.1 per cent of the Muslim household in rural Bihar took loan an average amount of outstanding loan per indebted household is Rs. 16,380.

The living condition of the Muslim both in urban and rural areas is deplorable. Their houses are smaller in size, they possess cheaper durable goods—bicycles, radios, tables, chairs and clocks etc and relatively expensive durable goods like scooters, motor cycles, refrigerators, television and telephone sets are worse off.

The Muslim population in Bihar has by and large remained deprived of benefits from the government poverty alleviation programmes, out of five such programmes that are essentially employment and income oriented, IRDP is the only one which has reached some rural Muslim house holds (5.3%). The others welfare oriented poverty alleviation programmes are practically non-existent for the Muslims both in rural and urban areas. Even the minority finance corporation (MFC) scheme specially designed to help Muslims and other minority practically does not exist for the Muslims in Bihar.

The average level of health standards of Muslims in Bihar is worse off than that of the general population. This is borne out by the figures of the birth rate, death rate, extent of immunization and intake of nutritious food and other related data. The estimated birth rate for the Muslims in Bihar was found to be 33.8 per cent in rural and 25.9 per cent in urban areas. The death rates among the Muslims in Bihar are also higher than that of the general population. The estimates from the present survey show the death rates among the Muslims to be 10.5 per cent and 7.7 per cent in the rural and urban areas respectively as compared to 9.8 per cent and 6.8 per cent respectively for the general population and so the life expectancy is lower among Muslims prefer to government health centers or hospitals but Muslim access to this public facility is practically absent in rural areas and extremely limited in the urban areas. According to the said survey 91.4 per cent of the rural areas and 78.5 per cent in urban areas the birth of the Muslims population in Bihar take place at home, with the traditional dais acting as the mid wives.

So far the participation in social institutions are concerned in spite of the per cent in combined Bihar and Jharkhand only 1.5 per cent of the rural households and 1.8 per cent of urban areas have a member participating in Panchayat a municipality administration.

So far the sense of insecurity is concerned they have a growing sense of insecurity due to the rise of majoritarian chauvinism. Quite a sizeable proportion of the respondents found the police trust worthy during communal disturbance or tension as only 28.2 per cent of the Muslim households in the rural areas and 23.9 per cent of them in the urban areas found the police to be unbiased during such happenings.

Due to poverty, poor living conditions, inferior health conditions and lack of investment have put Muslims at the bottom rung. Poverty alleviation programme have not helped them. So far the literacy rates is concerned in the rural areas the overall literacy rate among the Muslims in Bihar according to the present survey is 38 per cent which is lower than for the general population and 44.4 per cent and due to economic constraints they are not able to utilize the better educational opportunities as what so ever are available there. Due to their poverty a large number of students prefer to go to government schools that are not functioning better. About 17.7 per cent of the rural areas and 32.2 per cent in the urban areas go to private educational institutions but these are ordinary private schools not the expensive one which has come out like mushroom growth in every street and corners. Textbooks are must and minimum for every school going children but these are available to only about two thirds of the Muslims students both in the rural and urban areas. About one tenth of the Muslim students do not possess any textbooks, which cripple their educational development. The other facilities provided by the government in the form of financial assistance is reported to be received only by 24 per cent of the Muslim students in rural areas and much lower proportion of 13.8 per cent in the urban areas. In view of the wide poverty among the Muslim households this level of assistance is utterly inadequate. Private tuition has become a necessity for students these days mainly because of low quality of teaching in the schools. Only 22.7 per cent of the Muslim students in the rural areas and 29.2 per cent in the urban areas avail themselves of this opportunity. Another indication of the Muslims not being able to send their children to very good schools because low levels of their incomes is that only 2.6 per cent of the Muslims students in the rural areas and slightly more in the urban areas have English as their medium of instructions. The over whelming proportion of them (as much as 97.3%) in the rural and about 90 per cent in the urban areas receive their education through the medium of either Hindi or Urdu. It is significant that the number of Muslim students receiving education through the medium of Hindi is quite high both in rural (56.8%) and in the urban areas (71.2%).

Due to the poor condition of education in the state of Bihar practically all the bright and promising students from Bihar whose parents can afford to migrate for education outside the state after completing school education. Some of them migrate even earlier. However since the economic condition of the Muslims in Bihar is generally weak, this kind of migration is less among them. The present survey shows that out of every 100 Muslim house holds only 3.5 and 2.6 students from the rural and urban areas respectively migrate for education.

The gender differences in literacy rates much narrower among the Muslims than among the general population. Muslim of Bihar show a strong desire for educating their children, both boys and girls, in spite of their economical condition being much worse than that of the general population. There is a substantial improvement in school enrolment among the children of Muslim population and much of the increase in enrolment is because of the higher enrolment in schools for girls now is only marginally lower than for the boys. There is also a decline in the dropout rates of school going children of the Muslims of the present generation.

Quite a sizeable percentage of the Muslims households in Bihar particularly from the rural areas send their children to Madrasas. Many of the households do so because they either have no access to or find the conditions extremely in hospitable in the only other in expensive system of education i.e. government schools. The percentage of the households sending their children to Madarsas in the urban areas drops down to nine which is explained by the availability of other types of educational institutions and perhaps the relatively better functioning of the government schools in the urban areas, Only 3.4 per cent of the parents in the rural households and 3.1%in the urban house holds showed a preference for religious education alone for their boys. However a much higher percentage of the parents (26.3%) particularly in rural areas would like their girls to have religious education. The corresponding figures for parents in the urban areas is 12.2 per cent.

4

The Concept of Minorities and Situation of Indian Muslims

The problems of minorities are a universal phenomenon. Each and every state of the world today has some kind of minorities. The Encyclopedia Americana confirms, "The movement of peoples, Ideologies and political boundaries have meant that distinctive minorities have been common phenomenon through out history."[1]

Although existence of minorities is universal, the nature of minority problems is not always and everywhere the same. It has differed and taxed the brains of statesman, thinkers and social scientists so much that there have been wars as a result of wrong methods to deal with it. Number of national and international treaties have been concluded for the protection of minorities at different intervals of history. So one of the pressing and urgent tasks before the modern government is to secure adequate and effective protection to them and to associate them in the work of administration Since the beginning of the 19th century with the rise of democracy the problems of minorities have become a serious political question and has played a great role in national and international affairs. Hamayun Kabir in his lecture asserts, "There can be no question of minorities except in a democracy. Unless there is democracy the problem would not arise in that form at all."[2] The first and foremost criterion of a democratic system is the recognition of equal rights and duties for all irrespective of caste, creed, sex, place of birth, religion or language etc. it is only democracy that recognizes different minorities and provides them equal treatment. It is also often stated that the efficiency of democracy lies in giving fair treatment to minorities. On the other hand minorities have no place in a totalitarian setup where every thing exists for the state. So minorities cannot keep their separate identities their in. they have to submerge themselves in the state itself. The problem of minorities as such is essentially a problem of democracy.

Grammatically speaking, the term minority is compound of Latin word 'minor' and the suffix 'ity' meaning inter alia the smaller in number of two aggregates that together constitute a whole or "the smaller number out of a whole divided into two".[3] According to Webster Dictionary, "minority is a racial, religious, ethnic or political group that differs from the larger controlling group".[4] But the concept of minority in social context is difficult to define as before the world war I. American as well as European dictionaries defined minority only in its legal, arithmetical and political meaning. In the middle twenties the Encyclopedia Britannica had no article on minorities.[5] More as neither the treaty of Versailles nor the League of Nations ever gave an exact definition of a minority. They either mentioned by name the minority they intended to protect or simply referred to inhabitants of a country who differ from the majority of the population in race, language, and religion.[6] Even the U.N.O. gave an agreed definition of minority only in 1950. The earliest edition of Encyclopedia Britannica containing a detailed article on minorities appeared in 1953. It defined minority as a "group held together by ties of common descent, language or religious faith and feeling themselves different in these respects from the majority of the inhabitants of a given political entity".[7]

In this way, the definition stresses more on the word feeling, which is psychological in nature than to scientific. International Encyclopedia of social sciences says that "contemporary sociologist generally defines minority as a group of people differentiated from others in the same society by race, nationality, religions or language who think of themselves a differentiated group or are thought so by others with negative connotation". It further add that "the important element in their differentiation is a set of attitude of persecution mania within the group and of prejudice from without—and a set of behaviours—those of group identification and self preservation within and discrimination and exclusion from without".

J.A. Laponce provided two definitions, one purely objective and another purely subjective, according to the former "A minority group whose, race, language, or religion is different from that of majority".[8] The United Nation Sub Commissions on Prevention of Discrimination and Protection of Minorities furnishes followings definitions, the term minority includes only those non-dominant groups in a population which possess and wish to preserve stable ethnic, religious or linguistic traditions or characteristics markedly different from those of the rest of the population".[9] The main point in this definition is that minorities are those groups of people, which want to preserve their separate identities and are not willing to be assimilated with the rest of the population. Prof. Louis Wirth at the World Congress of Sociology, held in Switzerland in 1950, emphasized on the inferior status of minorities by defining them as groups distinguished from the rest of the society by racial or cultural characteristics (which have) become objects of differentials and inferior treatment and (have) develop(ed) a consciousness of their inferior status".[10] This idea of recognizing inferior status and giving inferior treatment to minorities is old which goes against the spirit of democracy and concept of equality and morality.

To sum up a minority usually possess the following characteristics:

- It is held together by common bond of ethnic, religious and linguistic characteristics distinct from the majority.
- Its numerical strength is less than the half of the total population of a given society.
- It has grievances regarding differential treatment meted out to it, and it has limited access to economic and political spheres.
- It considers itself as distinct from others and others also think it as a separate and distinct entity.

- It has a sense of insecurity, which finds expression in its physical, social, emotional and psychological behavioural pattern.
- It considers itself as under-privileged having inferior status.

Classification of Minorities

Minorities may broadly be classified as under:

(a) Political minority
(b) Economically dominant minority
(c) Cultural minority
(d) Religious and linguistic minority
(e) Racial minority

(A) *Political Minority* may further be segregated as:

(i) *Minority as a ruler*—Supreme upholder of power as it possesses the power of legislature, executive and judiciary. A distinct class in itself, through special prerogatives and privileges, which are denied to the majority. British Raj in India or white racial rule in the South Africa.
(ii) *Minority as equal partners*—Not enjoying any special privileges be on equal basis but having grievances ranged from physical insecurity to will full neglects in all walks of life.

(B) *Economically dominant minority*—The small minority owing the major slice of national cake, through manipulation and having control over the administrative structure, e.g. Parsis in India and Jews in USA.
(C) *Cultural minority*—A subgroup differentiating itself on the basis of cultural heritage and identities.
(D) *Religious and linguistic minority*—A group or subgroup with different religious faith or languages with its own

script, numerous in any society. Muslim, Sikh; Christian etc. are such minority in India.

(E) *Racial minority*—A group or subgroup considering race as the basis of differences e.g. Negroes in America, Whites of the South Africa or Rhodesia.

General Problems of Minority

Some major problems of the minority are universal in nature, faced by them in every day life. They complain of insecurity of life, honour and property as the occurrences of frequent communal, racial and linguistic riots are the common phenomenon and the minority suffers more losses in all respects. They have a feeling of discrimination in all walks of life and are afraid of cultural, religious invasion by the majority and want prompt redressel of their grievances which usually are not fulfilled or delayed, ultimately leaving them alienated, fatalist or react violently by losing faith in constitutional methods. A backward and segregated minority either rationalizes its present status as pre-ordained or unscrupulous leadership may exploit its injured feelings. As the minority loses faith in all government machinery it also loses aspiration to progress or prosper. Sociologically it has been proved by numerous studies that children of higher socio-economic origin are more likely to yearn plan for and achieve higher educational and occupational goals than the children of lower socio-economic origin (Ralph,[11] Pitirim,[12] Sewell, Orenstein,[13] Parsons[14] etc.)

Some Prominent Characteristics of Indians Muslims

In the political parlance of modern India the Muslims have been recognized as the religious and linguistic minorities as they follow Islam and majority of them speak Urdu as their mother tongue. They are not ethnic minority as racially Muslims in any part of India belong to the same ethnic stock as the rest of the population. The flesh and the blood are the same as there are close cultural affinities.[15] Muslims in India are the largest single significant minority and before the partition they stood in the ratio of one to four of the whole population. At present it is the home of 105,554,812 Muslims i.e. roughly 12 per cent of the total population of the country and next only to Indonesia (191 million) and Bangladesh (117 million) it has the largest Muslims concentration in the world. All other minorities in India put together (Christians 2.32%, Sikh 1.96%, Buddhist 0.77%, Jains 0.41%, Zoroastrians/Parsis 0.01% etc) account for not more than 5.46 per cent. Muslims are spread in almost every state and union territory in considerable number. In certain areas their population is larger than even national average e.g. in Lancadive Minicoy & Amindivi Island (94.31%), J&K (67.1 3 estimated) and the Assam, West Bengal, Kerala, UP and Bihar they are—28.43, 23.33, 17.33 and 14.88 per cent respectively of the total population of the country.[16]

The Muslims kings ruled over the country for more than seven centuries and according to Prof. Rasheeduddin Khan "Muslim mass psychology (however irrational and factually untenable) reveals a subjective awareness of their collective superiority, born out of seven hundred years of Muslims hegemony in the Indo-Gangetic Plains and Deccan".[17] This statement may be true for the very microscopic Muslim elite but the fate of Muslim masses was not better than their counter parts in the majority community as most of them are converted Muslim without any change in their socio-economic status and occupational pattern with same racial stock and common heritage. So far the Muslim elite is concerned, this group always enjoyed all the material comforts and social position, but is the most egoistic in thought and practice, opportunist to the extent of using their co-religionists for their selfish ends without identifying with them and contributing very little to the welfare of them. Muslim masses generally consider it as the mouthpiece of the party in power and feel that these are just a showpiece carved out to decorate the picture of secularism. Muslim masses are still a backward lot both economically and educationally and it appears that they have fallen in the vicious circle of poverty, depressions, frustration, educational backwardness and isolation.

To understand the genesis of Muslim self-estrangement, their fatalistic and despondent attitude, their frustration which has alienated them from the mainstream of national life and made them socio-economically and educationally backward. It is necessary to analyze the problem and grievances delicate and complex, real or imaginary, which the community is facing.

1. Frequent Eruption of Communal Riots and State Terrorism

The continued eruption of large-scale communal riots (an estimated 15,500 anti Muslim riots or an average of one and a half riots per day[18] erupted in the country between 1947-84) from time to time is one of the major problems the community is facing. Regarding the planning and execution of riots in post independent India, Pandit Nehru the first Prime Minister of Independent India once remarked "Generally speaking, the Muslims do not and cannot think of any deliberate aggressive activity, both by virtue of their numbers and their general position in the country, they are frustrated and weak and they know well that any aggression on their part will lead to their own suffering."[18A] Regardless of which side starts the riots, the Muslims are generally the worst losers in terms of lives lost and property destroyed.[19] Indian Muslims have an impression that the police and law enforcing authorities always operate particularly during riots under the influence of communal parties and politicians in a biased manner and they will never get any justice from them.[20] Government always tries to keep Muslims " defensive and demoralized atmosphere, tenterhooks and their family equilibrium instable."[21] Justice Krishna Iyer in his letter addressed to the Union Home Minister P.C. Sethi dated November 1982 wrote "The prima-facie feeling is strong that the PAC has got into the narrow living spaces of huddled Muslims families and shot several males in cold blood".[22] M.N. Buch a civil servant narrating his own experiences says "even today many highly placed Hindus still look upon every Muslims as potential Pakistani... As a District Magistrate I still remember the secret instructions we used to receive from the

Government not only to keep a watchful eye on Muslims in any law and order situation but also to seize even licensed weapons if the occasion demanded it, while no similar instructions were ever received about potential Hindu troublemakers.[23] N.C. Saxena in his report on Meerut riots (1982) maintained that "in riots it has been noticed that the presence of Administration and police forces suddenly disappeared for few hours when most of the (planned) incidents of looting, arson and murders took place ...in many places police forces behaved like mob and committed atrocities...The District Administration perceived threat to public peace only from Muslims and therefore they choose to take one sided action... The orders from the senior officers in the district to the police could be summarized in one phases i.e., Muslims must be taught a lesson. The Provincial Armed Constable (PAC) and other police forces faithfully implemented this policy".[24] The role-played by Bihar Military Police (BMP), Rajasthan Armed Constabulary (RAC) etc. during riot is also notorious. The role of BMP in the Jamshedpur riots of April 1979 described by an eyewitness is chilling, "11&12th the first two worst days of rioting the BMP and state police forces had a field. It looked as if some R.S.S. officer commanded the BMP. These forces went into action just a few hours after the outbreak of violence, driving into Muslim bustees in a deliberate pick and hit style.[25] Recent Gujrat riots was basically a massacre by the state armed police force.

Peter Van Derveer in his article 'Riot and Rituals: The construction of violence and Public space in Hindu nationalism', wrote "Riots in India I have witnessed or read about were more often well planned and well defined targets and rules. In some cases you know exactly when and where to expect them to begin and end as if they were rituals. Both rituals and riots play significant roles in the construction of social identities."[26]

Ravi Nair, Director of South Asian Human Rights Documentation Centre while reporting about the Bombay Program 1993 reveals that the over whelming majority of the people killed by police were Muslims. Some how the police bullet hits the Muslims, not the Hindus. It is this perception and policy direction of teaching Muslim a lesson, comments Iqbal A. Ansari, "which has caused the security force to act as a terrorist forces".[27] Muslim elites (Politicians, social activists, religious leader's, educationist, professional and journalist etc.) believe that anti Muslim violence is planned and executed to render Muslims economically, educationally and socially crippled and as a final outcome of that economic, educational and social backwardness assimilate them into the lower rungs of Hindu society. The official reports released from time to time regarding the casualties during communal riots reveal as following table shows.

Table 4.1: Casualties in Communal Riots in India.

		KILLED					*INJURED*				
Year	*No. of Incidents*	*H*	*M*	*O*	*P*	*T*	*H*	*M*	*O*	*P*	*T*
1954	84	N.A	N.A	N.A	N.A	34	N.A	N.A	N.A	N.A	512
1955	75	N.A	N.A	N.A	N.A	24	N.A	N.A	N.A	N.A	457
1956	82	N.A	N.A	N.A	N.A	82	N.A	N.A	N.A	N.A	575
1957	58	N.A	N.A	N.A	N.A	12	N.A	N.A	N.A	N.A	316
1958	40	N.A	N.A	N.A	N.A	7	N.A	N.A	N.A	N.A	369
1959	42	N.A	N.A	N.A	N.A	41	N.A	N.A	N.A	N.A	1344
1960	26	N.A	N.A	N.A	N.A	14	N.A	N.A	N.A	N.A	262
1961	92	N.A	N.A	N.A	N.A	108	N.A	N.A	N.A	N.A	593
1962	60	N.A	N.A	N.A	N.A	43	N.A	N.A	N.A	N.A	348
1963	61	N.A	N.A	N.A	N.A	26	N.A	N.A	N.A	N.A	489
1964	1070	N.A	N.A	N.A	N.A	1919	N.A	N.A	N.A	N.A	2053
1965	173	N.A	N.A	N.A	N.A	173	N.A	N.A	N.A	N.A	758
1966	144	N.A	N.A	N.A	N.A	45	N.A	N.A	N.A	N.A	467
1967	198	N.A	N.A	N.A	N.A	25	N.A	N.A	N.A	N.A	880
1968	346	24	99	10	N.A	133	445	45	403	240	1549
1969	519	66	558	49	1	674	796	1000	806	276	2877
1970	521	68	176	54	N.A	298	656	731	220	116	1723
1971	321	38	65	N.A	N.A	103	603	606	54	57	1330
1972	240	21	45	3	1	70	541	407	108	151	1207
1973	242	26	45	1	N.A	72	648	456	169	232	1500
1974	248	26	61	N.A	N.A	87	566	435	122	143	1266
1975	205	11	22	N.A	N.A	33	444	277	169	72	962
1976	169	20	19	N.A	N.A	39	391	330	40	33	794

(Contd.)

(Contd.)

Year	No. of Incidents	KILLED					INJURED				
		H	M	O	P	T	H	M	O	P	T
1977	188	12	24	N.A	N.A	36	563	385	63	111	1122
1978	219	51	56	1	N.A	108	752	711	212	126	1801
1979	304	80	150	31	N.A	261	N.A	N.A	N.A	N.A	2379
1980	427	87	278	10	N.A	375	N.A	N.A	N.A	N.A	2691
1981	319	N.A	N.A	N.A	N.A	196	N.A	N.A	N.A	N.A	2613
1982	474	N.A	N.A	N.A	N.A	236	N.A	N.A	N.A	N.A	3025
1983	500	N.A	N.A	N.A	N.A	1143	N.A	N.A	N.A	N.A	3652
1984	476	N.A	N.A	N.A	N.A	445	N.A	N.A	N.A	N.A	4836
1985	525	N.A	N.A	N.A	N.A	328	N.A	N.A	N.A	N.A	3665
1986	764	N.A	N.A	N.A	N.A	418	N.A	N.A	N.A	N.A	5321
1987	711	N.A	N.A	N.A	N.A	762	N.A	N.A	N.A	N.A	7653
1988	671	N.A	N.A	N.A	N.A	802	N.A	N.A	N.A	N.A	8762
1989	634	N.A	N.A	N.A	N.A	739	N.A	N.A	N.A	N.A	7438
1990	564	N.A	N.A	N.A	N.A	639	N.A	N.A	N.A	N.A	6892
1991	656	N.A	N.A	N.A	N.A	817	N.A	N.A	N.A	N.A	8920
1992	1601	N.A	N.A	N.A	N.A	3009	N.A	N.A	N.A	N.A	10417
1993	2292	N.A	N.A	N.A	N.A	952	N.A	N.A	N.A	N.A	2989
1994	179	N.A	N.A	N.A	N.A	78	N.A	N.A	N.A	N.A	794
1995	99	N.A	N.A	N.A	N.A	36	N.A	N.A	N.A	N.A	380
1996	728	N.A	N.A	N.A	N.A	209	N.A	N.A	N.A	N.A	2057
1997	725	N.A	N.A	N.A	N.A	264	N.A	N.A	N.A	N.A	2503
1998	626	N.A	N.A	N.A	N.A	207	N.A	N.A	N.A	N.A	2065

Sources:
1. Bureau of Police Research & Development. Ministry of House Affairs, Government of India.
2. P.R. Rajgopal, *Communal Violence in India* 1987, New Delhi Uppal Pub. House, pp. 16-19.
3. Syed Shahabuddin, *Muslim India*, New Delhi, No. 134 p. 156.

The Table 4.1 shows that there is not a single year since independence when communal peace was not disturbed in a big or small manner. It further shows that Government published the data of casualties only for 10 years i.e. between 1968-1978 and even during those periods casualty among Muslim were very high. Only in Bhagalpur riot (1989) out of 1481 casualty 1378 were Muslims and 35,000 Muslim families were rendered homeless, 3,000 Muslims were arrested where as only 700 non-Muslims were arrested.[28] While the majority member Commission report accused 14 police official including S.P., S.I. and other civil administration directly responsible for the riot. According to one I.P.S. officer Vibhuti Narain Rai in over half the riots the percentage of Muslim killed is over 90 per cent of the total casualties. In the Bhiwandi riots of 1970 for instance, a total of 78 people were killed in which according to Home Ministry own admissions only 17 were Hindus & remaining Muslims. In the subsequent Jalgaon riots 43 people were killed one Hindu & rest Muslim. Of the total property destroyed Muslim incurred a loss of Rs. 33.9 lakhs while Hindus suffered damaged of Rs. 83,725 only.[29] The story is the same of almost all the riots when the Muslims were butchered; even in Bombay riots eyewitness accounts from both the communities testify to the massacre of innocent Muslims. Another striking feature of the pattern of communal violence is that generally riots occur in the Muslim business and small industrial sector, for example they adversely affected Beri industries of Muslims of Jabalpur and Bihar Sharif, Brass industry of Moradabad or lock industry of Aligarh etc.

Table 4.2: Riot Prone Area.

Andhra Pradesh:	Adilabad, Hyderabad, Karimnagar, Karnal, Medak, Nalgonda, Nizamabad, Rangard.
Assam:	Cachar, Darrang, Golpara, Kamrup, Nowgong
Bihar:	Bhagalpur, Bhojpur, Champaran (East & West), Darbhanga, Gaya, Gridih, Gopalganj, Hazaribagh, Jamshedpur, Madhubani, Monger, Nalanda, Patna, Purnea, Ranchi, Santhal Pargana, Siwan, Singhbhum and Sitamarhi.
Delhi:	Central Delhi, East Delhi and West Delhi.
Gujrat:	Ahmadabad, Baroda, Banaskantha, Bharuch, Jamnagar, Junagarh, Kheda, Panch Mahal, Sabar Kantha and Surat.
Kerela:	Cannore, Mellapuram, Trichur, Trevandrum.
Karnataka:	Bangalore, Bidar, Dharwar, Gulbarga, Kular, Mysore and South Kanara.

(*Contd.*)

(*Contd.*)

Madhya Pradesh:	Bhopal, Chhindwara, Damoh, Indore, Jabalpur, Khandwa, Khargona, Mandsaur, Raigharh, Raisen, Ratlan, Sagar, Sahore, Scone, Shajapur, Ujjan and Vidisha.
Maharashtra:	Ahmadnagar, Akola, Amravati, Greater Bombay, Buldhana, Nasik, Parbhani, Pune and Thane.
Orissa:	Balasore and Cuttack.
Rajisthan:	Bhilwara, Chitorgarh, Jodhpur, Jaipur, Kota, Nagaur, Pali and Udaipur.
Tamilnadu:	Arcot (North & South), Coimbatore, Dharanpur, Madurai, Ramantapuran, Tiruneiveli, Trichi.
Uttar Pradesh:	Agra, Alighar, Allahabad, Azamghar, Badaun, Bahraich, Banda, Barabanki, Bareily, Basti, Bijnore, Buland Shahar, Deoria, Faizabad, Fatchnagar, Ghaziabad, Ghazipur, Gonda, Gorakhpur, Jaunpur, Kanpur, Lucknow, Mathura, Meerut, Moradabad, Muzaffarnagar, Nainital, Pilibhit, Partupgarh, Rae Bareilly, Rampur, Saharanpur, Shahjahanabad, Sitapur, Sultanpur, Varanasi.
West Bengal:	Calcutta, Murshidabad, Nadia & 24 Pargana.

Source: Muslim India April 83, p. 166—Quoting Govt. of India.

The table 4.2 shows that though anti Muslim riots is a common feature in the post independence India and spread throughout the country. But the district having very thin Muslim population like coastal Andhra hill, district of UP with Muslim majority etc. or Muslim majority area like Malapuram in Kerala or Murshidabad in WestBengal etc. has less case of riots. Further riots usually erupt in urban areas than the rural belt though recent trend show that it can be planned everywhere. Industrial cities like Bombay, Bhiwandi, Baroda, Surat, Kanpur, Moradabad, Meerut, Jamshedpur, Ranchi, Rourkela etc. where it was considered that the working class solidarity would be stronger have not been immune from the riots. The following table shows riot prone areas where communal violence erupts frequently.

In every riots since independence no matter when and how or where the riots take place; no matter who started the riots, in the end the victims are mainly and only Muslims who lose their lives, property and honour. "It has a big problem, has very bad and unhappy memories behind it," remarks Syed Hamid, "it continues to tarnish the fair image of this great country, have had an unsettling effect on the Muslims and have weakened their resolve to improve themselves educationally, socially & communally".[30] It is a common feeling that riots could, however be checked if the government and local administration took their duty seriously, lack of clear headed policy and determination on their parts are responsible for its wide spread as the rioters are not motivated like terrorist who could risk life or limb.

2. *Discrimination against Muslims*

It is a common feeling among the Muslim elites (Politician, Social activists, religious leaders, academicians, professional and Journalist etc.) as well as masses that state agencies discriminate against them in all spheres of life, be it law and order, welfare scheme, education or health etc. Bias against them started even before India got independence when Intrim Congress Government issued a secret circulars executive policy decisions and understandings have barred recruitment of Muslims from the rank of an ordinary peon to the position of chief secretaries in the ministries.[31] Union Home Ministry headed by Sardar Patel issued such circular to state Home Ministries not to recruit Muslims at all. Circumstantial evidences support this as during a meeting with Jawaharlal Nehru right after independence Chaudhry Khaliquzzama a veteran Muslim leader of UP informed the Prime Minister that in UP 8000 national guards were to be recruited with instructions not to take single Muslims, Nehru replied that Sardar Patel held the Port-folio and he would inquire from him about it.[32] In Madras too—state government issued a notice that Muslim should not be recruited to the police force at all levels matter was raised in the State Legislature, and then the Home Minister Dr. Subbaroyan admitted the presence of such Government Order (G.O.) which prohibited the recruitment of the Muslims.[33] "Muslim is a victim to double injury, remarks Prof. Ali Ashraf some inflicted upon them by others—this disorientation is reflected on the one hand by criticism against Muslim fanaticism, backwardness and even lack of patriotism and on the other hand Muslims complaint of discrimination in the field of public employment and cries of despair against threats to their life and property during riots.[34] Dr. Hasan Ahmad while enlisting the discrimination at various levels maintained that "out of total 405 industrial license approved in 1979 just 5 were given to Muslims i.e. 1.25 per cent Indian Oil Corporation has given a meager 4.05, 2.3 and 3.2 per cent of its dealership to Muslims in petrol, gas and kerosene oils. In Delhi the telephone connection to Muslims came to only 1.52 per cent".[35] It is a common feeling that Muslims are last to be hired and first to be fired.

In this way it is an established fact that Muslims are discriminated and their average level of living is lower than the others A.M. Khusro attributes it to the functioning of economic principle of which whenever there is a bias, large minority loses opportunities".[36] Gopal Singh in his report on high power panel on minorities SC&ST and weaker section rightly commented, "The sense of discrimination now prevailing among the minorities must be eliminated root and branch, if we want the minority to form an effective part of the mainstream".[37]

3. *Inadequate Representation in Various Services*

One of the most eloquent grievances of the Indian Muslims is inadequate representation in various services under central/ state government and other public or private sector unit and banking etc. Inspite of the fact that Indian constitution provided under the article 16 of Fundamental Rights equal opportunity to all irrespective of any discrimination on the basis of religion, caste, creed etc. in the matter of public employment, the number of Muslims being recruited to the various services has been dwindling. The following table will show the actual position.

Table 4.3: Employment of Muslims under Central Government Class-wise.

S. No	State	Total No. of employees	Muslim employees	% age	Class-I Total	Class-I Muslim	Class-I % age	Class-II Total	Class-II Muslim	Class-II % age	Class-III Total	Class-III Muslim	Class-III % age	Class-IV Total	Class-IV Muslim	Class-IV % age	Population Proportion of Muslim in sample Districts
1.	Andhra Pradesh	258	27	10.47	8	—	—	10	2	20.00	187	19	10.16	53	6	111.32	26.45
2.	Assam	3,135	255	8.13	2	—	—	470	22	4.68	2,205	192	8.71	458	41	8.95	36.72
3.	Bihar	6,617	359	5.43	28	—	—	995	27	2.71	3,950	237	6.00	1,644	95	5.78	—
4.	Gujarat	10,361	494	4.77	371	—	0.27	477	5	1.05	6,864	373	5.43	2,649	115	4.34	8.48
5.	U.T. of Chandigarh	1,479	8	0.54	33	—	—	28	—	—	1,200	6	2.50	218	2	0.92	1.45
6.	Haryana	897	6	0.67	27	—	—	28	—	—	750	4	0.53	147	2	1.36	33.62
7.	Kerala	8,898	337	3.79	1143	22	1.92	739	22	2.98	5,609	224	3.99	1,407	69	4.90	24.89
8.	Madhya Pradesh	2,811	179	6.37	20	—	—	69	8	11.76	1,942	119	9.12	781	52	6.66	5.34
9.	Maharasthra	4,384	184	4.20	17	1	5.88	27	—	—	3,230	121	3.74	1,110	62	5.59	9.93
10.	Orissa	13,040	205	1.57	30	—	—	513	16	3.12	10,031	160	1.60	2,466	29	1.18	1.07
11.	Rajasthan	6,674	229	3.45	401	—	—	132	6	3.03	4,821	199	4.14	1,330	26	1.95	11.54
12.	Tamil Nadu	200	8	4.00	3	1	33.33	25	1	4.00	133	5	3.76	39	1	2.56	7.02
13.	U.P.	12,307	929	7.55	134	11	8.21	335	15	4.48	7,295	550	7.54	4,543	353	7.77	17.29
14.	WestBengal	4,782	136	2.81	15	—	—	213	—	—	3,740	85	2.25	814	51	6.26	26.22
	GRAND TOTAL	75,951	3,346	4.41	2,232	36	1.61	4,060	122	3.00	52,000	2294	4.41	17,669	904	5.12	5.93

Source: Gopal Singh Panel Report on Minorities Vol II.

Table 4.4: Muslim representation in Lok Sabha.

Year	*Total Seat*	*Muslim members*	*% Age*
1947	252	31	12.30
1952	289	36	12.45
1957	494	24	4.85
1962	494	32	6.47
1967	520	29	5.57
1971	518	27	5.21
1977	543	32	5.89
1980	543	46	8.48
1984	543	41	7.55
1989	543	33	6.07
1991	543	28	5.15
1996	543	27	4.97
1998	543	28	5.15
1999	543	31	5.70
2004	543	36	6.62
2009	543	30	5.52

Source: Muslim India New Delhi.

Table 4.5: Percentage of Muslims in Central Government Services.

Services	*Year*	*Total Number*	*Muslims*	*Percentage*
I.A.S.	1981	3883	116	2.98
I.P.S.	1981	1753	50	2.85
Income Tax	1971-81	881	27	3.06
Railway traffic & Account	1971-81	415	11	2.65
Bank	1971-81	1377275	2479	0.17
Office of Central Services	1971-81	826669	3346	0.40
Indian Army	—	1100000	29093	2.64

Source: Mohibul Haque Radiance 11 July 1999.
Omer Khalidi Hindustan Times, New Delhi 19-2-06.

Several bodies and individuals representing the Muslims community had voiced this dismal state of affairs. With the population of about 12 per cent Muslim representation in parliament is 4.81 per cent (1996) and the numbers of States with zero Muslims representation are 14 as the following Muslim employment in government sectors is exceedingly low.

In 1981 Muslim constituted 3 per cent in the I.A.S. 2.85 per cent in I.P.S. 3 per cent in the income tax department 2.65 per cent in the Railways and 2.85 per cent in the Banks. In the case of the Central Government Muslim constitute 1.61 per cent of the class I cadre; they are 3.9 per cent in the class II cadre rising to 4.4 per cent in non-technical supervisory cadres. More than that there is no Muslim among the 5 members and 18 senior executives if L.I.C. and 19 members of Reserve Bank of India.[38] Rasheeduddin Khan comments, that "inadequate intake of Muslim in all India services and less than proportionate share in terms of population in their representation in the state legislature and parliament is exploited by the exclusivist parties playing what may be called passion politics.[39] As the Muslims are 12 per cent of the Indian population one can understand if they get 9 or 8 per cent of the job but what if they get 3 or 2 per cent. Does that represent the differences between talents or is it due to the biases of the kind that prevail in the society? Asked A.M. Khusro. He further observed that "I can perhaps understand why in the I.A.S. or I.F.S. they do not obtain 10 per cent of the post but what about the fact at the lower job levels is less than skilled or unskilled jobs as chaprasi, peons, army and police personals where few qualification are really necessary. The minorities are not getting their proportionate share."[40]

There is not a single Muslim at all in Union Home Ministry's two sensitive departments i.e. Intelligence Bureau (I.B.) and Research Analysis Wing (R.A.W.) since its inception and when asked to comment, Mr. Vijay Karan, a former C.B.I. Director remarked, "it is a sort of an unwritten code, every body knows about it and it is accepted as a fact."[41] According to one calculation, denial of government jobs particularly in the army and police only caused Indian Muslims a loss of about Rs. 4500 crore per annum as their share in wages alone.

4. Neglect of Urdu

The treatment meted out to Urdu in the post independence India is another source of the Muslim grievances. Urdu which was born and brought up in India and enriched by dialects such as *Brij Bhasa, Awadhi* & *Haryanvi* etc. finds recognition as one of the national languages in the 8th scheduled of the constitution having 6th position in the linguistic map of India spoken by 51.5 million people (2001 Census). There is unanimity among all the progressive moderate, orthodox and modernist Muslims on this issue. Syed Abid Hussain is of the opinion that the learning of Urdu for Indian Muslims is not only a vital cultural but also a religious necessity... It would be nothing less than intellectual and spiritual suicide to give up Urdu.[42] The declining fortunes of Urdu were meatly summed up by a leading authority an Islam Prof. W.C. Smith— The community is in danger of being deprived of its language than which only religious faith is deeper possession.[43] Muslims have a strong feeling that the preservation of Urdu is preservation of Deen[44] that to deprive them of the Urdu language and the spiritual inheritance.[45] They feel that Urdu is being denied the opportunity of development at the cost of Hindi with a deliberate attempt to throttle the language—a crime against humanity. (Mittal,[46] Shakis[47] Ghani[48]), or nothing less, than cultural genocide.

It is a fact that throughout the struggle for India's independence Urdu was the chief language of the leaders and masses, revolutionaries and statesmen alike irrespective of religious and parochial affiliation and was spoken and learnt by all Hindus particularly Keyastha, Khatris, Kashmiri Pandit and Punjabi's etc. Even in the early stage of the formation of the constituent Assembly it was decided that Hindustani written either in Devnagri or the Persian script shall be the national language, but later due to the influence of communal politics constituent Assembly adopted a motion on the 14th September 1949 with only casting vote (78/77) of Dr. Rajender Prasad that the official language of the Union shall be Hindi in Devnagri script.[49] This displacement of Urdu happens because it was identified with the new nation Pakistan Hindu radical right wing politician within the congress party like Sardar Patel, K.M. Munshi, Gobind Vallabh Pant Puroshottandas Tandan, Sampurnanand and Govind Das etc. did not want to give Urdu its rightful place as it was closely related with Muslim culture and was seen as a rival of Hindi. The following table shows the position of Urdu among the major Indian language spoken as mother tongue as well as Urdu speaking population of various states.

Table 4.6: Number of Speakers of Major Languages as Mother Tongue in India (2001).

Sl. No.	*Languages*	*Number of speakers*
1.	Assamese	13.2
2.	Bengali. (ii)	83.4
3.	Gujrati. (vii)	46.1
4.	Hindi. (i)	422.1
5.	Kannada (viii)	37.9
6.	Kashmiri	5.5
7.	Malyalam (ix)	33.1
8.	Marathi (iv)	71.9
9.	Oriya	33.0
10.	Punjab	29.1
11.	Sanskrit	0.01
12.	Sindhi	2.5
13.	Tamil (v)	60.89
14.	Telego. (iii)	74.0
15.	Urdu. (vi)	51.5

Source: Census of Indian 2001 Series I (languages) Registar General and Census Commissioner Government of India 2001.

As a table (4.6 and 4.7) shows that though it ranked 6th position and spread throughout the country but unfortunately it failed to occupy the basis of different languages. Further the census shows that Urdu is not the mother tongue of all Muslims, which is correct to the state of West Bengal, Orissa, Kerala etc. but certainly not with UP, Bihar, Andhra Pardesh, Karnataka, Maharashtra, Delhi etc. These states are Urdu belt and census officials do mockery of the census by falsely counting Hindi as the mother tongue of Urdu speaker[50] This undercount of Urdu is clearly motivated by the linguistic, rivalry, prejudice against Urdu a desire to inflate the number of Hindi speakers.

Table 4.7: Urdu Speaking Population (1991) State wise Break up and Status of Urdu Education.

States/U.Ts	*Total Muslim Population*	*Person declaring Urdu as mother tongue*	*No. of state run Urdu Elementary schools*
Andhra Pradesh	5,923,954	4,207,546	1,135
Bihar	1,27,87,985	7,286,870	5,500
Gujrat	3,606,920	643,926	161
Haryana	763,775	233,343	000
Himachal Pradesh	89,134	13,569	000
J&K	5,059,344	6,315	—
Karnataka	5,237,023	3,610,636	2,853
Kerala	6,788,364	12,350	—
M.P.	3,282,800	1,206,385	—
Maharastra	7,628,755	4,582,624	2,108
Orissa	577,775	386,857	—
Punjab	239,401	34,189	—
Rajisthan	3,525,339	764,565	73
UP	24,109,684	10,208,084	000
West Bengal	16,075,836	1,331,022	220
Delhi	889,641	367,458	95
Goa, Daman & Diu	73,563	29,263	—
INDIA	10,66,56,401	3,49,41,435	

The table further shows that though UP is the largest Urdu speaking state but there is not single Urdu Medium elementary school and when we compare it with the several thousand Urdu Medium schools immediately before independence it is a convincing genocide. Smith D.E. remarks, that the majority community and the state government have at times been most insensitive and even irresponsible in their handling of this issue.[51] In the post independence India the treatment according to Urdu symbolizes the ruling elites double faced ness, the gap between its assurances and action, promise and performance. Urdu has been thrown out from educational institutions, courts and government offices etc.[52] Muslims middle class has tended to be alienated from its mother tongue. "It has been forced into the ghettos, the Mushaira" remarks, Mani Shankar Aiyar, "and reduced to being the mother tongue of the most orphaned segment of Indian population".[52] The only demand and desire of the Urdu speaking Indians is, pleads Mohd. Hasan, "that the exile is ended and Urdu is rehabilitated in these places."[53]

Another tragedy with Urdu language is that it is largely associated (though language has no religion) with a particular religion of India i.e. Islam and considered a foreign language. This adverse propaganda is due to its script and some Arabic & Persian words in its vocabulary. But the fact is that the basic of this language is purely Indian though for its encroachment like a living language it has freely drawn from other sources too. Syed Ahmad Dehlavi in his famous 4 volumes Urdu Dictionary *Farhang-E-Asfia* published in 1918 used 54,009 Urdu words in it. The break up is as follows:

1.	The total number of words in dictionary	54,009
2.	Hindi, Punjabi & Purbi words	21,644
3.	Urdu word formed by the combination of Hindi etc.	17,505
4.	Arabic words	7,584
5.	Persian words	6,041
6.	Sanskrit	554
7.	English	500
8.	Portuguese, French, Spanish & Italian etc.	181
	Total	54,009

Source: Syed Ahmad Dehlavi *Farhang-E-Asfia*, Delhi, National Academy.

This is enough to dispel the concept that Urdu is an alien and Islamic language in India. Further whatever the word it has borrowed from Arabic & Persian has undergone metamorphoses, changes in meaning and phonetics that it has no relevance their common words like *Muqadama, Surat, Mihnat, Maloom* and *Zila* etc. are such examples spoken by common Indians lost their Arabic meanings and also sound-a case of total assimilation in Indian phonetic system.[55] But in India as every movement or efforts takes communal colour so any move taken up for the rightful status of the language was communalized by vested interest. As D.E. Smith remarked, "Despite all the efforts of the Urdu protagonists to refute this partly inaccurate identification, the demand for recognition of Urdu was popularly regarded as demand of the Muslim minority."[56]

6. Mass Media Campaign and Involvement in Non-Issues

Yet another grievance of the Muslim is that Indian mass media is projecting them as fundamentalist, terrorist, anti-national and foreigner and are being treated as the vote bank by ruling party, though these are merely a miss-information. Through misleading head lines and slanted stories they prove any point of view that are tutored to them. There is a campaign that Muslims will soon outnumber the Hindus as Muslim men are allowed to have four wives. Secondly Muslims in general are opposed to family planning so the birth rate is higher among them. But the fact is that though Indian Muslims are religiously permitted polygamy. It is very rare as in 1961 census a survey of polygamous marriage was conducted by the Government of India. It's finding was that the polygamous marriages were highest amongst the tribal, second highest amongst the Buddhists followed by the Jains and Hindus, Muslims figured last on the list.

So far the family planning is concerned it is a fact that Islam forbids abortion and permanent family planning measures but at the same time some Muslim countries for instance Turkey and Indonesia follow several methods with 63 per cent Turkish and 48 per cent Indonesian using the contraception. Further the growth rate between 1981-91 among the Muslims was 32.76 per cent while among the Hindu 22.78 per cent and if the same rate of growth continued it will take 200 years for Muslim to be 20 per cent of the total population reports the research conducted by the Pune based *Gokhale Institute of Politics and Economics.* More than that this higher rate of growth among the Muslims is due to the socio-economic and educational backwardness in comparison to Hindus, according to the survey conducted by *Operation Research Group* in 1990. It shows that the number of live birth depends upon fertility, substantially both amongst Hindus and Muslim women. Further, Muslim women also in large number use intrauterine devices, conventional contraceptives and oral pills etc. Regarding census figures experts pointed out to several factors: as over reporting or under reporting during census enumeration and migration etc.[57]

Table 4.7: Trends in Fertility Level.

Religion	*RURAL*			*URBAN*		
	1971	*1981*	*% Decline between 1971-81*	*1971*	*1981*	*% Decline between 1971-81*
All Religion	177	143	19.2	154	123	20.1
Hindus	174	141	20.0	149	119	20.1
Muslims	197	163	17.3	178	145	18.5
Christians	192	132	31.2	159	117	26.4
Sikhs	181	153	15.5	161	116	27.9
Buddhists	177	150	15.2	160	130	18.7
Jan's	168	135	19.6	146	111	24.0

Source: Census of India 1991.

So far the allegation that Muslims are fundamentalists, terrorists and anti-national with the images of masked men wielding Kalishnikov's attacking peace loving people and stock pile of assorted arms are concerned. According to Asghar Ali Engineer, "the violent image of Islam is limited mainly to the North India where the religion was introduced by conquering rulers. In south, however, Islam was brought by the trading Arabs along the coast of Kerala."[58] But even no Muslim invader of the north even came into this country with the sole intention to propagate Islam rather their motive was always political and economic like any other rulers. In India, the bulk of conversions from the oppressed and subjugated classes amongst Hindus to Islam took place under the influence of the peaceful Sufis. Further Namita Bhandare and others argue, "Despite their militant image Muslims masses have not organized themselves to defy the law and raze a place of worship to the ground as assorted Hindu organization did in Ayodhya on the 6th December 1992". They further comment, "compare the reaction of the fundamentalist Muslim after the

Babri Masjid demolition with that of the tolerant Hindus after Indira Gandhi's assassination when over 1,000 innocent Sikhs were slaughtered in Delhi and a number of Gurudwaras were razed to ground by Hindu mobs".[59]

Muslims have a strong feeling that, "regarding their faith and ideology, the role of our national media is very distressing... they (mass media) appear united on one point that is to oppose tooth and nail Islam and Muslims. If any where in the world some thing wrong is committed by any Muslim or a Muslim Government our national media makes a mountain out of a mole hill... if the country happens to be Pakistan it is a God sent opportunity to blame Islam and Muslims".[60] They further have a feeling that some motivated groups and interested political parties which benefit from Hindus/Muslim discord, keep finding non issues in order to further alienate Muslims such as cow slaughter, A.M.U. minority character, banning of the Holy Qura'n or Azan, Shah Bano case, uniform civil code, case of Ameena a Hyderabadi girl, Babri and other mosques, Status of Urdu, Kashmir and growth of Muslim population etc. The aim is to keep Muslims forever on the defensive in order to divert their attention from their real problems. Thus they are likely to remain a poor, illiterate and exhausted community. This class remarks P.C. Punnen are potential collaborators with rank Communalist at a Pinch it might even portray the V.H.P. as a band of arch-angels[61]

7. Interference in Muslim Personal Law

Another major problem confronting the Muslim mind that of their personal law under the Directive Principles of State Policy Article 44 has been incorporated which says that the state shall endeavour to secure for the citizens a uniform civil code through out the territory of India. During the debate of the constitution assembly it was said that it is to make the country a strong and consolidated nation. Indians Muslims have been opposing the very concept of the enactment of a uniform civil code with all their might, right from the enforcement of the constitution and the representatives of Muslim organization throughout the country passed several resolutions passed in

December 1970 says that, "parliament had no right to interfere in the personal laws of Indian Muslims which are based on the Qura'n and Sunnat."[62] Muslims opposed the move as they consider that marriage and personal laws of their community are part of their religion. Taking any such step will be infringement of the fundamental rights they are believed to enjoy. The Government of India's policy since its independence is to respect the view of Muslims and not to interfere in their personal law. Dr. B.R. Ambedkar, father of the Indian constitution, as a law minister had said in Lok Sabha that, "in our country... the profession of a particular religion carries with it the personal law of the person. You can not get away from the position."[63] Similarly Govinda Menon speaking as the law minister had remarked that, "article 44 of the constitution... should be read along with Article 25—a fundamental right which is laid down that the existing religious right of all communities should be allowed to continue."[64] Different Prime Ministers of India right from Pandit Jawahar Lal Nehru to the present repeatedly assured the community that, "the Muslim personal law in no case will be changed (and) Indian Muslims should have no apprehension on the score."[65] But despite all these assurances, Muslims have apprehension as Judiciary, mass media, pressure group and certain political parties are working in this direction. It is the time, remarks, Abdul Moghni, that, "the patriotic elements of Indians nation should realize that the real problem of the Muslims in democratic India is to reassure them of the preservation of their identity.[66] The champions of uniform civil code should realize that multiplicity of family laws in the U.S.A. has not come in its way of developing a united political nationhood.

REFERENCES

1. *The Encyclopedia Americana.* Vol. 19 (New York, Americana 1961), p. 206.
2. Hemayan Kabir—*Minorities in Democracy* (Calcutta, Mukhepadia, 1968), p. 45.
3. *The Concise English Dictionary* (London, Blackie 1918), p. 432.

4. *The Webster New world Dictionary* (Delhi, Pitamber 1976), p. 309.
5. J.A. Laponce—*The Protection of Minorities* (California Borkeler 1960), p. 3.
6. Art 86 & 93 of treaty of Versailles quoted by C.A. Macartuny—*National States and National Minorities* (London, Oxford 1934), p. 4.
7. *The Encyclopedia Britannica* Vol. 15 (Chicago, Benton 1968), p. 542.
8. J.A. Laponce—*Op cit.*, pp. 3-4.
9. *The year book on Human Right for 1950* (New York, U.N.O. publication 1950), p. 490.
10. *The Encyclopedia Americana, Op cit.*, p. 206.
11. Turner Ralph—H Sponsored and context mobility and school system, *American sociological Review* Vol. 25, (December 1960), pp. 855-867.
12. Sorokin P.A. *Social Mobility* chap. ix (New York, Harper 1927).
13. Sewell & Alan Orenstein—Community of Residence and Occupational Choice, *American Journal of Sociology* vol. 70 (March 1959), pp. 551-563.
14. Parsons T.—The school classes as social system some of its Functions in American society, *Harvard Education Review* vol. 29 (1959), pp. 551-563.
15. Publication Division—*Muslims in India* (New Delhi Govternment of India 1964), p. 1 and also K.L. Gauba, *Passive voice* (Bombay Thacker 1973), p. 13.
16. Census of India 1991 series—*I India paper I of 1995 RELIGION*. The Register General & Census Commissioner of India.
17. Rasheedudin Khan—*Minorities in nation building*—A seminar Address, New Delhi, 31st March 1970.
18. Abdul Moiz Manzer—*The Radiance* Vol. xx No. 38 (New Delhi, 27.1.1985).

18A. Jawahar Lal Nehru—*Letters to Chief Ministers* Vol. IV (New Delhi, 1985), p. 39.

19. D.E. Smith—*India as Secular State* (London, Princeton 1967) p. 414.
20. Syed Hamid—*The Tehzibul Akhlaq* No. 19 (Aligarh, 1983).
21. Ausif S. Vasfi—*The Radiance* Vol. xix No. 35 (New Delhi, 8.1.84).
22. Hasan Ahmad—*Startling Revelations.* Nations and the World No. vi (New Delhi).
23. M.N. Buch—*Muslims in India.* The Statesmen (Calcutta, 12.12.1990).
24. Iqbal A. Ansari—*State terrorism and communal violence.* The Radiance Vol. xxvii No. 24 (New Delhi 5-11, April 1992), p. 81.
25. "Jamshedpur Riots as a Cover for Land Grabbing." *Economic and Political Weekly* (19 May 1979), p. 870.
26. Paul R. Brass—*Riots and Pagrams,* New York Macmillon, 1997, p. 116.
27. *Ibid.* p. 81.
28. Riaz Azimabadi—*The Bhagalpur riots.* The Secular Democracy (New Delhi, July 1995).

29. Namita Bhendari, L. Fernandes & Minu Jain—The Appeased Minority. *The Sunday* (Calcutta, 13.2.1993).
30. Syed Hamid—Educational Status of India Muslim. *Muslim India* Vol. III, No. 36 (New Delhi, December 1985), p. 553.
31. Moin Shaker—*Islam in Indian Politics,* Delhi, Ajanta, 1983, p. 45 & Sheikh Mohammad Abdullah—*Autobiography Aatish Chinar*—(Srinagar Ali Mohammad & Sons, 1988, p. 576) and Shahabuddin—Shahabnama—(Karachi, 1982, p. 535)
32. Chawdhri Khaliquzzama—*Path Way to Pakistan* (Lahore, 1961) p. 325.
33. Mohammad Reza Khan—*What Price Freedom* (Madras, 1969) p. 386.
34. Ali Ashraf—Presidential Address 7th All India Muslims Educational Conference (New Delhi, 1984).
35. Hasan Ahmad—*Op cit.,* p. 47.
36. K.D. Sharma—*Education of National Minority* (Delhi, Kalamkar 1978), p. 27.
37. A.G. Noorani—On minorities. *The Statesman* (Calcutta, 14.6.1995).
38. Hasan Ahmad—*Op cit.,* p. 47.
39. Rasheeduddin Khan—*Op cit.,* p. 17.
40. A.M. Khusro—*Economic & Cultural problems of Muslims.* Intellectual Meet on Problems of Muslims, (New Delhi, June 1983).
41. Murli Krishna—No Muslim in I.B. & RAW. *The Telegraph* (Calcutta, 18.3.1994).
42. Syed Abid Hussain—*The Destiny of Indian Muslims*-London Asia 1965, p. 219.
43. W.C. Smith—*Islam in a Modern History*—Princeton, 1957, p. 266.
44. Ashraf Ali Thanvi—quoted Ashraf Ali Engineer—*Indian Muslims—A Study of the Minority Problems in India,* New Delhi, Ajanta Publication 1985, p. 318.
45. Abul Hasan Ali Nadvi—*Muslim in India* (Lucknow, Nadwa), p. 139.
46. Gopal Mittal. The Muslim Minority's Problem and Secularism. *The Swarajya,* Vol. xiii, No. 20. (November 10, 1968), pp. 13-14.
47. Moin Shakir—*Muslim in Free India* (New Delhi, Kalakar 1972), pp. 95-138.
48. A.M. Ghani—Cause of Urdu goes by default. *The Mainstream* (New Delhi, January 1968), p. 17.
49. Lok Shaba secretariat—*The Constituent Assembly Debates* Vol. ix (New Delhi, Government of India 1966), p. 1487.
50. Syed Hamid—*Mardum Shumari Ya Mardum Bezeri* (Nadai Millat 24 March 1991), p. 11-12.
51. D.E. Smith—*India as a Secular State* (London, Princeton 1967), p. 224.
52. Mohd. Hasan—*The Sunday World* (Delhi, 9th October 1972).
53. Mani Shankar Aiyar—Root cause of Muslim Backwardness. *The Sunday* (Calcutta, 5-11 November 1995).
54. Mohd. Hasan—*Op cit.,* p. 15.

55. Syed Ahmad Dehlvi—*Muqadama Farhang-e-Asafia* Vol. I (Delhi, National Academy), 1974 p. 10.
56. D.E. Smith—*Op cit.*, p. 427.
57. Kalpana Jain—Convergence of Hindu and Muslim Growth rate with Education and Economic status. *The Times of India* (New Delhi, 25th October 1995).
58. Asghar Ali Engineer—*The Sunday* (Calcutta 7-13 February 1993).
59. Namita Bhandare and others—*Op cit.*, p. 16.
60. Mufti Shamsuddin, *National Media and Muslim passivity.* The Radiance (Delhi, 5-11 April 1992).
61. P.C. Punnen—Shades of Animals Farm. *The Hindustan Times* (Delhi, November 6, 1998).
62. *The Hindustan Times* (Delhi, 22.12.1970).
63. *Parliamentary Debate*, Volume VIII (1951). 2949 quoted by Kamlesh Kumar Wodhwa—Minority Safeguards in India (Faridabad, Thomson 1975), p. 157.
64. *The Times of India* (Delhi, 6th May 1970).
65. *The Times of India* (Delhi, 21st May 1973). *The Hindustan Times* (Patna, July 30, 1995).
66. Abdul Moghni—Islamic Identity in Peril. *The Radiance* Vol. XXVII No. 24 (New Delhi, 5-11 April 1992).

5

Educational Backwardness of Muslims: Explanation and Causes

William W. Hunter while writing a book after the first war of independence (1857) on the Indian Muslim, which was published in 1871 maintained that, "In the case of Muslim's, mosque preceeded school even in the sphere of education and that regardless of his worldly means, the Muslim often chose his son's education which would secure for him an honorable place among the learned of his community in preference to an education which would open the gates of success in the modern profession or in the official line.[1] He further commented that Hindus easily accepted the English education as they did in the case of Muslim rule but for Muslims it was altogether different as they were not only the political but also the intellectual power... The ancient conquering race cannot easily divest itself of the tradition of its nobler days.[2]

The publication of the said book created a great stir with regard to its different aspects of finding. *Sir Syed Ahmad Khan* (1817-1898) too earnestly endeavored for years to trace the reason for avoidance of English Education by the Muslims. In 1871 just after the publication of Hunter's book he constituted a committee to investigate into the causes and to suggest measures by which education could be spreaded among the Muslims. The Committee in order to investigate, announced three prizes for the best essays by the educated Muslims, thirty-two essays were received and fully discussed at a larger body of the educated Muslims... and the dislikes to English Education and this antagonism was not merely a matter of chance but having some reasons.

During the reigns of the Caliphs of Baghdad the Greek Sciences such as logic, philosophy, mathematics, chemistry, medicine, astronomy and geography etc. were translated into Arabic, they were named as rational (*aqlia*) Sciences and were accepted by the whole Muslim world without any hesitation and with slight modification and alteration, they gradually found their way into the religious discourses and later on they were identified with Islam and its sacred tradition of faith. Muslim also contributed a lot to the development of these sciences even before the dawn of Europeans Sciences and its Renaissance.

But when the European learning was introduced, Muslims world reacted sharply to it. Their antipathy and antagonism gone up so far indeed that they began to look upon the study of these learning by a Muslim as little or less than embracing of Christianity. This reaction was due to several factors. In India; Europeans entered basically with commercial motives but when they settled down with the active cooperation of *Mughal* rulers and found political condition in chaotic state they soon revised their aims and began to aspire at first to replace the Muslim power and then to remove the main obstacle viz. Islam and its culture from the way of progress of Western civilization.[3] In attacking Islam the idea was to denounce Islam and its impact due to long drawn war of crusade. Thus right from 1765 AD onward the British carried out intelligently and imperceptibly their policy removing the obstacle i.e. Islam, and eliminating its impact from society in order to impose their own progressive civilization. This is confirmed by the following observation made by W.W. Hunter. "The truth is that we hastened by a single decade, our formal assumption of sovereignty. we should have been landed in a Mohammedan (sic) rising infinitely more serious than the mutiny of 1857. The admirable moderation of the East India Company's government and their determination to let Mohammedan (sic) power expire by slow and natural decay without hastening its death by a single moment averted this danger. India passed from a country of Islam into a country of the enemy, by absolutely imperceptible gradations".[4]

Historically Christian mentality and European attitude towards Muslims in general and Islam in particular is rooted in certain wrong assumptions. They regard Islam as responsible for erecting fanatical barriers in the way of progress of humanity. They also hold that the followers of Islam are averse to any change and progress. In their opinion Islam, which provides a compromise between materialism and spiritualism, is the main obstacle in the progress of Western civilization and human progress. For instance, according to Andre Servier, "Islam is the secretion of the Arab brain" and he has no hesitation to declare that, "it is the religion that is the chief obstacle between them (i.e. the Muslims) and us."[5] He further maintains, "Islam is the enemy not because it is a religious doctrine different from our own philosophical conception but because it is an obstacle to all progress and to all evolution".[6]

Muslims on the other hand are very proud of the popularity of Islam. No religion has ever maintained so strong hold over the people of the world as Islam. It is the Muslim psychology that whenever they fail in other fields of life they tend to withdraw to their religious defenses and justify their failures and stagnation on religious ground.

The suspicions of Muslims in adopting the European knowledge were also due to several other factors. Externally the destruction of Baghdad, Bukhara and Damascus in 1258 AD by the Mongols and of Muslim rule in Spain were also an important reason in these places which were the center of learning, educational institution and laboratories etc. were completely destroyed and a large number of scholars were killed, many of them scattered as they left for other places. But the internal factors had played more important role such as Ibn Khalidoon (1332-1406 AD) one of the great Muslims scholars and historians divided knowledge into two groups, Divine and Worldly. While commenting on philosophy, he remarked that it is a useless thing as it may lead us go astray. Though he considered magic as real science as it is related with the spiritual power of human being but as chemistry has nothing to do with spirituality, so it is worthless".[7] Further Ibn Khalidoon in his famous book *Muqaddama* wrote—"we heard that in the country of Firangee (Europeans) in the northern coastal area of the Mediterranean sea people are talking much about the natural philosophy, it is taught and explained in details in various classes, and a great number of students are attracted to it. But as it is not going to add in our religious Knowledge so it is better to avoid it".[8] This is a case of intellectual indifference or alienation from the intellectual world, remarks Dr. Abdus Salaam—a Noble laureate, "by a great intellectual and scholar of history which ultimately was the intellectual death of the Muslims world. While ignoring Alkndusy "Acquire Knowledge wherever you get it".[9] Hafiz Ibn Qaim Aljuzi comments that, "our religious leaders stood firmly on the pulpit and with full authority and pride command that this world is Heaven for Infidels and a prison for a Muslim; meaning that the prosperity of this world may curtail the share in the Here after."[10]

Mujaddid Alf Thani (1564–1626 AD) wrote about the philosophy that, "they are non sense and idiots and those are more silly and idiots who consider them wise, as pirating some knowledge from the Divine books they propagate their pseudo and fake Knowledge". He further wrote, "when the teaching of plato Jesus Christ reached Plato, the leader of these unfortunate, ignored it considering that as he himself is enlightened so he is not in need of it, but the poor fellow should have thought that the miracle performed by him is also against the natural law before commenting it".[11] Is it not strange that the persons like Hazrat Mujaddid Alf Thani was not aware that both were not contemporaries as Plato (427–347BC) was about 350 years before Jesus Christ.

While on the contrary, Hujjatul Islam Imam AlGhazali (1058–1111AD) commented that, "the knowledge of medicine, mathematics and industrial sciences are obligatory as it is essential for life. Mathematics helps us in the distribution of wealth and inheritance." Further he commented, "in many cities Jews and Christians are physicians, though their evidence according to Islamic tenets are not valid inspite of that we see that Muslims are not learning medicines and what they learn is jurisprudence so that they may loot the property of orphans, *Awqaf* (trust) and *Wasiyat* (last will) etc. They wanted the post of judges to boast upon others and accumulate wealth". He further maintained, "some foolish friend of Islam contradicted the discovery and theory of science and philosophy as against Islam and considered it as services rendered to Islam. Consequently the people who have the faith on the logical and scientific discoveries consider Islam based on ignorance ultimately ignoring Islam itself".[12]

In India, due to the loss of political power, antagonistic and discriminatory attitude adopted by the British rulers Muslims tended to array themselves in the deepest distrust of the British and western culture".[13] The Indian Muslims started retiring into their cell. They developed exclusiveness and everything modern particularly coming from the west was looked at with suspision. The leadership of the community had passed almost decisively into the hands of intensely nationalistic but deeply conservative section of Mullahs. The fundamentalist movement gained momentum and many found solace in the mystic orders. In the philosophical arena the universalistic approach of Ibn-sena (Avicenna) who adopted science and philosophy to Muslims theology appeared now to be largely abandoned.

In the above-mentioned situation Syed Ahmad Khan thoroughly studied the reasons, which prevented Muslims from joining educational institutions providing European learning. He discussed the problems with his other contemporaries and concluded that in India Muslim abstention was due to the following several reasons.

1. Absence of religious instruction and practices.
2. Dearth of Muslim teachers and other teacher neglecting Muslim students.
3. Alien system of education, medium of instruction, unnecessary subjects and more than that the notion being full of defects.
4. Director of education ignoring the feeling of Muslims.
5. Neglect of oriental language and books containing objectionable materials.
6. Wrong examination system as it encourages cramming.

7. Aristocratic pride of race for not mixing their children with the commoners.
8. Having no friendly term with the British.[14]

Sir Syed further maintained that since the Muslims are not acquainted with modern education so they are prejudiced and have no respect for it and consider mean and degraded, to their own learning this feeling was further strengthened by false religious superstitions.[15]

Having analyzed the causes that prevented the Muslims from joining the Govt. educational institutions Sir Syed decided to start a campaign popularly Known as Aligarh Movement and founded Mohammedan Anglo Oriental College at Aligarh in 1870. After 12 years i.e. in 1882 Government of India appointed a Royal Commission on education with Sir William W. Hunter as its chairman to inquire into the causes of backwardness of Indian Muslims and to ascertain views of responsible Indians. Some of the Muslim intellectual held that the absence of Islamic instructions and still more the injurious effects of English education in creating a disbelief in their religion and thus corrupting morals and manners was the main obstacle in their progress. The commission maintained while summarizing its impression that the reasons are numerous.

(a) The small proportion of Mohammedan (Sic) teachers in Government intuitions.
(b) The unwillingness of government educational officials to accept the counsel and co-operation of Mohammedans (Sic).
(c) Numerous minor faults in the departmental system.
(d) The comparatively small progress in real learning made by the pupils in government schools.
(e) The practice among well to do Mohammedans (Sic) of educating their children at home.
(f) The indolence and improvidence 100 common among them.
(g) Their hereditarian love for the profession of arms.

(h) The absence of friendly intercourse between Mohammedans and Englishmen.
(i) The unwillingness felt by the better born to associate with those lower in the social scale.
(j) The poverty nearly general among Musalmans.
(k) The coldness of the govt. towards the recess.
(l) The books used in government schools whose tone was hostile or scornful towards the Mohammedan (Sic) religion.
(m) A great stress on the teaching of the Qura'n and religion during the school going age, which they carried so far that they object to their children being taught, even the secular subjects by non-Muslim teachers.[16]

In this way a variety of other causes were also put forward at different times by members of the Muslim community.

The Royal Commission, however, was inclined to lay greater emphasis on some other factors such as pride of race, a memory of by gone superiority, religious fears and unnatural attachment to the learning of Islam. J. Muray Mitchell put this point of view more graphically, "They are convinced of the infinite superiority of Arabian and Persian literature to the *Kaffir*, in things external must submit to his hated sway but they scorn the thought that their minds also should be enslaved by this miserable books. What is Shakespeare and Milton compared with Hafiz or Saadi? ... They see simple Hindus rush forward to imbibe the ideas of Christianity and so vault into the fat pastures of Government employer let him, it is worthy of an idolater but no true believer should stop so low".[17]

Besides, there were also many causes of a strictly educational nature; the time spent by Muslim boys in memorizing text from the Holy Qura'n or learning of the Persian language or receiving laborious religious instructions at the *maktabs*. More over, a few Muslim parents could afford the luxury of English education for their children and therefore, preferred them to become learned in Islam, which did not cost much while at the same time it gave them a place of honors among the faithful.

Al Panch, Urdu daily in its editorial dated 27th August, 1886 while commenting on way the Muslim boys lose interest in education held extreme poverty as the main reason of educational Backwardness. It, remarked, "The officials of the department of Education generally complain that the Muslim boys so long as they are in lower classes show great promise—they top the list of successful boys in annual examination, some of them even secure double promotion... but the same students show a slower progress and become dull as they go up... The reason is that most of the Muslim students came off from the poor families; with the advance in school their requirements also increase but their income is static. They are unable to purchase costly books and to pay school fee and maintain themselves. It pours cold water on their enthusiasm as the cruel destiny is laughing at their back".[18]

One another important reason of educational backwardness was the fact that Muslim rulers, nobles and wealthy persons made the endowment trust for educational purposes, which in the word of James Grant was not less than one fourth of the area of Bengal, was confiscated by the British government in 1838 under land resumption Regulation, which in the word of Hunter was the starting point of the decay of Muslim education.[19] "It was another severe blow to the cause of education of the Muslim community" remarks Siddique, "as it had deprived the Muslim educational institutions the sources of their sustenance."[20]

The replacement of Persian with English in 1837 as the official language was fully utilized for the elimination of the Muslims from the government post, while the doors of the Hindu college (established in 1817) the main center for learning English were closed to the Muslim ... the language policy of the rulers further eliminated the Muslim from government services and forced backwardness on them."[21]

All these factors kept Muslim boys away from the English medium schools and colleges, the Hindus had no reason to be hostile to British rule while the Muslim realized that material progress was necessary but not at the cost of their religion and culture. Later Hindus also realized it. Besides that very small number who managed to join them did so at a much more advance age than the Hindus. Further while Hindu boys were being encouraged by their community to take whole-heartedly to secular studiessuch as English and mathematics etc. Muslims even while attending these schools were required to devote considerable time to religious instruction. "On some of them this dual ordeal had almost a demoralizing effect," As Syed Abul Fazal, pointed out, "I think it is the neglect of English education and this neglect is the consequence of their prejudices." He added, "They used to show hatred towards the English education, they did not make themselves qualified and they even supposed that the English education would greatly demoralize their character... The Mohammedans (Sic) of India have lifted their hands against themselves."[22]

Justice Syed Mohmood while writing the educational alienation of Muslim traces four important reasons i.e. political tradition, social customs, religious beliefs and poverty. He maintained that an insight into the political causes could be obtained by studying the history of the last two centuries.... The government schools and colleges included among their pupils some of those whom the Muslims with an undue pride and unreasonable self-conceit and vanity, regard with it worthwhile to associate with persons whom they considered inferior to themselves in social position. The same self-conceit and prejudice of Muslims led them to attach an undue importance to their own literature, metaphysics, philosophy and logic and in the same spirit; they regarded the English literature and modern sciences as quite worthless and productive of no mental and moral good. They did not tolerate these persons being called learned men, who acquired respectable knowledge of European literature or science. They could never be brought to admit that sound and useful learning existed in any language except Arabic & Persian, further the poverty of the Muslims community is only too obvious to require any comment.[23]

While comparing the European learning with prevalent traditional Islamic education or Asiaticised Greek dogmas Syed Hussain Bilgrami commented, "now the situation has completely changed. The art of rhymester of the calligraphists has ceased to be remunerative, the physics of Aristotle and Avicenna is antiquated, and the *IlmaSysat* of Tusi is useless; the algebra of Khayyam has lost its value; the chemistry of Jabir is mere a jugglery; the metaphysics of Averross is of no use; the Platonism of Farabi is of little account".[24]

Lord Macaulay commented, "the backwardness of Muslim is due to the lack of good English school for Musalmans (sic) and one of our first duty is to establish one."[25]

According to O'Leary, "the survival of antagonistic spirit of Muslims and Christians, the tendency of natural science to breed irreligiousness, are the real cause of Muslim reluctance to learn English and acquire western learning". To Muslims their religion was not just a set of opinions or speculative ideology; it implied a social order of life, which differed vastly from that of the Christians, the Jews and the heathens.[26]

With the passage of time and due to the sincere attempt by Sir Syed Ahmad Khan, his comrades and colleagues and the Aligarh movement the situation has gradually changed positively as Muslims realized the importance of modern western education and they almost caught up with the rest, around 1947 as most of the data indicate that Muslims were not particular behind others in modern education and employment but slightly ahead of the others. For instance in 1931-32 the Muslim percentage in school was 27.7 per cent compared to their population in India of 25.1 per cent[27] further on January 11, 1939 Pandit Gobind Vallabh Pant, the then Prime Minister of UP met the press consultative committee and placed the actual position of Muslims of UP as follows.

..."The Muslims form 14 per cent of the population. Generally the Muslims presentation in Services is far in excess of what it should be on the population basis. Take for example some important services. In the provincial executive services the Hindus are 52.5 per cent and the Muslim 39.6 per cent among the tehsilder Hindu 54.9 per cent and Muslim 43.6 per cent, in the provincial judicial services Hindu 72 and Muslims 25 per cent, among Dy. SP's Hindus 56 per cent and Muslims 28 per cent, among police Inspectors Hindus 54.2 and 43.8 per cent among Head constables Hindus 35.3 per cent and Muslims 64.4 per cent...etc".[28]

The same was the condition with regard to Bihar as during the period 1895 to 1898 total appointment made as Deputy and sub. Deputy Collectors was 71 and only 20 were Biharis out of these 20, thirteen were Muslims and only seven were Hindus.[29] But since independence as the various report of survey and study confirmed the Muslims had again fallen badly behind others as there has been slow, sure and continuous process of degeneration of Indian Muslims. The present educational backwardness of Muslims is not the same which was at the time of Sir Syed as he had almost put an end to that, remarks A.R. Shirwani, it is second and new chapter of Muslims educational backwardness which opened in 1947.[30]

Prof. A.M. Khusro pointed out that in analysis made some time back (after the riot of Ahmadabad) by Dr. Gopal Krishna of Center for Developing Societies, it was found that Muslims as a group were poor, their social performance, their involvement in national matters, their level of saving, their educational performance are invariably lower, school dropout rates among them are higher and success rates are lower and this is so without exception in every region and in every category.[31] In the same manner the Congress M.P. ...Mani Shanker Aiyar comments, "on every index of development, income, education, health, share in Government services, share in private enterprise, role in self employment, memberships in legislature, the level of their achievements is substantially below their share of population. The only index on which they figure higher than 12 per cent is poverty".[32]

In this way the educational backwardness of Indian Muslims as a social group is a universally recognized fact. Though no precise statistics are available but it emerges clearly from every field survey undertaken in recent years, however limited howsoever measured whether in terms of literary level of enrollment at primary level or secondary level, the dropout rate over school years, the proportion of those who have a done high school or of those who are graduates or post graduates or hold a professional qualification. Even the National Policy on education 1986 recognized Indians Muslims as an educationally backward and deprived community.

The educational backwardness of Muslims is at the root of every problems, which Indian Muslims are facing. The declining trend in education are due to two important reasons.

(a) A few Muslim children are joining school, and
(b) Out of those who are joining a large number are dropping out.

The extent of this backwardness is staggering, as a statement of a famous Gandhian historian and Scholar can understand it, Dr. B.N. Pandey that, "Muslims are more educationally backward than even to scheduled caste and Tribes".[33] Even the minority Commission in its report of 1983 accepted that Muslims are 10 times more educationally backward than any other community.[34] Delhi based philanthropist and educationist; Shirwani remarks, "according to all available indications Muslims lag very badly behind the rest of the Indians, they are five to ten times behind others in most places while in some places they are even twenty to fifty times behind others".[35]

On the plight of Indian Muslim, Ashrafi, comments that, "if one wants to see how a community from its economically well to do, educationally developed and culturally dominating status (in relevance to its contemporary society) has turned into one of the economically down trodden and educationally the battered community within the same society in a span of just a couple of decades he should have a look at the present condition of Indian Muslim".[36]

Hakeem Abdul Hameed, Chairman, *Hamdard National Foundation,* Delhi wrote an article on 30th May, 1980 entitled Crisis of Intellectual leadership among Muslims and held a series of discussions between 30.09.1980 and 19.04.1983 with educationists and social workers in Delhi, Bombay, Patna and Nitarhat (Bihar) etc. On January 23, 1981when Prof. Abdus Salam, noted Scientist and Nobel laureate met Hakeem Abdul Hameed, both of them discussed at length the educational backwardness of Indian Muslims and felt the need of a sound reliable and authentic data for the same. For this *Hamdard Education society* was founded and on a fact finding mission. Three all India survey projects were taken up namely—Muslim managed schools and colleges; Arabic/Dini Madarsas and All India Economic Survey of Muslims. To achieve the maximum participation of all concerned and to get quick neat and clean responses, it announced an incentive of cash awards worth Rs. 35,000 for the best-filled questionnaires/Responses in October 1981. The responses were quit satisfactory as 72.8 per cent school responded and on the basis of the responses *Hamdard Education Society* published 225 pages survey report in 1984.[37]

The said report is based on the survey, analysis & synthesis of the observations and suggestions received from the head of 430 Muslim managed schools and 44 collages from 16 states including 44 schools and 6 colleges from Bihar. It has identified the following four important common problems of all Muslim managed Male/Female/Co-education, educational institutions of India.

1. Intramural Problems of the Institution
2. Financial Problems of the Institution
3. Problems concerning Muslim community
4. Problem concerning Educational system

1. Intramural Problems of the Institutions

Under the head come the issues like lack of physical infrastructure, non availability of good/trained teachers particularly lady teachers and science teachers, admission/availability of Muslim students, management of school, Urdu medium school, residential facilities in schools and shortage of text books.

In addition to the problems, availability of good trained science teachers we also find that facilities to teach science have to be improved further. Concerted efforts have to be made for the procurement of proper apparatuses in these schools, laboratories from the community resources as government science grants are given to only 3.7 per cent schools and they are too meagre, insufficient, and rather negligible.

2. *Financial Problems of the Institutions*

These problems mainly cover the issue like lack of financial resources, aid of students, incentive to teachers, funds for science education and development programmes.

The survey report indicates that the majority of the institution (above 70%) are given grant in aid but the amount is meager e.g. 3 to 10 per cent of total requirements (like grant received by 3.7% of these schools for science/lab apparatus etc.) A good number of schools are unaided and community fund and schools own resources constitute the major source of income.

Lack of financial resources has impinged upon the quality and quantity of schools hostels, playgrounds, libraries, science laboratory apparatus and equipments, trained teachers, science books etc. On one hand and on the other there have been other manifestations also like increasing numbers of drop outs as the students go up further classes due to financial factors of the students/parents as at least 3 major economic factors are responsible for the massive rate of dropout of Muslim students at school level.

Table 5.1: Economic Factors Resulting in Increasing Number of Drop Outs at School Level (out of 14 Reasons).

Sl. No.	*Economic reason for dropouts*	*Mean value on 4 point scale*
1.	Financial difficulty of parents	2.6 point
2.	Child needed as earning member	2.1
3.	Teachers lack enthusiasm	1.3

Sources: Based on the response of the survey conducted by Hamdard Education Society, New Delhi 1984.

Another manifestation of financial crisis in these Muslim managed schools is the fact that while 61.6 per cent schools have their own buildings other 35 per cent are in rented buildings. The number of classroom is not sufficient, a total of 6,294 rooms are available in 430 schools. Limited financial resources allow very little aid to students or grant/incentive to teachers or adequate rise in the salary of teachers and all these combined together have affected growth and quality of education, especially science education in these schools.

3. Problems Concerning Educational System

The third major problem area is the educational system in vogue as education not being job oriented, problems of science education, languages, nursery, primary education, co-curricular activities and physical education, problems of Urdu teaching, lack of parental cooperation, high dropout ratio, minority character of the institutions, curriculum and teaching methods etc.

4. Problems Concerning Muslim Community

These problems include female education, lack of paternal concern about their children education, illiteracy, ignorance, poverty, economic backwardness, apathy, inhibition and other complexes, negative socio-psychological factors lack of economic support, absence of intellectual leadership, lack of adequate number of schools etc. Social factors like superstition of the family, purdah system; early marriage, non-availability of lady teachers etc. are some hindrances in the way of girl's education.[38] The Muslim managed degree and post graduation colleges are also facing several problems. Some of them, which were identified, are same as in schools and impinge upon the educational productivity of school and colleges. They were (a) Medium of instruction (b) admission of students (c) receiving Grants in aid from university/U.G.C./Govt. (d) obtaining parents cooperation (e) finances (f) recruitment of teachers and (g) dealing with educational authorities and local bodies etc.

As the survey report indicate the drop out rate among the Muslims are higher than to any other group and it keeps increasing as the Muslims students go up further classes. In this survey an attempt was made to review some co-agent factors responsible for high rate of drop out in these schools. Opinions of the Heads of the institutions were sought to mention, as to what extent the different reasons were responsible for drop out. The responses were as follows:

Table 5.2: Reason for Dropout of Students in Muslim Managed Schools.

Sl. No.	*Reasons*	*Mean value on 4 point scale*
1.	Parent not serious about education	2.7
2.	Financial difficulty of parents	2.6
3.	Child needed as earning member	2.1
4.	Too heavy curriculum	2.1
5.	Frequent absence of child	2.1
6.	Bad company of the child	1.9
7.	Teachers lack enthusiasm	1.8
8.	Unsympathetic parents	1.8
9.	Early marriage	1.6
10.	Too much homework	1.6
11.	Mentally retarded child	1.4
12.	No teaching in school	1.3
13.	Teacher's frequent absence	1.3
14.	Too severe punishment at home/school.	1.3

Sources: Based on the response of the survey conducted by Hamdard Education Society New Delhi.[39]

In this way educational backwardness of Muslim in post independence era is due to religious, social, economic, political, psychological and purely educational reasons. Religious factor includes belief and tradition while social factors include social customs, lethargic attitude of parents, community and school culture, working condition of Muslim managed institutions, majority community attitude, and Muslim leadership. Economic factor include poverty, lack of facilities. Psychological factor includes inferiority complex and lack of motivation while educational factors include heavy curriculum, problems due to language, medium of instruction, defective examination system and purposeless education etc. these are as follows:

1. Religious Beliefs and Social Customs

This includes Islam being not tolerant to modern scientific knowledge and out look or its tradition of avoiding secular education, parents' fear of becoming irreligious due to secular education or indoctrination of Hindu mythology in textbooks and school culture or due to the lack of religious education in general schools. The social custom includes dislike of parents for co-educational institutions or male teachers in girl's schools or purdah system, early marriage of boys/girls its after effects, difficulty in getting suitable matches for educated girls or marriage at older age, education or non education but expenditure on marriage is unavoidable. The girls don't have to do jobs so education is meaningless for them or the girl will leave the parents house so it is of no use for parents to spend on girl's education.

Maulana Sadruddin Islahi maintained that cooperation with the evil system is strictly forbidden in Islam." He went to the extent saying that participation in legislation; present Banking system, services in court etc. are directly in clash with the Islamic tenets while postal, transport, health and education services, though not in direct clash with Islam but are also to assist the Nizam-e-Jehalat (evil system) in various ways and degrees so it is also anti Islamic. During the British rule a fatwa (religious decree) with the signature of five hundred Ulemas was issued that participation in the council (legislature) is Haram (forbidden) for Muslims as if any un Islamic law is being legislated to initiate, to support or even to keep silence without opposing it is not justified. So far the present banking system based on interest is concerned, to participate in it in any form even auditing or witnessing is Haram (forbidden). The same is the case of the defense services as Prophet said that those who are fighting for Mushrik (idolaters) is one among them. Maulana Ashraf Ali Thanvi allowed services only in education provided that there is no direct clash with Islam and there is no other means of survival.[40] Both Maulana Hussain Ahmad Madni & Abul Aala Maudoudi advised a Deputy Tehsilder to resign from the job as it was unIslamic provided that there is some other means of livelihood.[41]

N.C. Saxena remarks" it is not without significance that wherever Muslims are sharing a territory with other communities they are economically more backward than non-Muslims." even in the Muslim countries like Malaysia, Nigeria, Lebanon, Egypt & Indonesia, they are far behind in education, industry and modern professions as compared to Chinese or Christians in those countries. The condition of Muslims where they are in minority is worse. Example may be given of Muslim in Thailand, Mauritius, Philippines, and Soviet Union & SriLanka etc. where they have done very poorly in modern profession—and all this is not a matter of sheer coincidence."[42]

M.R.A. Baig traces the roots of Muslim stagnation to general orthodoxy, which is perpetuated upon Muslim community because of the hold of Islam over them. According to him "the traditional orthodox super naturalism of Islam preaches submission to authority rather than critical examination of ideas and institution. He is therefore convinced that unless social reform takes place within the community, Muslim will continue to suffer from communal and social degeneration, economic stagnation and educational backwardness.[43] Najma Amin comments, "Muslim loyalty to their traditional learning fails to develop creative intellectual faculties."[44] Maxime Rodinson argues, "As ideology for social-economic enlistment Islam is impracticable. Therefore if a Muslim society wishes to progress it will have to undergo a radical conversion where old interpretation of Islam will have a synthesis of religious and humanist values from which both the economy and society will be benefited."[45] The educational backwardness is also because of the fact that the teaching of Islam insists much on Akhirat (Hereafter) than to the worldly affairs. "This world is only a preparatory ground for the next world i.e. Akhirat", is a common sermon given by so-called clergymen from the pulpit of the mosque or in any religious congregation.

Numerous scholars of Islam have challenged these ideas. They deny that there is any dichotomy in Islam as it advocates for the scientific discovery and temperaments and basic teaching of the Qura'n approves it. (Azmi[46] Hussain,[47] Ali,[48] Siddiqui,[49] Asad,[50])

2. Economic Factors

This is a very important factor, which affects the growth of education of an individual, society or community. There have been the basic reasons, which created a major obstacle in the way of Muslim education in the post independent period. A study of the economic conditions of Muslims of India was conducted by Gopal Krishna on the basis of the fieldwork in 35 districts spread over 16 states. Among the several variables one was study of the occupational status of Muslims and non-Muslims classified as low; lower middle; middle, upper middle, and high. The percentage distribution of these two communities in the sample survey was as follows:

Table 5.3: Occupational Classes.

Community	*Low*	*Lower Middle*	*Middle*	*Upper Middle*	*High*
Muslims	32.3	30.8	21.8	14.6	0.7
Hindus	23.0	33.0	11.9	27.6	4.4

Sources: Gopal Singh Panel Report on Minorities, Vol. II.

The families were also classified on the basis of per capita annual income and the result was as follows:

Table 5.4: Per Capita Income.

Community	*Up to Rs. 250*	*Between Rs. 251 and 700*	*Above Rs. 700*
Muslims	57.1	29.7	13.2
Hindus	4.5	29.9	29.6

Sources: Gopal Singh Panel Report on Minorities.[51]

In this way 13 per cent of Muslims families had monthly income of Rs. 700 and above as compared to 30 per cent non-Muslims. Therefore general poverty of an average Muslim family prevents Muslims children in availing the facilities of higher education. In a competitive situation such groups that have initial advantages of resources, talent and jobs continue to enjoy an edge over other groups.

According to S. Navalakha of the institute of economic growth "the percentage of elite Hindus is 85.3 per cent as against their population share of 82.6 per cent. But in the case of Muslims the percentage of elite is 4.5 only as against a population percentage of 11.12 per cent. In case of Christians it is 1, ½ times higher than that of their population percentage".[52] A survey of the Indian economy further show that out of 200 top industrialist none are Muslims. Only 3.7 per cent Muslims took loan from the Bank while 43 per cent Muslims were debarred from their land while among the Hindus the percentage is less than 20 (The Times of India 11th June 1999). The Muslims representation in Government Services, industries, public sector undertaking, private firms, banks, police, armed forces, railway, educational and postal services on the whole is less i.e. 2 to 5 per cent Muslims artisans and small scale manufactures are also not in a better position and so they have made a very little progress in contemporary India.

An estimation has been made that in India about 4.5 crores of people are getting salaries either from Government department or from private enterprises including factories, commercial banks, educational institutions etc. this mean that about one third of India's population is living on the salary income. Of these employed in the above services as on an average an employed person is expected to support four or five other members of his family. This shows that a low representation in the services by a community is the reason of lagging behind in the economic field.

In the case of Muslim artisans and small-scale manufacturers, due to poverty not only the areas of abode of Muslims shrank and their population got compressed in the remaining space under their occupation but also the traditional sources of their livelihood started eluding their grasp. This was either the indirect consequence of government policies or as a result of tough and unfair competition from the more resourceful new entrants into the field or through large-scale organizer of trade by Government and non-government powerful agencies. Combinations of these factors are responsible for the speedy retreat of the Muslims in various areas of their economic activities.

So far the reasons of poverty are concerned, in addition to rampant unemployment and under employment income inequalities also is a menace. Poverty is also traceable to the so called vicious circle of poverty i.e. low level of income generates low level of saving which in turn keeps the level of investment low. Low level of investment yields low level of income and thus the circle is completed.[53]

In this way it is poverty, ignorance, illiteracy, conservatism and hard choices between earning and learning of the Muslim community in general which creates hindrance and obstacles in the path of education and others fields. Mehdi Hasan comments, "Indian Muslims have fallen in the vicious circle of poverty—depression—frustration—educational backwardness and isolation".[54] If the child is intelligent but the atmosphere at home is not conducive to learning due to poverty it is of no use. The community will be better off if it works for social and economic reforms and send children to school instead of sending them to shops and workshops or providing them laissez-faire to astray in the street.

3. Muslim Community

In the post independence period Muslims are lagging far behind in education both quantitatively as well as qualitatively, even in the Muslims managed educational institutions Muslims students are in minority. Many social scientists and Muslims scholars are blaming the Muslims community for this. "If the Muslim children are not joining educational institutions in proportion to their population," asks Ali Ashraf, "who is responsible for this failure"? He further observes,"I would make bold to say that Muslims generally want to reach the destination without making the journey. This is a fact of the community's own colossal failure that no amount of conceptual or factual twist and turns can demolish".[55] The Indian Express in its editorials also commented" that although government can not be absolved of responsibility for its neglect... it is evident that each community can do much more to its educational backwardness".[56] N.C. Sexena and Ms. Anoie Thavil too blame the Muslim community for the same.[57] Syed Shahabuddin remarks, that "the community does not feel the need to invest human energy and resources in pursuit of modern knowledge of science and technology, of new vocation and professions and tread new path, the result is intellectual stagnation".[58] According to Shirwani, "Instead of hazarding this guise or that, instead of shooting off this opinion or that, instead of putting the blame to this factor or that, Muslims have to make a concerted effort to bring their children forward in education, whenever and, where ever they have made such an effort it has succeeded". He further commented that "the government is apathetic, the nation at large is disinterested, but the biggest pity is that Muslims have not so far paid due attention to their education".[59] While Syed Hamid remarks, "it seems we are not eligible to do some big project with a patient or in a manner".[60]

So if the Indian Muslims have to survive as a self-respecting segment of the country's population and they have to march into the 21nd century with responsibility, full confidence & respectability they have to introspect themselves and develop an understanding of their own problems and of the methods of their solution to come out from their intellectual stagnation. The community as such should realize that "God helps only those who help themselves", as the Holy Qura'n said centuries ago. Further Muslims should inculcate a sympathetic appreciation of their problems among their countrymen with whom their fate is inextricably linked and seek a device in cooperation with all. This is gigantic as well as a challenging task, which Indian Muslims are faced with.

4. Non-chalant Attitude of Muslim Parents

This includes parents not inclined to teach their children as they are illiterate and careless for the education of their children or content with their present lot or have no aspiration to improve. It may also be due to their poor economic condition as they have no money to pay school fee or purchase books and other reading/writing materials or they are required as earning member of the family so they consider education as a kind of luxury beyond their reach. It may be due to the fact that father is busy earning bread while mother is illiterate and busy in house hold affairs. Too severe punishment at home or unsympathetic parents or having no rapport with the teacher to know the problems or progress of their children may also be the factor for the same. These all lead to the conclusion that as parents do not take interest so students lack initiative.

According to the survey conducted by the Hamdard Education Society, New Delhi, the most important reason for stagnation and dropout of students in Muslim managed educational institutions is that the parents are not serious about the education of their children. According to the said survey 381 out of 430 Heads of the institutions considered it as one of the important factors of dropouts. Out of 381, 102 Head considered it 76 to 100 per cent responsible for dropout while for 123 it has 52 to 75 per cent responsibility and 80 and 76 Head considered as 26 to 50 per cent and 0 to 25 per cent respectively responsible for the dropout so their mean value on 4 point scale is 2.7.[61]

In this way parent's casual attitude and unsympathetic parents or too severe punishments at home were also considered responsible factor for dropout by many.

As the Muslims share in public and private enterprises is ridiculously very low due to prevailing hostile discrimination or what so ever. It has become disincentive for Muslim parents, as the prospect appears to be bleak. So why to waste time, money and energy? It is not easy to counter this line of reasoning remarks Syed Hamid,[62] "once the parent will perceive that a reasonable opportunity and fair competition exists they will surely pay due attention".[63] Even those parents who are educated though their number is not adequate run pillar to post to get their children admitted in the schools. But after that they have little time and inclination for helping out their children with the homework and have any rapport with the concerned teacher or school authorities regarding the performance of their children. These children are deprived of the environment and the guidance needed at the early age of education. Indian Express put the blame on Muslim students being the first generation learner so deprived of an atmosphere of learning and encouragement at home. It further comments, that "low paid white collar jobs for their offspring's do not seem attractive to Muslim parents".[64]

Nasim Zaidi places it in a better manner when he comments, "Which factor pulls back Muslim students to achieve academic distinction? It is generally low priority given to educational development and career making of children. The attitude of Muslim parents and guardians and their approach to education makes the real differences. The children are not inspired to aspire for higher academic standard and are not reminded of their present task and future target. Consequently the Muslim lack initiative and do not make the best use of their potentialities that really counts in education is not well sought for."[65] Dr. Qidwai appeals the Muslim parents to realize that investment in education is as rewarding as investment in any other sector like agriculture or industries etc, there is a need for change of approach towards education.[66]

5. Muslim Management

One important aspect of the educational backwardness of Indian Muslim that we should not ignore is working condition of Muslim managed educational institution itself, particularly in Northern India. Indian Constitution guarantees the fundamental rights to its Citizen, under which article 29&30 deals with the Minorities right to establish and manage educational Institution. Various religious and linguistic minorities established educational institutions of their choice. Indian Muslims also established such institutions though their number is not enough but there is a common and strong feeling that these institutions specially established by Muslims are not in a good condition rather they are ill administered. These institutions were setup with the laudable purpose to promote education among them. Most of these institutions are not properly managed and are least bothered to upgrade their standard both qualitatively and quantitatively and lack work culture "the apathy and Callousness of the Muslim managed educational institutions is the main reason of educational backwardness." remarks A.R. Shirwani as "conscious, honest and earnest effort resulted in improvement".[67] These institutions have become a dumping ground for the employment of kith and kin. The performance of any institution depends upon the combination of the managing committee, the principal, teachers, students and the community at large, and their cooperation and coordination etc. Usually in these committees such persons get memberships who have neither interest in education due to their preoccupation nor have any formal educational background. Even such examples are not rare that in these schools and colleges, the secretary or members of the committee are either high school pass or dropout but they get the place due to financial power or numerical strength. The Secretary or committee members work in a despotic and autocratic manner, humiliate the teaching and non-teaching staff and interfere in almost all the academic and day to day activities of the institution. During teachers interviews they may ask such questions which have no relevance with the subject and appoint such persons with whom their personal petty interest is attached. They are guided by local, religious, caste or sectarian considerations. The tussle for power, funds and ego clashes among the committee members and influence groups, old and new teachers, professional and non professional staff, secretary/principal/teaching staff etc. are very common and perhaps the most rampant factors harming the cohesion, culture and educational productivity of the institutions. Managing committee particularly its principal or secretary considers such institutions as their personal property. Teachers and other employees are treated as domestic servants.[68] Misappropriation of funds, irregularities from admission to examination is a common phenomenon. In such institutions teachers may be warned, mentally tortured, harassed, humiliated, suspended, terminated and even liquidated if they refuse to fall in line to tame them so that they could not raise voice against any grievances or wrong doings. Instead of being governed by any rule of law they are governed by whimsical ideas and rule on the plea that as being a minority institution—a holy cow, government or any other agency can not interfere in its affairs. Under such circumstances staff become sycophants to keep their bosses in good humour and take least interest and enthusiasm in teaching learning process. Such institutions lack educational initiative and environment of mediocracy prevails leading to mere some tricks or tamashas[69] or as Shaukat Ali observed, "except educational activities all types of activities flourish there."[70]

Syed Hamid observes that "with some exceptions Muslim managed schools and colleges have been faction-ridden and stagnant. Unfortunately many of those among us who are associated with the pernicious habit of flying at each other's throat, succumbing to the dictates of a bloated ego and sacrificing the institutions to selfish motives".[71] He further comments that the biggest weakness, which pushes us backward, is that we are incapable of running institutions. All our institutions are the area of mutual clashes. Not only this the admissions and appointments are more on the basis of the pulls, pressures and favours and less on the consideration of the merit which affects equally the levels of the students as well as the teachers in an adverse manner.[72]

6. Muslim Leadership

Mani Shankar Aiyar and lots of other social scientists consider Pakistan as the root cause, basic & primordial cause for Muslim backwardness as "the partition robbed the community of its leader—from grass root level to upward, with the migration of Muslim elite".[73] The Indian Muslims have been named as a cephalous and anthropologists define the cephalous society as one without leadership. It literally means without a head—a chief to get through them at the time of emergency. After partition the dearth of dynamic leadership of the community to lead it out in a comfortable position in the social, educational and economic fields free from communal and political ill-feelings together with the base of strong organization and committed to the cause of the community had strongly been felt.

But it does not mean that there is a dearth of Muslims leadership. Akbar S. Ahmad, a Pakistani journalist and bureaucrat divided the Indian Muslim society in three strata upper, Middle and lower classes. The first in the strata belongs to princes; *Nawabs* and landlords who could not cope with the rapidly changing social order, some of them drifted to Pakistan while most of them sank into oblivion. The middle class consisted of lawyers, doctors, teachers, and other professionals who had migrated en—block to Pakistan. A dynamic middle class at its best has provided leaders, ideas, continuity, stability and strength to the community. (Maulana Azad, Allama Iqbal and Mohd. Ali Jauler etc. belonged to this class). The migration of the middle class devastated the social structure of Indian Muslims and was largely responsible for their cephalous conditions. The third category belonging to general public scattered in urban, Slums and villages comprising of the peasants, artisans and domestic servants remained in Indian and continued life as best they could. They clang to their traditional dress and languages in spite of pressure and in some place become easy fodder for communal disturbances.[74]

K.A. Kadeer classifies Muslim leadership in the post independence period in the following three categories, some lustre of their own, like Maulana Azad and Zakir Hussain and others but lost in their luster without for the community. Other Muslim ministers and Governors—by and large are men of mediocre talents lifted to power by virtue of their ability to satisfy their masters, while a third group consists of M.C. Chagla, M.H. Baig etc. distinguished in their own professions who stayed in politics only to betray the community for their personal glorifications. Of the three types thrown into the vortex of power, the first category is harmless, the second is useless and the third a positive danger to the community.[75]

Due to lack of proper and enlightened leadership there is confusion and chaos. Enlightened leadership means men of integrity who enjoy the confidence of all including the core of majority community and of the country as a whole endowed with sincerity of purpose. They should be able to obtain due share of goods and resources and the lackeys who are happy with the crumbs they get from the tables of the haves and not ask for more.

Kis ko yeh fikr hai ke qabiley ka kya hua
Sab ko yeh fikr hai ke Sardar kown ho.

(No one is bothered for the condition of the community but all are thinking that who will be its leader.)

Muslim intellectuals have a feeling that the post independent Muslim leadership belongs to above mentioned classification. The first group had more or less vanished from the political scene with a few at state level. The second group is dominating the socio-political scene but they lack integrity of purpose. They do have less influences on the society and make sensational and cheap talks at the time of election and the voting pattern of the community at large is so built up that they are able to extract the Muslim support leading to their victory and ultimately ignoring the Muslim cause for at least another five years. The third group is small but enjoys all the government patronage. They don't face the community, as the community by and large is sensitive on these issues. In this way Muslim society in post independence period is a rudderless ship tossing and turning at the whims of the wind. They are in search of a good honest and sympathetic leader. They want a leader who can tell them that Islam is not pillow to rest upon but a belt to be girdled round the waist so that they are better able to strive for excellence in a highly competitive society.

Muslim community will be better off if its leaders and intellectuals work for social reforms and play a creative and constructive role for its welfare and create a general awareness regarding the importance of education. "But Muslim leadership", remarked Syed Hamid, "had seldom been alive to the importance of education...the infatuation of Indian Muslim with politics and the habits of their leaders to make rational attitude and educational progress impossible."[76] N.C. Saxena also blames "the Muslim leadership who had done nothing to ensure that the community gets rid of the feeling of integrity and despair."[77] Bihar state Minorities Commission in its report submitted to the State Govt. in January 2005, suggested that enlightened leadership and their efforts to organize their community could only improve the condition of the Muslim as they can play a stellar role in promoting wider and more effective participation by the community in social and political organization.

7. Government Attitude

This includes that central, state as well as local Government and its various agencies are not at all interested in the education of Muslim as it failed to provide an atmosphere of security and has been consciously trying to keep them economically and educationally backward so that they may not be aware of their rights and raise voice against any exploitation or social injustice. The educational backwardness is also due to the biased bureaucracy, as the government scheme of Muslim welfare does not reach the common people.

In a democratic set up it is the duty of the government to look after the prosperity of its citizens. Indian constitution has clearly ordained that there will be no discrimination among its citizens on what so ever ground. But the Muslim masses, their intellectuals and leaders have a feeling that government is apathetic and consciously trying to keep the Muslim backward. "There is a plan to corner the Muslim and lamentation about it is only an act of window dressing. The guilty man of the state of affairs knows the fact too well."[78] Ausaf S. Vasfi comments, "Muslim backwardness in education is not due to the aversion to education but it is due to the atmosphere of insecurity which is all pervading among Muslims. Their insecurity, which haunts and threatens them day in and day out particularly in northern states, keeps them on tenterhooks and their family equilibrium unstable. It keeps Muslims in the defensive and demoralized atmosphere and in this situation what positive or concrete action can be expected."[79] The life, honour and property of Muslim are not secure. Their plight is miserable and they are worst victims in the frequent outbursts of communal violence. They are the target of attack not only by the misguided elements of majority but of the armed police, the guardians of law and order who let loose a reign of terror on Muslims by turning their guns against them, violating their indiscriminate arrests. "On purely educational ground in many places," remarks A.R. Shirwani, "education of Muslim is being throttled due to official neglect, apathy and even hostility of certain petty-minded officials".

He further comments, there are many Muslim majority villages and areas where the government has not opened any school while adjoining Hindu areas have many".[80] Instead of opening schools whatever the schools Muslim had opened do not get recognition and grant in aid. Their files get storm of dust in spite of all persuasion and are ultimately closed down. N.C. Saxena a senior I.A.S. & former secretary, Minority Commission and Director Lal Bahadur Shastri National Academy of Administration, reported that "during" field work he founded that 99 per cent of the schools were located in Hindu majority areas while 95 per cent of the police stations are located in the Muslim majority areas." Does this imply, asks Shirwani, that the Hindus deserve to be educated while the Muslims deserve DANDA?[81] Syed Shahabuddin a former member of LokSabha from Kishan Gunj constituency (Bihar) narrates that Urdu speaking people dominate Deghal bank area of Kishan Gunj but surprisingly in all 68 schools located, there is hardly Urdu teacher though Urdu enjoys the status of second official language of Bihar.[82] In Bihar and Jharkhand such cases are also numerous, when Urdu unit of a school is filled by Sanskrit and Hindi teachers even in the Muslim dominated areas.

It is also a fact that the constitutional rights of Minorities are at the mercy of biased bureaucracy. They hardly exercise them without going to the courts of law. Scores of educational right cases are still awaiting verdict of the Supreme Court, High court and other law courts, where however court verdict has been given in favour of the minorities, the Government machinery, which has to implement them knows ways and means to stall the process.

So far the minority commission is concerned it was appointed by the Janata party government to review the various existing safeguards provided in the constitution for minorities against the discrimination, denial or deprivation of rights and to recommend legal administrative and other measures to ensure their implementation for betterment of the minorities (especially the Muslim) Mrs. Indira Gandhi former Prime Minister and then opposition leader commented that "it was appointed just to shelve Muslim problems, instead to solve them." Feelings of Muslim intellectuals were not different from it, S.N. Fardi remarks, "these cells and commissions are merely patch work shooting a show as it does not help in spirit.[83] As once a British Prime Minister had commented that if one finds difficulty in entertaining the grievances of the victims he should immediately appoint a committee.

Though Muslims constitute about 15 per cent of the total population of combined Bihar they are not represented even to the extent of 3 per cent in the educational administration, in subordinate educational set up Muslims are not more than 2 per cent, same is true of the Ministerial staff and class IV employees. In general schools and colleges including the Government institutions the Muslim representation is not even 2 per cent and discounting the language teachers the percentage is even less than one.

A committee with Syed Hamid (former V.C.A.M.U & present Chancellor of Jamia Hamdard New Delhi) as its chairman was constituted to make on the spot study of the Programme of Action (POA) under 1986 Educational policies and 15-point Programme for the welfare of minorities. The committee after studying the ground situation in three states i.e. UP, Bihar and Delhi concluded in its report that "the provision relating to education of minorities in the programme of action have not been implemented or any instruction have never been issued to district authorities nor the 15 point programme received any attention and no steps for educational advancement of minorities were ever initiated, further they were neither monitored nor even reviewed and though state governments were fully aware of the educational backwardness, they never cared to probe into reasons for the backwardness. Muslims were kept in dark about their educational status and the nation which was kept in the dark all the time continued to consider the majority of the Muslims as obscurantist, reactionaries and fundamentalists". "What more can one expect from a community kept in total dark about its ignorance and illiteracy? Questions the report".[84]

Though the National Policy on Education 1986 identified Indian Muslims as an educationally back ward and deprived community but the progamme of action it adopted is not adequately remedial, remarks Syed Shahbuddin. Educational development is not a matter of opening a few community polytechnics and industrial training institute in selected districts or establishing coaching classes in selected urban centers or modernizing Madarsa education.[85] But educational development means providing more primary schools, more secondary schools, more vocational training centers, more industrial training institutes, more polytechnics, more general and professional colleges all over the country on the basis of national norms so that the Muslims mohallas villages, panchayats, wards, blocks and towns are not left out. The mother tongue must be used as the medium of instruction at least at primary and secondary stages. The text books should not include any offensive or derogatory materials, the school culture should not reflect the religious ethos of the majority community so that the student of other community do not run the risk of loosing their cultural and religious identity. And only the promise of gainful employment in due measure can beacon the parents to sacrifice the present for the future.

"The remedy for backwardness of Muslims as a social group at the national or the state level lies in social justice", comments Syed Shahabuddin "Give the Muslim his proportionate share in every welfare or development scheme at all levels panchayats, upwards no more no less...Muslim will transform within a generation."[86]

8. Text Books and School Culture

One of the important reasons for the antagonistic relationship between the two major communities i.e. Hindus and Muslims in India and Muslim avoidance to modern and secular education is the feeling of the Muslim Community as such that school text books and school culture contains materials which are against the religious faith and tends to proselytize their younger generation. They contend that it militates against the very foundations of Islamic faith i.e. its concepts of a monotheism and apostleship etc. (Nigam[87] Smith[88]). They suspect that in this way educational institutions through its text books, comics, additional supplementary reading, school culture and other co-curricular activities seek to inject religious beliefs and cultural values of the majority community into the minds of Muslim children and youth (Latify[89] Nadvi[90] Hasan[91] Hamid[92] Shahbuddin[93] and Khan[94]). Through comics and supplementary readings children's mind is biased and prejudiced against Muslims who are painted as tyrants having lust for wine and women and no respects or regard for values and morals, (ever) fighting Hindus, killing them and tyrannizing over them.[95]

In these textbooks Muslim and their rulers are referred as jubians (unclean) melachas and turks (alien).[96] It indoctrinates the young mind with a particular ideology or tilt towards a particular way of thinking. An over weightage is given to the Hindu's rites, rituals, mythological, cultural and historical figures. The history, social science and language textbooks still follow the tradition of British Raj that was based on the distortion of history to justify the norms of Divide-et-empira. These books are full of objectionable materials, derogatory references, distorted and fabricated information and humiliating approach to Muslims. According to K. Ram Chandra Rao, "as the trend of the text books and school culture is, the future would see further alienation and increased animosity between the Indian Muslim and Hindus as they depict Muslim as thieves and murderers, bereft of ethical values etc. which influenced the immature minds of innocent children promoting further communal antipathy instead of harmony and with the advances age steeping them in communal poison.[97] O.P. Gupta reports that school culture is full of Hindus religious practices and is visible in the dramas that are enacted in the schools prayers and Pujas that are organized.[98]

Such examples are numerous as one book *Hamare Purvaj* has been prescribed for High school in three parts containing 65 lessons, the description on religious and historical personalities are as follows.

As the table 5.5 shows 47 religious and 12 historical personalities totaling 59 of Hindu faith have been incorporated while only 5 historical personalities of the Muslims have been included. Further among the Muslims, names of Akbar, Dara Shikoh, Chand Bibi etc. are there. Almost all the picture plates selected for the book depict Hindu religious faith and culture. Under the chapter Kabir, there is a block depicting Kabir in Turkish cap and Tehbund lying at the feet of Swami Ramanada.

Table 5.5: Religious and Historical Personalities.

	Religious personalities	*Historical personalities*	*Total*
Hindus	47	12	59
Muslims	Nil	05	05
Christians	Nil	Nil	Nil
Sikhs	01	Nil	01
Jains	Nil	Nil	Nil
Total	48	17	65

Besides this derogatory reference highly objectionable materials and lessons concerning the rites, rituals, mythology and religious beliefs of the majority community, a new trend is also emerging i.e. ignoring the heroes of Muslim phases of Indian history and if presented in most unflattering and even positively disgusting colour. Even the role of the Muslim freedom fighters and martyrs during India's National Movement has completely been ignored in the textbooks prescribed for the various classes in schools and colleges. References of Maulana Azad whose contribution is not less than any one else is only to abuses and counter the effect of Mohd. Ali Jinnah and his demand for Pakistan while Sir Syed & Allama Iqbal were held fully responsible to provide ideological base for Pakistan and partition of the country.[99]

"The fear of Muslims is not imaginary," comments Maulana Ali Main, "as the new educational system is rapidly throwing their children in the lap of religious and intellectual apostasy."[100] Parthasarthy Committee appointed by Ministry of education to review the text books in 1970 went on record that 3 per cent of books need immediate withdrawal from use, 20 per cent needed to be revised while 9 per cent books required deletion of certain portions.[101] In India the forces of chauvinism and of assimilation are at large whose main aim is to exploit education to spread disinformation about Islam and the Muslims to de-Islamise the Muslims youth. They want to impose an alien culture upon them in the name of national unity or integration, in brief to assimilate and adsorb them. "Why should" Muslim parents asks, "we send our children to schools? For deIslamization or Hinduisation, for brain washing, for developing an inferiority complex or for being subjected to humiliation and mockery." "The state should guarantee it," remarks Syed Shahabuddin "that education under a secular order is not a vehicle for cultural assimilation and for imposition of cultural or even a religious norms of one community over another."[102] There is an urgent need of some machinery to monitor the content and methodology even in this sensitive field.

9. Attitude of the Majority Community

This includes the conscious or unconscious approach of the majority community i.e. Hindus keep Muslims educationally backward so that the latter should take the position of SC & ST and *Achhuts* (Dalits) who are moving upwards. Some Hindu organizations want them to assimilate and absorb them in Hindu culture and are not prepared to accommodate them in India with a distinct identity or they fear that with the educated Muslims job opportunities will further diminish or they may lose cheap skilled or semi skilled labourers or there is phobia some where in their sub conscious that educated Muslims will rule or dominate them as they did in the past.

Nirad. C. Chaudhry narrated the Hindu perception of Muslims in the first decade of the last century in the following words " first we felt a retrospective hostility towards Muslims for their one time domination on us the Hindus, secondly on the plane of thought we were utterly indifferent to them: thirdly we had friendliness for the Muslims of our own economic and social status with whom we come into personal contact, our fourth feeling was mixed concern and contempt for Muslim peasants... as our live stock."[103] With a change of few phrases even after a century there are the same feelings among most of the members of majority community as the Muslims consider it.

Social Scientist believes that the main sources of conflict and tension are permanently rooted in the collective Hindu psyche." The Hindu elite visualizes the 700 years of Muslim rule in India as a period of forced conversion to Islam, destruction and conversion of temples into mosques and other symbols of humiliation. Muslims as a community are supposed to be exclusively responsible for the partition of the country. They consider Muslim as an outsider with extraterritorial loyalties, who is incapable of belonging to the country as a patriotic citizen. The Indian Muslims are treated as the fifth column of Pakistan.[104]

Islam is devouring Hinduism; Islam is a militant religion. It preaches brutality. Muslims believe in one God, one book and are more organized. They are orthodox and fanatical. Muslims continue to be aliens and don't adhere to the Indian civil code... and so they will have to pay the penalty of leaving India.[105]

The very concept of a nation is opposed to the Qura'n. Therefore if they do not have any feeling of affection for the country it is because of the Quranic Shariat i.e. Islamic System of governance is opposed to our constitution and law. If we have faith in our constitution we will have to ban Qura'n and Islamic System of governance.[106] On every Friday Muslim priests raise their hands and pray loudly from the Qura'n "Fansurna Ala quamil Kafreen (2.286) give us victory over the non believers, the Kafirs and millions of faithful say Ameen in thunderous supplications.[107]

A significant number of the majority community stresses on "the total loyalty to the nation as a condition to live in this country harmoniously"[108] and this "total loyalty means that the Muslims must in all aspect i.e. speech, dress, behaviour, sentiments and feeling etc. adopt Indian Culture which is Hindu culture. This is the only way to unity and Muslims must understand it".[109] Even the magazine like the Illustrated weekly of India in its editorial suggested that the Indian Muslims should adopt the Hindu name such as Ram & Sita if they wish to live peacefully in India. Indonesian Muslim do this so why Indian Muslim hesitate.[110] It asked:

Muslim as well as non-Muslim secular intellectuals and leaders have a feeling that anti Muslim forces have decided to push the Muslims down to the position of second class citizen to the lowest level to perform the menial tasks once reserved for Achhuts, to the hewers of wood and drawers of water, as it were to replace the adivasis, the Achhuts and the shuddras, as the latter rose one by one in the social and economic scale. One such intellectual K.R. Rao observes "I feel extremely sad to learn that Indian Muslims not only feel frustrated but also insecure in their own motherland. Muslims of India shed their blood like other Indians in defense of the country. They made great contribution to Indian civilization. They are as much part of Indian society as Hindus and so the latter have no right to order the Indian Muslims as they are in India in their own right, but not by mercy of Hindus. Unless this truth permeates the consciousness of every Indian, we can not have a harmonious or prosperous society in India." He further comments that, "Indian Muslims are unable to understand the demand by some Hindus that the Muslims should join the mainstream. They would like clarification and specification of the applications of this demand. Does it mean that they should give up their mother tongue and renounce their personal laws and social customs and habits? These are not demanded by the constitution from any citizens",[111] while Syed Shahabuddin comments that "how far back in history can you go and how far in future will you carry your burden of bitterness, why must you preach the doctrine of perpetual hatred, of constant confrontation."[112]

India is a multi-lingual, multi-religious, multi-racial and multi-cultural country based on the principle of peaceful coexistence. It has adopted a constitution, which is secular in its nature as it provides all freedom known to modern civilization. In spite of this, communalism is reasserting in its body politic. Though legally and constitutionally Hindus are in a dominating position. Political power is in their hands by virtue of their number and this has given them the leverage to monopolize economic resources as well. There is a need that minority should be protected from the permanent tyranny of religious majority against absorption and assimilation, against coercion and violence, against fear and hatred incited by the unchecked articulation of the religious right, the extremist fringe, the chauvinist groups and fundamentalist parties through their anti secular, anti democratic, anti constitutional ravings and ratings. Majority community should realize that the Muslims are as much part of the Indian society as they are. A changed atmosphere, attitude and point of view with a sympathetically and cooperative approach is needed towards Muslim problems.

10. Medium of Instruction and Examination System

Educationists all over the world agree that the medium instruction for the younger children must be their own mother tongue as the subject other than mother tongue required double labour one to know the language while other in knowing the subject matter or acquiring proficiency. Education through mother tongue has been accepted as the educational and psychological requirement, which helps the children to blossom and his mind to open up and become a tuned receiver of knowledge and information, so it is the basic right of the children. First All India Provincial Education Ministers Conference held in Delhi in August 1949 adopted a resolution that the medium of instruction and examination in the junior stages must be the mother tongue of the child and where the mother tongue is different from the regional or state language arrangement must be made for instruction in the mother tongue by appointing at least one teacher provided there are not less than 40 pupils speaking the language in the whole school or 10 such pupils in a class. The mother tongue will be the language declared by the parent or guardian to be the mother tongue.[113] In 1956 two articles 350 A&B were incorporated in the constitution (7th Amendment Act 1956) which states "it shall be the endeavour of any state and every local authority within the state to provide adequate facilities for instruction in the mother tongue at the primary education to children belonging to linguistic minority groups and the president may issue such direction to any state as he considers necessary or proper for securing the provision of such facilities."[114]

According to 2001 census Urdu ranked sixth position (i.e. 51.5 million person spoke Urdu as their mother tongue) among the major languages spoken as mother tongue in India while in combined Bihar 11.8 million persons spoke Urdu as their mother tongue. After independence deliberate efforts were made to oust Urdu from Indian soil especially in UP where it was attempted to convert it into a monolingual state and destroy Urdu in its land of birth by digging at its very roots. In Bihar situation was a bit different as due to public pressure and constant efforts of Urdu wallas it had been declared as the second official language of the state. But unfortunately no effective step had yet been taken for education of Urdu speaking children in their own mother tongue. The resolution of the Education Ministers Conference or the constitutional guarantee and the feeling of educationists turned out to be nothing more than a pious declaration. No arrangement has been made to implement the constitutional or other agreed schemes for learning and acquiring proficiency in mother tongue at the middle/high school level. There are some Muslim managed Urdu middle/and high schools in the state though they have their own problems like recognition, affiliation, grants in aid and internal feud etc. but as the several survey reports indicate that Muslim students with Urdu medium are doing well in comparison to Hindi medium students. Take the example of Bihar in 1985 the average result of all mediums indicates that pass percentage was 72.43 per cent while the result of Muslim schools with the Urdu medium was 86 per cent in Bihar Secondary School Examination Board.[115]

Problems with Urdu medium Students are numerous, as most of the institutions exist in almost sub human conditions. Their buildings are old, dilapidated, sparsely lit and unhygienic. Most of these schools do not have laboratories etc. And if any of them have it lacks proper equipment.[116]

Text books in Urdu are also not available in most of the cases as N.C.E.R.T. or state agencies stopped or delayed publication of most of the text books particularly science, mathematics and social sciences in Urdu for various classes. If some books are published it is approximately four to eleven months late so student could not get its benefits, even they become outdated since the books or courses are changed without any rhyme or reason. Further in the government school medium of instruction is either Hindi or other regional languages and so after getting some education in Urdu medium if one desires to enter in other medium school get it difficult to complete with other students. Those who cross the schooling threshold the disincentive to raise their knowledge of Urdu to university education in any subject other than Urdu language and literature is virtually unavailable. Thus weak foundation in Hindi or English further adversely affects Muslim students at college and University level as there is no text book or learning materials in Urdu, and lectures are delivered either in Hindi or English. More than that student are allowed to answer in Urdu scripts but there are no provisions of script examiners. Usually these answer books are evaluated by those examiners who do not even recognize a single alphabet of that language and if a few honest examiners return such copies without evaluating them the secondary school examination board, intermediate council or university will not bother to get it evaluated but either the result will be declared by providing an average marks or be put pending and to get the pending result cleared is not an easy task. During the centralized evaluation answer books are summarily evaluated. 'Copy kati jati hai,' is a term generally used to indicate the non seriousness in evaluating the answer books where no real effort is made to judge the merit of the answer books. Moreover Muslim students have to learn some more languages as compared to their counterparts. Besides English and Hindi they are also supposed to learn Urdu, Persian or Arabic, their mother tongue and cultural or religious language as well as the language of the holy Qura'n.

The chapter under review discusses the causes of educational backwardness of Indian Muslims in general and Muslims of Bihar in particular. The revolt of 1857 was devastating in its nature as it affected almost all the spheres of Indian Muslims the publication of William Hunter's book—"the Indian Musalman" (1871) highlighted their deteriorating condition created a storm with regard to its different aspects of finding. Sir Syed Ahmad Khan earnestly investigated the reason for avoidance of English education by the Indian Muslims and reached to a definite conclusion with the determination to start Mohammedan-Anglo-Oriental College at Aligarh and publication of social reform magazine "The Tehzibul Akhlaq" popularly known as the Aligarh movement. It showed a healthy trend throughout the country as the socio-economic; political; cultural and educational condition changed sharply and in a very short span of period Indian Muslims were well ahead to others.

In the post independence period, once again, the Indian Muslims are facing deprivation and backwardness in almost all aspect of life particularly in education. Hakim Abdul Hameed sincerely attempted to know the reasons of educational backwardness by surveying the Muslim managed educational institutions of India (1980) and identified financial and intramural problems of these institutions. Social scientists and workers consider some more reasons responsible for the educational backwardness of Indian Muslims in general and Muslim of Bihar in particular. Besides, very poor economic condition, the general lethargy of the parents and community, discriminatory and biased attitude of the government, unfriendly and indifferent attitude of the majority community, objectionable materials in text books and school culture, poor educational environment in Muslims managed educational institutions, lack of proper & sincere Muslim leadership, absence of text books in Mother tongue and faulty examinations system etc. are considered as some major causes which arrested the progress of education among Muslims of Bihar in the post independence period.

REFERENCES

1. W.W. Hunter—*The Indian Musalmans* (London, 1871), pp. 132-33. A reprint of this book was issued in 1964. (Delhi, 1969).

2. *Ibid.*, p. 148.
3. Mujeeb Ashraf—*Muslim Attitudes towards British Rule and Western culture in India* (Delhi, 1982), p. 18.
4 W.W. Hunter—*Op cit.*, p. 102.
5. Andre servier—*Islam and Psychology of Musalmans* (London, Chapman1924), pp. VII-IX.
6. Andre servier, *Op cit.*, p. 12.
7. Irfan Ahmad—Islam Aur Science. *Tahzibul Akhlaq*, vol. 4 No. 13 (Aligarh, July 1985), p. 5, quoted from Taha Hussain, *Ibn Khaldum* pp. 229-30.
8. Abdus Salam—"Arab aur Alam Islam mein science ka Ahya". *Tahzeebul Akhlaq*, Vol. 20 No. 2 (Aligarh, October 1983), p. 5.
9. Abdus Salam (*Ibid*), p. 5.
10. Hafiz Ibn Qaim—"Musalman Ke Pasti Ke Asbab". *Tahzeebul Akhlaq*, Vol. 4, No. 13 (Aligarh, July 1925), p. 7.
11. Sheukh Mohd. Akram—*Raud Kausar* (Delhi, Abid Dunya), 1986 p. 171 quoted from Maktubat Imam Rabbani 3/23, p. 170.
12. Shibli Nomani—*Al Ghazali* (Aligarh, March 1956), p. 176.
13. Abu Hayat—*Musalman of Bengal* (Calcutta, Rabi 1966), p. 16.
14. Shan Mohammad—Introduction—*Writing and Speeches of Sir Syed Ahmad Khan* (Bombay, Nachiketa 1972), p. 8.
15. Sir Syed Ahmad Khan—Speech at Meerut on 14/3/1888, Shan Mohammad, *Op cit.*, p. 199.
16. W.W. Hunter—*Report of the India Education Commission 1882-1885*, pp. 483-507; Rafiq Zakaria *Rise of Muslims in Indian Politics—An Analysis of Development from 1885-1906* (Bombay, Somaiya 1970), pp. 174-76.
17. J. Murray Mitchell—*Musalman of Bengal*. Report of the General Missionary Conference held at Allahabad (1872-73).
18. *The Alpanch*—Daily News paper (Kanpur, 27th August 1872) p. 3.
19. Syed Tufail Ahmad—*Musalmano ka Raushan Mustaqbil* (Delhi, Azizia 1945), p. 158.
20. M.K.A. Siddique—*Educating backward Minority* (Calcutta, Abadi 1984).
21. *Ibid.*, p. 19.
22. Syed Abul Fazal—*On the Muhammadan of India* (Calcutta, 1872), pp. 14-15.
23. Shan Mohammad—*Op cit.*, p. 5.
24. Syed Hussain Bilgrami Presidential address at 14th Mohammadan Education Confererence held at Rampur—*The Pioneer* (Allahabad, January 5, 1901), Rafiq Zakaria, *Op cit.*, p. 5.
25. Azizur Rahman Malik—*The British Policy and the Muslims in Bengal* (Dacca, Asiatic 1961), p. 200.

26. Ram Gopal—*Indian Muslims* (Bombay, Asia, 1984), p. 19 and also Ninian Smart—The Religious Experiences of Man kind (New York, Charles 1969), pp. 421-23.
27. R.U. Shaikh—*The Radiance* Vol. XIX No. 52 (New Delhi, 6/5/1984).
28. Syed Shahabuddin—"Position of Muslims in UP Services before Partition", *Muslim India* No. 141 (Dekgu Sep. 1994), p. 413.
29. V.C. Chaudhary—*The Creation of Modern Bihar* (Patna, Motilal 1980), p. 72 and Ali Ashraf—*The Muslim Elite* (New Delhi, Atlantic 1982), p. 29.
30. A.R. Shirvani—"Assessing educational backwardness a right approach" *The Radiance,* Vol. XX, No. 32 (Delhi 16/12/84).
31. A.M. Khusro—*"Economic and Cultural Problem of Muslim"*, Address-Intellectual Meet on the Problems of Muslims (New Delhi, June 5, 1983).
32. Mani Shankar Aiyar—"Muslims backwardness the root causes" *The Sunday,* Vol. 22, No. 44 (Calcutta 5/11/95), p. 60.
33. Khalid Sabir—*"How much educationally backward Muslims are?"* News from India (New Delhi, June 5, 1983).
34. N.C. Saxena—*The Radiance* XIX No. 35 (8/1/84 & vol. XX, No. 4, 8/6/84).
35. A.R. Shirwani—*The Radiance* vol. XX No. 25 (New Delhi, 28/11/84).
36. Hasan Shahiullah Ashrafi—"Educational Problem of West Bengal Muslim". *The Radiance* XIX No. 51 (29/4/84).
37. S. Shamim Shah—*Educational Survey Report on Muslim Managed Schools and Colleges in India* (New Delhi, 1984), pp. xiii-xxiv.
38. *Ibid*—pp. 129-131 and also S. Shamim Shah—*"Major Problems of Muslim Managed Schools"* Paper presented at Problem of Employment and Education of Muslims (Aligarh, August 5 & 6 1983).
39. *Ibid*—pp. 71 and also Shamim Shah *"Educational and Economic Problems of Indian Muslims"*; Intellectual Meet on Problems of Muslims (New Delhi, June 5, 1983).
40. Sadruddin Islahi—"Nizam Batil ke Sath Taawun" *The Maarif,* Vol. 59 No. 1 (Delhi 1950), pp. 47-48.
41. Sadruddin Islahi—"Nizam Batil ke Sath Taawun". *The Zindagi,* Vol. 7 No. 2 (Rampur 1915), pp. 72-85.
42. N.C. Saxena—Public Employment and Educational Backwardness Among Muslims in India—A discussion paper A.M.U. Seminar (Aligarh 1983), pp. 10-11.
43. M.R.A. Baig—*The Muslim Dilemma in India* (Delhi, Vikas 65), p. 36.
44. Najma Amin—A.M.U. Conference 15/6/1986.
45. Maxime Rodines—*Islam and Capitalism* quoted by N.C. Saxena, *Op cit.*, p. 15.
46. Altaf Ahmad Azmi—*"Qura'n Majeed and Sciencce Uloom"* conference on science ki Talim Musalmano Mein. (Aligarh A.M.U. 15/1/1986).

47. Afzal Hussain—"Dichotomy of Religious and Secular Education" *The Rediance* XX No. 23 (Delhi 14/10/84).
48. Shahid Ali—"Problems of Education in Muslim World." *The Radiance* XIX (Delhi 7/3/1984).
49. M.K.A. Siddique—*Faryad-e-Jaras* (Calcutta Abadi 1987), pp. 27-32.
50. Mohd. Asad—*Islam at Cross Roads* (Lahore Arafat 1937), pp. 68-78.
51. M. Abdus Salam—"Socio economic Problems of Muslim of India" *The Radiance*, XX No. 1 (Delhi 13/5/1984).
52. M. Abdus Salam, *Ibid. The Times of India* 11 June, 1999.
53. Hasan Mujtaba Kamonpuri—"Poverty & Planning India." *The Radiance*, Delhi 31/7/1983.
54. Ali Ashraf—*"Perspective on the Educational Problems of Indian Muslim"* Address at the 7th All India Muslim Educational Conference (Delhi 1984).
55. Mehdi Hasan Quated by M.K.A. Siddique—*Educating Backward Minority* (Calcutta, Abadi 1984), p. 37.
56. Editorial—"Root of Backwardness"—*The Indian Express* (Delhi April 4, 1984).
57. Ms Anoice—*The Indian Express* (Delhi February 8, 1984).
58. Syed Shahabuddin—"Educating a Community". *Muslim Indian* No. 91 (July 1990), p. 292.
59. A.R. Shirwani—*The Times of India* (Bombay 1/4/84).
60. Syed Hamid—"Musalman Hind Ki Talim Samaji Aur Tehzibi Masail" *The Tehzibul Akhlaq*, Vol. 3, No. 16 (Aligarh A.M.U. August 1984), p. 3.
61. S. Shamim Shah, *Op cit.*, p. 71.
62. Syed Hamid—"Educational Status of Indian Muslim"—*Muslim India*, Vol. 3, No. 36 (New Delhi, December 1985), p. 553.
63. Syed Shahabuddin—Educating the Muslim Community. *Muslim India*, No. 145 (New Delhi, January 1995), p. 3.
64. Editorial—Root of Backwardness, *Op cit.*, No. 55 and also N.C. Saxena *Op cit.*, p. 10-11.
65. S. Niasim A. Zaidi—"Employment of Muslim in Public services". A case study of A.M.U. Alumni (Aligarh) A.M.U. 1983, p. 7.
66. A.R. Qidwai—Inaugural address seminar on Employment and Education of Muslims, A.M.U. Aligarh 5/8/83.
67. A.R. Shirwani—*The Times of India*, Bombay 1/4/84.
68. Shakeel Ahmad. *"Working of Muslim Managed Educational Institution of Bihar"* Paper presented at Bihar Muslim Educational Conference Patna 10/3/1986.
69. Ziaur Rahman Azmi—"Hamari Talim Aur Talimi Darsgeahein". *The Tehzibul Akhlaq*, Vol. 14, No. 13 (Aligarh March 95), p. 46.
70. Shaukal Ali—"Muslim Zeer Intizam School Ki Halat". *The Tehzibul Akhlaq* vol. 9, Syed Hamid, *Op cit.*, p. 553.
71. Syed Hamid—*Op cit.*, p. 553.

72. Syed Hamid—"Paper at all India Muslim Educational conference" Ghalib Academy, New Delhi, 24/10/93.
73. Mani Shankar Aiyar—*Op cit.*, p. 60.
74. Akbar S. Ahmad—*Religion and Polities in Muslim Society* (Lahore, Cambridge 1983), p. 65.
75. K.A. Kadeer Shah—"The Muslim Problems in India". *The Radiance* XIX No. 42 (Delhi February 26, 1984).
76. Syed Hamid—*Op cit., Muslim India,* Vol. 3, No. 36, p. 553.
77. N.C. Saxena—*Op cit.*, p. 10-11.
78. S.N. Faridi—"Orthodox Muslim Outlook". *The Radiance,* Vol. XIX No. 45, (Delhi, March 18, 1984).
79. Ausaf Saied Vasfi—*The Radiance,* XIX No. 35 (Delhi, 8/1/84).
80. A.R. Shirwani—*The Radiance,* XIX No. 38 (Delhi, 29/1/84).
81. A.R. Shirwani—*Interview the Surya* (New Delhi, April 15, 1984), and also Young Muslim Digest Vol. 8 No. 2 and 3 (Banglore, June 1984).
82. Syed Shahabuddin—*Interview Nai Dunya* (Urdu) Vol. 41, No. 28 (Delhi 28/12/85).
83. S.N. Faridi—*The Radiance* XIX No. 45 (Dated 18/3/84).
84. Joseph Maliakan—"Situation Report on Education for Minorities" *Muslim India,* No. 154 (New Delhi October 1995), p. 75.
85. Syed Shahabuddin—"Towards a New Action Plan for Minorities" *Muslim Indian,* No. 93 (New Delhi September 90), p. 387.
86. Syed Shahabuddin—"Response to Mani Shankar Aiyar" *Muslim India* No.156 (New Delhi, December 95), p. 573.
87. Nigam—*"Laying Secular Foundation through Education"*. The Secular Democracy (Delhi, April, 1964). p. 24.
88. D.E. Smith—*India as a Secular State* (Bombay, 1963), p. 211.
89. Danial Latifi—*"Redressal of Minority Grievances"—Mainstream,* Vol. 3 and 35.
90. Abul Hasan Ali Nadvi—*The Muslim in India* (Lucknow, *Majlis-e-Tahqiqat*).
91. S. Noorul Hasan—*"Presidential Address, Intellectual meet"* (New Delhi, June 5, 1984).
92. Syed Hamid—*"Syed Abid Hussain Memorial Lecture"* (Delhi, August 1984) and also *"Educational Status of India Muslim"*, *Op cit.*
93. S. Shahabuddin—"Educating a Community" *Muslim India,* No. 91 (New Delhi, July 1990), p. 292-293.
94. R.S.A. Khan—*The Radiance* (Delhi April 25, 1982).
95. A. Rahman—*"Historical and Sociological Back Grounds of Riots"*. Azad Academy Journal (Lucknow, March 1995) and& N.A. Makki, *Hindustan mein Gumrah Kun Tarikh Nawesi*—Jamshedpur 2005.
96. Through it is not our tasks to just defend the medieval rulers but analysis made by a man like K.R. Malkani editor of The Organizer will not be out of place to mention—"Muslim rulers did not establish

Islam as the State religion of India. Through many of them came from rough steppes of central Asia and gave India a Harsh administration they were basically political rulers and not a religious Zealots ...even the (mush maligned) Aurangzeb trusted only Hindus to guard his private apartment—K.R. Malkani—*The Statesman* (Calcutta August 30 1980).

97. K. Ramchander Rao—"Indian Muslim are Feeling insecure" *Manju Wani,* English Telgu Weekly 1983.
98. O.P. Gupta—Research Project *"Why Muslim Community Shuns Government School in UP"*.
99. M.A. Makki—*"Muslim Mojahideen Azadi our Hamiri Nisabi Kitabeen" The Tehzibul Aklaq*. (Aligarh June 1995) p. 35 and also *"Hindustan Chhuro Taahrik our Bihar ki Chand Muslim Shuhda". The Azad Hind* (Calcutta 18/9/74).
100. Abul Hasain Ali Nadvi—*Op cit.,* p. 130.
101. K.D. Sharma—*Education of a National Minority* (Delhi Kalamkar, 1978), p. 28.
102. Syed Shahabuddin—*"Educating a Community"* Muslim India, No. 91, *Op cit.,* p. 293.
103. Nirad C. Chaudhri—*Autobiography of an Unknown Indian* (Bombay, Jaico 1951), p. 2251.
104. Iqbal A. Ansari—*Muslim Situation in India,* New Delhi. Sterling Publishers 1989, p. 176.
105. Moin Shaker—*Islam in Indian Politics* (Delhi, Ajanta 1983), p. 45.
106. P.R. Rajgopal—*Communal Violence in India* (New Delhi, Uppal Publication House 1978), p. 25.
107. *Ibid.,* p. 26.
108. S.P. Singh—*The Hindu* (Madras, 27/10/1980).
109. R. Parthasarathy—*The Hindu* (Madras, 8/11/1980).
110. Editorial—*The Illustrated Weekly of India* (Bombay, 16/12/79).
111. K. Ramchandra Rao—*"Indian Muslim are Feeling Insecure" Op cit.* and also *The Radiance,* March 13, 1983.
112. Syed Shahabuddin—*The Radiance* (Delhi, 2/11/1980).
113. S. Abul Hasan Ali Nadvi, *Op cit.,* p. 130.
114. *Constitution of India* (Lucknow, Eastern Book 1980), p. 124.
115. A.R. Shirwani—"Are Muslims of UP lagging behind due to Hindi Medium" Stencil No. 449 Dated 15/5186.
116. Syed Tausif Ausaf—"Urdu Medium Education" *The Radiance,* XXXI No. 13 (New Delhi, 3/3/1996), p. 15.

6

Action Programme for Educational Development among Muslims: Conclusions and Suggestions

Islam has associated immense importance to the acquisition and extension of knowledge so much so that the very literal meaning of the word Qura'n is read or recite and 750 verses i.e. approximately 1/8 part of the holy Qura'n exhort the believers to study nature. In hundreds of saying prophet Mohammed (P.B.U.H) urged the followers to cultivate scientific temperament and sprit of reasoning, inquiry and investigation as seeking of knowledge is obligatory for every Muslim men & women. It was not merely for the sake of fun when about 1400 years ago he asked the believers to undertake a hazardous journey as from Arabia to China for the acquisition of knowledge. This all resulted into education which was considered as a divine command, Reading and writing rapidly spread not only in Arabia but in the whole Islamic empire. During Turko—Afghan and Mughal rules in Bihar education was a matter of right for all its citizens. The rulers, nobles and other officials considered it as a religious duty or *Sawab—jaria* and took keen interest in the spread of Knowledge. As religion formed the backbone of education so most of Maktabs and Madarsas were attached to *Masjid, Khanqah or Dargah* etc. William Adams in his reports on the state of education in Bihar and Bengal (1835-38) admits that during the above mentioned period there were about 1,00,000 indigenous schools in Bihar and Bengal i.e. roughly two school for every three villages. During the British period we found that as a trader they wanted to earn more and more profit so they adopted a policy of neglect and indifference. The antagonistic attitude of the British towards Muslim further arrested the progress of education among them. This policy continued till Sir Syed Ahmad Khan started his campaign popularly known as Aligarh Movement to change the British attitude and for social and educational regeneration of Indian Muslims. Consequently a number of social, literary, cultural and educational societies were established through out the state. Gradually Bihari Muslims realized the importance of western education and in a short span of time as the contemporary records indicate, the educational condition of the Muslims of Bihar improved to a significant extent. In the beginning of the present century Muslims were once again well advanced in comparison to Bihari Hindus.

In the post independence period we find that the Muslim were by passed in the development process of India, educational condition of the Muslims has once again deteriorated very much. This phenomenon is usually attributed to two commonly prevalent explanations—i.e. particular attitudes or cultural ethos, as there is close linkage between religious and secular spheres of life in Islam and emphasis is more on religious education. Further reluctance to secular education is also due to acute psychological complex as they coiled themselves up into their cultural shell. While another explanation refers to an invidious discrimination practiced against them, which is reducing them to the status of hewers of wood and drawers of water. In Bihar educational deterioration of Muslim is also attributed to the partition of the country and its after effects when about 3.5 lakh middle class Muslim families of north and central Bihar had migrated to the East and the West Pakistan for security and in search of greener pastures, leaving behind a large populace which was leader less and rudder less, educationally bankrupt, socially uprooted economically deprived and with an acutely depressed morale. But even after the 50 years of India's independence whatever the micro or macro studies were conducted reveals that the community, as such suffers from a number of disadvantages. Majority of whom are afflicted by low income, wide spread illiteracy and many other socio-economic disadvantages. Commission like those of High power panel on Minorities, the Mandal Commission and the individuals like Gopal Krishna, N.C. Saxena and others unmistakably pointed out the relative backwardness. Muslims are educationally handicapped, deprived and are not responding adequately to contemporary educational development and expansion. They have fallen in the vicious cycle of poverty—unemployment—illiteracy—conservatist attitude and lack of motivation etc.

In India Muslims have been recognized as religious and to a great extent a linguistic minority. They are the largest single significant minority as their number is 13,81,88,240 i.e. roughly 13.4 per cent of the total population of the country and only after Indonesia and Bangladesh has largest concentration of Muslims in the world. They are not ethnic minority as racially they belong to the same ethnic stock as the rest of the population, with common flesh and blood as most of them are converted Muslims. In spite of that they have a feeling of discrimination in all walks of life and are afraid of cultural and religious invasion by majority community and want prompt redressal of their grievances, which usually are not fulfilled or delayed. This ultimately leaves them alienated, fatalist or react violently by losing faith in the constitutional methods. A backward and segregated minority either rationalizes its present status as pre ordained or unscrupulous leadership may exploit its injured feeling. As they lose faith in all government machinery, also lose aspiration to progress or prosper. There is an urgent need that their grievances must be eliminated root and branch, if we want the minorities to form an effective part of the mainstream.

The most important complaint of Indian Muslim is the safety of life as frequent eruptions of planned communal riots and state terrorism when usually law and order enforcing authorities behave in a partisan manner have very much demoralized the morale of Muslims in the country. Several survey and study indicate that a very small portion of the Muslims find the police trust worthy and a very few find the role of the police to be unbiased during communal tension. The fascist forces have succeeded in their design to reduce Muslim stature to a pitiable size. They are discriminated in almost all spheres of life. Their representation in various services is inadequate, their mother tongue i.e. Urdu which is spoken by a population of 51.5 million has been forced into the ghettos and reduced to being the mother tongue of the most orphaned segment of India's population. Muslim considers it nothing less than cultural genocide. They complain that Indian mass media project them as fundamentalists, terrorists, anti-national, and foreigners and spread misinformation about Islam and Muslim and voice against their personal law. These are just to keep them forever on the defensive in order to divert their attention from their real problems.

A study conducted by the Bihar State Minority Commission reveals that the over all socio-economic status of the Muslims of Bihar is generally inferior to that of the others sections of population. Out of 1,74,53,356 Muslims in Bihar, about 87 per cent Muslims live in rural areas while remaining 13 per cent live in urban areas. Though Islamic ethos is basically egalitarian, and in its religious texts no division of the society ordained by birth but due to long interaction with the Hindus, 43 castes among the Muslims of Bihar were identified. Their economic condition both in rural and urban areas are worse so a large majority of them migrate out side the state in search of job or livelihood. The average annual income of Muslim household is meager so about 49.5 per cent of them live below the poverty line and nearly all the poverty alleviation programmers of the government by pass the community. The death rates are higher due to inferior health care for them. The over all literacy rates for the Muslims are lower than the general population, secondly the gender differences in the literacy rates are narrower among the Muslims. About 1/5 of the Muslim children in the school going age do not attend school in both urban and rural areas. The majority of Muslim students receive their education through Hindi more so in the urban areas. The use of Urdu as a medium of instructions is rather limited.

The result of the socio-economic status scale, conducted by the present researcher, of the Muslims of Bihar shows that the students studying at various schools and colleges of the state belong to the lower and lower middle strata, which is higher among the Muslim i.e. 70.4 per cent while among non-Muslim it was 52 per cent, a difference of 18.4 per cent. So far the upper middle and upper strata is concerned their percentage were 29.6 per cent and 48 per cent respectively. This means that those Muslim families who can afford to teach their wards in schools and colleges are poor in comparison to those non-Muslim students who are either their class mates or are studying in more or less same types of educational institution in the surroundings.

Chapter proceeding deals with the causes and explanation of educational backwardness of Indian Muslims in general and Muslims of Bihar in particular. The revolt of 1857 was devastating in its nature as it adversely affected almost all the spheres of Indian Muslims. The publication of William Hunter's book, *The Indian Musalman* (1871) highlighted their deteriorating condition and created a storm with regard to its different aspects of finding. Sir Syed Ahmad Khan founded Mohammedan Anglo Oriental College in 1875 at Aligarh and started the publication of a social reform magazine, *Tehzibul Akhlaq*. The movement started by him is known as Aligarh Movement which showed a healthy trend throughout the country as the socio-economic, political, cultural and educational conditions of Muslims changed sharply and in a very short span of period Indian Muslims were well ahead than the others.

In the post independence period whatever the information and statistics are available through macro or micro studies clearly indicates that the Muslim community as such suffers from a number of disadvantages. Mani Shanker Aiyer report that "on every index of development, income, education, health, share in Government services, share in private enterprise, role in self employment, in legislatures—the level of their achievement is substantially below their share of population. The only index on which they figure higher than

12 per cent is poverty". Even the Government of India in its report National Education policy 1986 accepted that Muslims are educationally deprived and backward lot. There is no need to delve deep into the historical and other reasons, which can be attributed to this sad state of affairs. The general lethargy of the parents and ethos of the community, discriminatory and biased attitude of the Government, unfriendly and indifferent attitude of the majority community and attempt of some communal organization to assimilate and absorb them in Hindu culture through objectionable and indoctrinated text books and school culture, defective examination system and absence of text book in Urdu, wounds of the partition which are not yet healed, lack of proper and sincere leadership, priorities and too much stress on religious institution, undue importance given to emotional and non issues at the expense of educational and economic activities, too much involvement in petty politics, lack of strong social and educational organization etc. are some of the relevant factors which lead Muslim communities into the darkness of backwardness in every field of human endeavour in Bihar. Now there is no use of just crying over split milk or blaming this factor or that but the need of the hour is time bound Programme of action on a war footing to remedy the situation. The following suggestions can be adopted for educational advancement and expansion of Muslims of Bihar.

The main difficulty in studying the educational status of Indian Muslims particularly in Bihar is unavailability of community wise accurate and authentic data, which is regarded as potentially an act of repression. The various agencies of the Government like Registrar General of Census, Ministry of Home Affairs, National Sample Survey and Minority Commission etc. should be approached to conduct and publish from time to time the cross tabulated literacy and educational statistics of the various communities. Further the Centre for promotion of Muslim Education and Cultural Development of A.M.U. Aligarh, Hamdard Education Society New Delhi, Institute of Objective Studies New Delhi, All India Muslim Educational Conference and recently established

Forum for Literacy Awareness and Muslim Education (FLAME) at Patna etc. should also sit together to collect and disseminate information. The deficiencies and trends should be brought out to facilitate action; regional variation and rural urban differences should also be taken into consideration.

As the study conducted by the Bihar State Minorities Commission shows that the socio-economic condition of the Muslim in Bihar, practically in all aspects is much lower than that of the general population of the state. It is therefore extremely important to take urgent, effective and where possible special measures to enhance there incomes and expand their employment opportunities.

As the vast majority of the Muslims live in rural areas measure should be adopted to improve the condition in the rural areas like improving agricultural productivity, building the rural infrastructure, processing of primary products and reviving rural based industries. Further as the poverty alleviation programme of both the Central and State governments, it is important to issue specific instruction to those responsible for implementing these programmes to make a conscious effort to ensure that the benefits of these programmes reach the Muslim population. In this connection priority should be attached to programmes design to enhance incomes, provide employment, develop skills and provide assets for undertaking productive activities. Secondly loan from the Minority Development and Finance Corporation should be given to the needy.

Social Stratification and often out right discrimination is the predominant, if not the sole reason for the insignificant presence of Muslims in Bihar in the organized sectors and for their much less than proportionate share of government jobs. Special measures are called for to over-come this segmentation of the labour market. These include setting target for the recruitment of Muslim in these jobs and monitoring their progress on a regular periodical basis.

To free Muslim from their siege mentality and to counter attempts to their ghettoisation a radical change in their social life style is needed, which is possible just to explore a sense of mission in them. It will provide a cure for many of the ailments the community suffers from including the siege mentality and sectarian divisiveness and pursuit of vanity.

The Muslim should not let the state abdicate its responsibility for educating the Muslim boys and girls. Central as well as state Government should be approached to fully implement Article 45 of the Indian Constitution for introducing free and compulsory education for all children till they attain the age of fourteen years. As the Supreme Court in its recent judgment accepted the right of education as a fundamental right, the Muslim Community must exercise it on equal terms.

This universalisation of education automatically implies that every slum, village, mohalla should have centre for elementary education. It should provide nutritious mid day meals, apart from uniforms and reading writing materials as an incentive. It should have a playground, recreational and extra curricular facilities etc. The poor parents should be compensated by the state for the loss of their earning of their children to schools; they must do this so that a new crop of happy, confident and articulate children comes up.

More schools should be opened in Muslim localities with suitable teachers. There is also a need to open technical institutions in large number for dropouts as well as for those who do not make the grade for professional courses taking into account their aptitudes, interest and availability of local resources.

The Minorities Commission should be given statutory status both at centre and state and should be transformed into chief machinery as envisaged in the Gopal Singh High Power Panel Report which should supervise and guide the steps taken by the Central and State Government and Muslim organization and institutions for their social, economic and educational advancement. The minorities cell should be created in every departments and ministry at central, state and local levels and it should be made more effective. The various recruiting agencies, board and admission committee should have Muslim representative to watch their interest and to eliminate all possible influence of prejudice and discrimination. The system should not only be fair but also appear to be fair so that psychological indifference of community towards education is over come.

The Muslim Community should invest their own resources i.e. *Zakat, Khairat* and other donation in establishing standard Maktabs or Qur'anic schools in every mosque for religious instructions so that every children can learn and those who goes to school spends an hour or so everyday in his local Maktabs to learn about Islam or attends intensive weekly courses on Sunday or closed holidays as a part time religious instructions like Kerala or Gujarat. The general Maktab education should also have the provision for the teaching of social studies, elementary science and simple arithmetic.

Beyond Maktabs full time religious or theological education should be organized in a planned manner through Madarsa, Darul-uloom and Jamia to train the future *Muhaddis, Muftis, Alim, Hafiz & Qari* etc. to meet religious needs of the community. In fact it would be ideal to have the nation wide system of affiliation to the central body of various school of thought like Darul Oloom Debond, Nadwatul Ulooma Lucknow or Madarsa of Bareilly or Banaras etc. the Madarsa syllabus should rationalize itself by including Modern Indian languages like Hindi, English, Science and Social Sciences, like Physical Science, Biological Science, Mathematics, History, Geography and Social Studies etc. without over loading the students or destroying the essentially religious feature of the Madarsas. The teacher of such institution should have proper qualification and training, which should further be enriched by providing regular orientation and refresher courses and workshop in their specific field by eminent scholars to further enrich it. So far the financial aspects are concerned in Bihar it self several crores of Rupees are collected annually by these Madarsas from the believers as *Zakat, Fitra or Atiya* etc. There is need to have proper financial management so that these amounts are not misappropriated.

The modernization of Madarsa education is the need of the hour as their graduate should not merely be a religious scholar but should have a modern mind, scientific temperament and broader outlook to understand the spirit of time and appreciates our rich cultural inheritance, global tendencies. The contribution of science and technology can regulate the flow of social energy in the proper and desirable direction. It is also needed that Madarsa education should be organized in suitable stages and segments so that at any stage the students may switch from the religious to the general education and vice-versa to bridge the two system of education. At equivalent to higher secondary or +2 stage a vocational input may by introduced to respectable livelihood and do not necessarily end up as a *Muazzin or Imam* of a mosque or teacher of a Maktab/Madarsa.

As there are two systems of education, religious and secular, the secular education can further be subdivided into two on the basis of whether this education is imparted by the government institution or minority institutions under articles 29&30 of the Indian constitution.

Indian Muslim's must take the advantages of the constitutional provision of Fundamental rights to establish and administer educational institutions of their choice in a large number as a means to maintain their religious, cultural and linguistic identity. The Government should adopt liberal, simple and clear-cut procedure to recognize, affiliate and provide financial assistance to such institutions if they fulfill the requisite criteria. There should be a time bound Programme of recognition and these institutions should follow the common syllabus and come up to the requisite standards. But at the same time they should be free to adopt their own school culture of the establishing community. The Article 29&30 should not be misused with the commercial motives as well as for satisfying the personal ambition. There should not be commercially mining educational planning and subverting educational regulations. Since they should meet a felt need of the minority community they should not be recognized as Minority institution unless at least 50 per cent of those enrolled are from the establishing minority community while the authorities should have the option to raise it up to 75 per cent (leaving 25% for other students). They should be free to, and in fact should recruit the best teachers irrespective of their caste or religion, without affecting their minority status. The examination Board or University must affiliate them if they fulfill academic standards. It is also needed that Muslim must resist any move to erode, dilute or abolish 29&30 and at the same time a watch should also be kept so that the management should not be capricious, fractious and irresponsible. It should not become the centre of exploitation; arena of mutual clashes and rivedries or din of corruption and mismanagement. It should be subject to reasonable regulation with regard to the service condition of the teaching and non-teaching staff, disciplinary rules be in consistent with the principle of natural justice and principle of sound administration should be observed. The management of such institution should be in the hands of selfless, sincere, and benevolent and undisputed leaders of the community. The problem, the deficiencies and the needs of such institution should be published in the local and regional papers so that the tendencies of withdrawal and attitudes of the closed society should be avoided. The residents of the catchments area of the school should contribute generously for its developmental needs. Teachers and Headmasters of Muslim managed educational institutions should have liaison with developed school of the area, hold free discussion, observe their working condition, communicate and consult with them for improving their own standard. Frequent orientation, refresher courses and workshop for teachers, principal and secretary or manager are very much needed to improve the working of Muslim managed educational institutions. Further scheme for remedial coaching should also get due attention and priority should be given. These institution should introduce at primary and secondary level the socially useful productive work/work experience while at the post secondary level vocational courses should be introduced.

The Supreme Court has recently ruled that every child must be instructed at the primary level through his/her mother tongue. Instructions through the mother tongue are the basic educational and psychological needs of every child so it is needed that the existing numerical limitation must be scrapped even if the students with particular mother tongue is spread over a panchayat or a village have to be horizontally aggregated. At the Secondary and College level mother tongue i.e. Urdu need not be the medium of instruction but it must be the first language as envisaged in the original "three language formula". But if the mother tongue (Urdu) is the medium of instruction and examination at secondary and college level, adequate arrangement should be made with regard to the availability of teachers & text books and other reading materials, particularly in sciences and evaluation of answer books be done by script examiners.

The state should guarantee that education under secular order should not be a vehicle for cultural assimilation and for imposition of cultural or even religious norms of one community over another. The syllabus, textbooks, school culture and the education method do not in anyway do injustice to Muslim or to their faith or degrade their social personality or distort their religious identity. An alien culture should not be imposed upon Muslim youths in the name of national unity or integration, submergence in the name of harmony, in brief, to assimilate and absorb them. Therefore a constant monitoring and regular screening of educational materials and school culture by the secular forces is needed.

In order to achieve the educational goals, to plan, to organize, coordinate and to guide educational activities and to constantly monitor its efforts there is need to have a net work of local, district and state level monitoring cell affiliated to national organization (Apex body). Such committees should include representative of all Muslim educational institutions as well as eminent and acknowledged educationists, thinkers, philanthropists, irrespective of political affiliation to guide individual institutions, the executive, the judiciary and the political parties. However the constitution of a parallel body bringing together at the district, state and national level, all minorities educational institutions of all communities would also be useful. A federation of Minority Educational Institutions will represent the collective will of all minorities at each level, which is necessary to protect and clarify the ambit of Article 30.

Educational facilities like books and Government financial assistance available to the Muslim students to pursue their educational goal should be provided. Central and state governments must provide books free of cost up-to at least the primary level to all students and up to secondary levels to poor students and increase technical assistance to Muslim students.

As about 60 per cent of the present generation of Muslim students have Hindi as their medium of instructions and extremely small per cent of them attend English medium schools/colleges and of remaining nearly 40 per cent of the current students are being educated through Urdu medium. Efforts should be made so that facilities for education through Urdu are at par with that through Hindi from the primary stage onwards so that Muslim parent can exercise their option regarding the medium of their children.

All India Muslim Educational Conference established in 1886 by Sir Syed Ahmad Khan should be revived to work as a central or national body with its branches in all districts and state head quarters as a think tank or "Brain Trust". This old organization has a decent past when it had played the pioneering role in promoting education among Indian Muslims directly inspired by the Aligarh Movement. Various regional organizations like Al Ameen Education Society Banglore, All India Muslim Education Society (A.I.M.E.S.) Calicut, Hamdard Education Society New Delhi, Anjurman-e-Islam, Bombay & UP Co-ordination committee etc. should operate as usual. The Aligarh Muslim University (A.M.U.) Old Boys Association spread through out the country should also be revived and motivated. All these organizations should act as catalyst to propagate the message of education and to serve as a forum to develop consensus on common educational problem, to interact, periodically review educational situation with other voluntary organizations and government representative's and to learn from each other experiences.

To motivate the Muslim Parents to send their children to school and to create an education consciousness in Muslim community, every opportunity should be exploited through various forums, gathering, conferences, and congregation of *Juma* or *Idd* prayers etc. It should properly be campaigned, a cadre of young men uncontaminated by politics should also take up drive for mass literacy in every mahalla, village and town with the help of Imams of mosques, respectable persons of the society, irrespective of their religious faith door to door campaign should also be carried out. To create an urge, Muslim leaders, educationists, religious scholars *(Ulema)* having credibility among Muslim masses should move in Educational Caravan from town to town, in different Mahallahs & Villages and addresses the gathering of the people giving it a shape of mass movement for education to highlight just one slogan 'EDUCATE OR PERISH'. Recently established forum for literacy Awareness and Muslim Education (THE FLAME) for promoting education among the Muslim community in Bihar and Jharkhand should take lead in this direction. Students and Old boys of A.M.U. spread through out the state should also mobilize such scheme in their respective areas. It should also have the support of enlightened and broad minded members of other community as there is no dearth of such people in our society. Our country needs good an enlightened Muslim and not the alienated opportunists, fanatical illiterates. But such Programme should be worked out methodically and after due consultation, preparation, untidily and executed with care, mission and zest.

Local, regional and national press, Urdu newspapers and magazine should extend the hospitality of their columns to this campaign. It should also publish the facilities, incentive, encouragement and other endeavours available in the field of education by Muslims and others. The opportunities provided by the government, the problem faced by the institution and experience gained in tackling them etc. the magazine and journal like Tehzibul Akhlaq, Radiance & Muslim India etc. should take initiative in this direction to provide proper guidance.

An assessment should be made of the entire *waqf*/Trust property of the state. Their control should be put in the hands of professionally qualified persons. The revenue from *waqf* properties should be solely devoted to general & technical education while donation from generous people should be used for scholarship and loans to be sanctioned to meritorious as well as poor and needy students. Such revenues can also be used for opening new school or technical institutions in Muslim concentrated areas or to supplement government grants in schools and colleges to provide better physical and teaching facilities. Such donation should also be exempted from Income Tax.

Apart from general expansion of education an effort should be made to pick up bright students at a fairly early stage and for them new type to model school should be opened in various parts of the state. Further influential Muslims of the area should cultivate the heads of the best school of the locality or town and persuade them to be liberal in giving admission to Muslim students. Scheme for the remedial coaching should also be initiated for below average students.

Primary and Secondary schools of the Muslim localities should be used out side the school hours or in evening for teaching adults and other earning children. Special courses have to be devised to make learning meaningful to the illiterate adults. It should give the capacity to speak up for their rights, to counteract cheating, exploitation and injustice, which an illiterate person faces at every step in our society.

The state and central government should liberally provide funds for opening of information, coaching and counseling centres in Muslim areas for providing academic and vocational guidance and for seeking and exploiting various opportunities spread through out the country and abroad to prepare the candidates for various competitive examinations.

Female education should be accorded top priority as the education of a girl means education of a family while a boy education is merely an individual education, further plan of action should be prepared at different levels for implementation within a specific period of time.

Reservation for the Muslim as a socio-economic and educational backward community should be instituted in admission into various courses of study particularly higher and professional education with a view to bring them at par with other communities. The quota should be in proportion to their population and level of their backwardness with the provision that the candidates of the Muslim sub communities notified as other backward community (OBC) should have first preference.

APPENDIX I

Prime Minister's 15 Point Programme on Welfare of Minorities (1984)

I. Communal Riots

1. The state governments are being advised that in the areas which have been identified as communally sensitive and riot prone. District and police officials of the highest known efficiency, impartiality and secular record must be posted. In such areas and even else where the prevention of communal tension should be one of the primary duties of district magistrate and superintendent of police. Their performances in this regard should be an important factor in determining their promotion prospects.
2. Good work done in this regard by District and police officials should be rewarded.
3. Severe action should be taken against all those who incite communal tensions or take part in violence.
4. Special courts or courts specifically earmarked to try communal offences should be set so that offenders are brought to book speedily.
5. Victims of communal riots should be given immediate relief and provided prompt and adequate financial assistance for their rehabilitation.
6. Radio and TV must also help in restoring confidence, communal harmony and peace in such affected areas.
7. It is unfortunate that certain sections of the press some times indulge in tendentious reporting and publication of objectionable and inflammatory material, which may

incite communal tension. I hope that editors, printers publishers and other concerned will cooperate in finding a way to avoid publishers of such materials.

II. Requirement to State and Central Services

8. In the recruitment of police personnel state Government should be advised to give special consideration to minorities. For this purpose the composition of selection committees should be representative.
9. The central Government should take similar action in the recruitment of personnel to the central police Forces.
10. Large scale employment opportunities are provided by the Railways, Nationalized Banks and public sector Enterprises. In these cases also the concerned department should ensure that special consideration is given to recruitment form minority communities.
11. In Many areas recruitment is done through competitive examinations often minority group have been handicapped in taking advantage of the educational system to compete on equal term in such examinations. To help them to over come these handicaps steps should be taken to encourage the starting of coaching classes in minority educational institutions to train persons to compete successfully in these examinations.
12. The acquisition of technical skills by those minorities who are today lagging behind would also help in national development. Arrangements should be made to set up ITI s and polytechnics by government or private agencies in predominantly minority areas to encourage admission in such institutions of adequate number of persons belonging to these communities.

III. Other Measures

13. In various development Programmes including the 20

point Programme care should be taken to see that minorities secure in a fair and adequate measure the benefits flowing there from. In the various committees members of those communities should be actively involved.

14. A part from the general issues to which I have referred there are various local problems, which develop into needless irritants to minorities. For instance encroachment of Wakf properties and no graveyards have let to protects and grievances in some places. Suitable steps should be taken to deal with such problems on an expeditious and satisfactory basis.
15. Problems relating to minorities need to be attended to on a continuing basis so that apprehensions are allayed and genuine grievances redressed. To facilitate this a special cell will be created in the ministry of home affairs to deal with matters relating to minorities.

APPENDIX II

Extract from New Education Policy and Programme of Actions (1986)

Minorities Education

Articles 29 and 30 guarantee the right of minorities to conserve the language script and culture and to establish and administer educational institution of their choice whether based on religious or language. So far as the religious and linguistic minorities are concerned the following to articles relating to fundamental rights in part III of the constitutions.

(I) Article 29. Protection of interest of minorities.

(a) Any section of the citizens residing in the territory of India or any part there of having a distinct language script or culture of its own shall have the right to conserve the same.
(b) No citizen shall be denied admission into any educational institution maintained by the state or receiving aid out of state funds on grounds only of religion, race, caste, language or any of them.

(II) Article 30. Right of minorities to establish and administer educational institutions.

(a) All minorities whether based on religious or language shall have the right to establish and administer educational institutions of their choice.
(b) The state shall not in granting aid to educational institutions discriminate against any educational institution on the ground that it is under the management's of minority's of minority, whether based on religion or language.

(III) Article 350A. Facilities for instruction in mother tongue at primary stage.

(a) It shall be the endeavor of every state and of every local authority within the state to provide adequate facilities for instruction in the mother tongue at the primary stage of education to children belonging to linguistic minority groups and the president may issue such direction to any state as he considers necessary or proper for securing the provision of such facilities.

1. The implementation of the above guarantees has been uneven although the various conferences of education ministers. Government of India memorandum of 1956 as also the statement of language in 1958 etc. have been laying emphasis on the special treatment to linguistic minorities.
2. According to 1981 census the religious minorities constitute about 17.4 per cent of the population of which Muslim are 11.4 per cent Christians 2.4 per cent Sikhs 2 per cent Buddhist 0.7 per cent and Jains 0.5 per cent Ministers of Home affairs have identified Muslims and Neo Buddhists as educationally backward at national level. It was agreed that the state government may also identify other groups which are educationally backward at the state level. Special affords need to be taken to bring those educationally backward minorities on par with the rest of the society and to make them participate fully in the national developmental activities.
3. The National policy on Education 1986 states the following regarding education of minorities vides para 4.8 of the document "Some minority groups are educationally deprived or backward. Greater attention will be paid to the education of these groups in the interest of equality and social justice. This will naturally include the constitutional guarantees given to them to establish and administer their own educational institutions and

protection to their language and culture simultaneously, objectivity and all possible measures will be taken to promote an integration based on appreciation of common national goals and ideals, in conformity with the core curriculum."

Phasing of Targets, Strategy Envisaged and Priority Measures

(b) Programme for 1986-87

The ongoing Programmes of the department of education, which would continue in 1986-87 are:

I. Imparting of technical skills through the ten community polytechnics set up in areas of predominant minority concentration.
II. Programme of evaluation of textbook from the standpoint of national integration currently undertaken by N.C.E.R.T.
III. Orientation programmes for principals/Managers and training programmes for teachers of minority educational institutions to be taken up by N.C.E.R.T. in a phased manner.
IV. University grants commission scheme of giving assistance to Universities/Colleges for starting coaching classes for students belonging to educationally backward minorities.

(c) Programme to be implemented during remaining three years of the Seventh Plan viz 1987-88 to 1989-90

The above scheme with supportive funding will be extended during the remaining years of the Seventh plan. The N.C.E.R.T., Ministry of welfare and the Dept. of Education have been having dialogue with the Vice Chancellor of the University of Aligarh, Jamia Millia Islamia, Kashmir, Marathwada and Osmania Universities, For setting up of Resource centers which would provide training and guidance to minority educational institution situated near these centers. The scheme for setting op of such centers is at present under consideration of the Ministry. A proposal mounting to Rs. 65 lakhs has been made for the seventh plan period for setting up of these Resource centers. The scheme of community polytechnics in the minority concentration areas during the seventh plan period.

(d) Long term Programmes

Early Childhood and Traditional School Education

Effort will be made to teach science mathematics and English on Voluntary basis in institutions imparting instructions in Traditional school. Early childhood education centers wherever possible will be set up in these school and in areas predominantly inhabited by educationally backward minorities. Socially useful productive work will also be introduced in these institutions. The Department of education will prepare a scheme of assistance for this purpose.

Primary Education

I. Institutionalize system for compilation of statistical information required by commissioner for linguistic minorities regarding educational facilities. This would be done by state Governments.

II. Eliminating delay in sanctioning of linguistic minority teachers posts and appointment of teachers by delegation of powers to district Collectors Action will be taken by the state Governments.

III. Survey on availability of textbook in minority languages and setting up of printing facilities in minority languages— Action will be taken by the state Governments.

IV. Survey an availability of teachers training facilities for teachers in minority languages and measures to enhance such capacity wherever necessary. Action will be taken by the state Government.

V. Efforts will be made to utilize 15 per cent of the curricular time for training in local craft/trades and to arrange evening classes for children of artisans/ agricultural labourers.

Middle and higher Education

I. A scheme for in service training from minority

institution to teachers in science, mathematics, Social Sciences English and career guidance through S.C.E.R.T and other resources center and state career guidance institutions. At present the N.C.E.R.T has a scheme for such training courses. The proposal is to extend this activity through S.C.E.R.T's to other above mentioned institutions.

II. A scheme for orientation courses for Managers and principals of minorities. Institutions in modern educational techniques by S.C.E.R.T. This is being done by N.C.E.R.T at present on a small scale.

III. Schemes of appointment of regional language, teachers in minority institution for national integration and for implementation of the three language formulas. This will be done by state Government.

IV. A scheme for remedial coaching in minority managed educational institutions. This will be done by state Governments.

V. Minority managed educational institutions will be given a fair representation in the scheme for computer literacy in school education.

Vocational and Technical Education

I. Provision of vocational course in higher secondary schools specially catering to educationally backward minorities.

II. Ensuring that in all the Programmes on technical and vocational education included in the policy, minority run institutions derive full benefit.

III. Setting up Craft Training Institute in identified minority artisan concentration blocks, with 80 per cent seats for artisan's children.

Women's Education

I. As the women literacy and the girls enrollment is lowest among educationally backward minorities, in the schemes of opening of girls schools, appointment of lady teachers, opening of girls hostels and providing of incentives in the form of mid day meals uniform etc. minorities needs should be fully met.

II. A production cum training center for crafts exclusively for girls preferably with women instructors with the extent possible in each of the identified minority concentration districts. This will be done by state Governments.

Voluntary Efforts in Adult Education and Early Childhood Education

Orientation course for professionals from minority communities to motivate voluntary efforts attaching one center to all minority institution, to create awareness of this schemes and to train supervisor for multiplier effect. This will be done by the state Governments.

Libraries, Reading Rooms and Extension Work

Scheme for encouraging setting up of libraries reading rooms etc. in minority areas pilot project for educational extension work in a few blocks on an experimental basis. This will be done by the state Governments that will provide adequate finances for the purpose.

Minority Managed Educational Institutions

I. Clear guidelines for recognition and for timely disposal of application. Each state Government to formulate its recognition policy and giving wide publicity to this.

II. Effective monitoring arrangement should be made to see the proper implementation of the programmes.

III. Schemes for setting up of state wise federation of minority institutions, to help in seeking cooperation of minority institution in effective implementation of educational uplift measures, in ensuring minimum infrastructure facilities, maintaining academic standards and protecting the interest of teachers, these bodies to be officially recognized and assisted.

Area Approach

Special attention to the illustrative list of minority concentration districts in locating school so that minority children have access in matters of admission. The list of 40 districts is appended. The state Government may include other districts on the basis of the concentration of other educationally backward minorities.

Schemes for Scholarship etc.

Schemes for scholarship for weaker section on merit cum means basis, with in built system of placement in good institution, fee exemption/fee concession/compensation for opportunity cost for artisan and other weaker section: such help could be routed through voluntary societies of all India repute. To be implemented by state Governments.

Organisation and Management Issues

I. Bench mark survey and research studies: Arranging Bench mark survey and periodical survey to assess the in crease in literacy and in educational attainments scheme for periodical research studies on various aspects to improve the effectiveness of remedial measures, specially relative availability of schools in minority concentration areas. This will done by the state governments

II. Association of educationally back ward minorities with boards of education and other advisory bodies: Educa6tionally backward minorities to be associated with a various education Board and advisory committees at central and state levels.

III. Monitoring arrangements: A cell will be created in the union education department and in the state education department to monitor effective implementation of these measures.

IV. *Review*: There shall be a review of all minority education programmes every Years.

(*Source*: National policy on education 1986 programme of action Ministry of education Government of India August 1986.)

APPENDIX III

Educational Rights of Minorities: Supreme Court Judgement (2002)*

Introduction

Article 29 and *Article 30* of the Constitution of India lay down certain safeguards/directions for the establishment and running of minority educational institutions. These articles arc given below to have a background of the issue under reference.

Article 29. *Protection of Interests of Minorities:*

(1) Any section of the citizens residing in the territory of India or any part thereof having a distinct language, script or culture of its own shall have the right to conserve the same.

(2) No citizen shall be denied admission into any educational institution maintained by the State or receiving aid out of State funds on grounds only of religion, race, caste, language or any of them.

Article 30. *Right of Minorities to Establish and Administer Educational* Institutions:* (1) All minorities, whether based on religion or language, shall have die right to establish and administer educational institutions of their choice.

(1A) In making any law providing for the compulsory acquisition of any property of an educational institution established and administered by a minority, referred to in clause (1), the State shall ensure that the amount fixed by or determined under such law for the acquisition of such property is such as would not

* P.D. Mathew S.J., *'The Landmark Judgement of the Supreme Court on Educational Rights of Minorities'*, Indian Social Institute, New Delhi, 2002.

restrict or abrogate the right guaranteed under that clause.

(2) The state shall not, in granting aid to educational institutions, discriminate against any educational institution on the ground that it is under the management of a minority, whether based on religion or language.

From time-to-time several cases came up before the High Courts and the Supreme Court. The judgement given by a Constitutional Bench of the Supreme Court on October 31, 1992 is considered as a landmark judgement as regards the educational institutions run by the minorities. The Constitution Bench consisted of eleven judges. Main judgement was given by seven judges. Four judges gave different interpretations.

Highlights of the Judgement

- All citizens have right to establish and administer educational institutions.
- The right to administer minority educational institutions is not absolute.
- State can apply regulations to unaided MEIs (Minority Educational Institutions) to achieve educational excellence.
- Aided MEIs should admit certain percentage of non-minority students.
- Percentage of non-minority students to be admitted to an aided MEI is to be decided by the State or University.
- Fees to be charged by unaided MEI cannot be regulated but no institution can charge capitation fee.
- State can prescribe minimum qualifications for teachers and the principal in an unaided MEI.
- Tribunal headed by District Judge should be constituted for redressal of grievance of employees of MEI.
- Stale can provide the manner of admission in case of an aided MEI to ensure that it is done on the basis of merit.
- Merit could be determined through common entrance test.
- Unaided MEI could have their own procedure for admission but the same had to be fair and transparent.

APPENDIX IV

The National Commission for Minority Educational Institutions Act, 2004

Functions and Powers of the Commission

(a) To advise the Central Government or any State Government on any question relating to the education of minorities that may be referred to it

(b) To grant minority status to any educational institution with prejudice to the provisions contained in the National Commission for Minorities Act, 1992.

(c) To enquire, *sua motu*, or on a petition presented to it by any Minority Educational Institution, or any person on its behalf into complaints regarding deprivation or violation of rights of minorities to establish and administer educational institutions of their choice and any dispute relating to the affiliation to a University and report its finding to the appropriate Government for its implementation;

(d) To intervene in any proceeding involving any deprivation or violation of the educational rights of the minorities before a court with the leave of such court;

(e) To review the safeguards provided by or under the Constitution, or any law for the time being in force, for the protection of educational rights of the minorities and recommend measures for their effective implementation;

(f) To specify measures to promote and preserve the minority status and character of institutions of their choice established by minorities;

(g) To decide all questions relating to the status of any institution as a Minority Educational Institution and declare its status as such;

(h) To make recommendations to the appropriate Government for the effective implementation of programmes and schemes relating to the Minority

Educational Institutions; and

(i) To do such other acts and things as may be necessary, incidental or conducive to the attainment of all or any of the objects of the Commission.

Appeal Against the Order of the Commission

1. Any person aggrieved by the order of refusal to grant no objection certificate may prefer an appeal against such an order of the Commission.
2. An appeal under sub-section (1) shall be filed within thirty days from the date of the order referred to in sub-section (1) communicated to the applicant:
   Provided that the Commission may entertain an appeal after the expiry of the said period of thirty days, if it is satisfied that there was sufficient cause for not filing it within that period.
3. An appeal to the Commission shall be made in such form as may be prescribed and shall be accompanied by a copy of the order against which the appeal has been filed.
4. The Commission, after hearing the parties, shall pass an order, as soon as may be practicable, and give such directions as may be necessary or expedient to give effect to its orders or to prevent abuse of its process or to secure the ends of justice.
5. An order made by the Commission under sub-section (4) shall be executable by the Commission as a decree of a civil court and the provisions of the Code of Civil Procedure, 1908 (5 of 1908), so far as may be, shall apply as they apply in respect of a decree of a civil court.

Power of Commission to investigate matters relating to deprivation of educational rights of minorities

(1) The Commission shall have the powers to investigate complaints relating to deprivtion of the educational rights of minorities.

(2) The Commission may, for the purpose of conducting any investigation, pertaining to a complaint under this Act, utilise the services of any officer of the Central Government or any State Government with the concurrence of the Central Government or the State Government, as the case may be.

APPENDIX V

Prime Minister's New 15-point Programme for the Welfare of Minorities (2006)

The 15-point welfare programme for the minorities was announced by the Prime Minister and approved by the Cabinet in 2006. The programme has the following components:

1. Enhancing Opportunities for Education
2. Equitable Share in Economic Activities and Employment
3. Improving the Living Conditions of Minorities

Enhancing Opportunities for Education

(1) *Equitable Availability of ICDS Services:* The Integrated Child Development Services (ICDS) Scheme is aimed at holistic development of children and pregnant/lactating mothers from disadvantaged sections, by providing services through Anganwadi Centres such as supplementary nutrition, immunisation, health check-up, referral services, pre-school and non-formal education. A certain percentage of the ICDS projects and Anganwadi Centres were to be located in blocks/villages with a substantial population of minority communities to ensure that the benefits of this scheme are to be equitably available to such communities also.

(2) *Improving Access to School Education:* Under the Sarva Shiksha Abhiyan, the Kasturba Gandhi Balika Vidyalaya Scheme, and other similar Government schemes, it will be ensured that a certain percentage of such schools are located in villages/localities having a substantial population of minority communities.

(3) *Greater Resources for Teaching Urdu:* Central assistance will be provided for recruitment and posting of Urdu language teachers in primary and upper primary schools that serve a population in which at least one-fourth belong to that language group.

(4) *Modernising Madarsa Education:* The Central Plan Scheme of Area Intensive and Madarsa Modernisation Programme provides basic educational infrastructure in areas of concentration of educationally backward minorities and resources for the modernisation of Madarsa education. Keeping in view the importance of addressing this need, this programme was to be substantially strengthened and implemented effectively.

(5) *Scholarships for Meritorious Students from Minority Communities:* Schemes for pre-matric and post-matric scholarships for students from minority communities was to be formulated and implemented.

(6) *Improving Educational Infrastructure through the Maulana Azad Education Foundation:* The Government was to provide all possible assistance to Maulana Azad Education Foundation (MAEF) to strengthen and enable it to expand its activities more effectively.

APPENDIX VI

Sachar Committee on Social Economic and Educational Status of Indian Muslim 2005-06

Main observation and Recommendation

1. Education

(a) Present State of Excess

Access to education is critical to benefiting from emerging opportunities that go with economic growth. The right to education is a fundamental right; the Report established the extent of educational deprivation experienced by the Muslim community. Muslims are at a double disadvantage with low levels of education combined with low quality education. Their deprivation increases many-folds as the level of education rises. 25 per cent of Muslim children in the 6-14 year age group have either never attended school or have dropped out. At the level of higher education, less than 4 per cent Muslims are graduates or diploma holders as against the national average of 7 per cent for the age group 20 and above. At the postgraduate level, only one out of twenty students is a Muslim.

(b) Recommendations

(i) Regular affordable school education that is available to any other child in India should be made available to Muslims in all localities.

(ii) Primary education in mother tongue is equally important.

(iii) Access to government schools for Muslim children is limited. This is particularly so in regard to girls for whom the non-availability of schools within easy reach hampers access to education at the primary level.
More schools for girls should be set up in localities of Muslim concentration, particularly for the 9-12 standards. This would facilitate higher participation

of girls in school education. Induction of more female teachers, provision of hostels for girls and transport facilities would be helpful.

(iv) Institution of more scholarships for professional and technical courses would encourage students to avail greater measure of opportunities in higher education.

(v) Skill development initiatives for those who have not completed school education may also be particularly relevant for some section of Muslims given the occupational structure. The pre-entry qualifications for admission to ITI courses should be reduced to Class VIII. The scope of ITI courses should be expanded to focus on emerging market needs. The eligibility of such programmes should also be extended to Madarssa educated children.

2. *Economy and Employment Opportunities*

(a) Present Status

The participation of Muslims in regular salaried jobs, especially in the government or large public and private sector enterprises, is much less than workers of other SRCs (Socio-religious Communities). Instead, Muslims have higher than average reliance on self-employment, home-based work and are concentrated in self-employed manufacturing and trade activities. Given the informal nature of their work participation, they tend to be more vulnerable than other workers with regard to work related industries in terms of type of contract, availability of social benefits and method of payment.

Since a large section of the Muslim workers are engaged in self-employment, improvements in employment opportunities for them requires a sharpen focus on skill development and related matters.

(b) Recommendations

(i) Specific programmes for self-employed or home-based workers to provide skill, credit, technology and market support in backward districts are needed. These programmes should effectively combine modern managerial, technical and design skills with artisanal skills to create effective intervention strategies.

(ii) ITIs, polytechnics and other Institutions, that provide skill training to non-matriculates, need to be located in backward and minority concentration districts.

(iii) Alternative mechanisms, including but not confined to micro financing bodies, should be identified and charged with the task of providing institutional support like market linkages, skill upgradation and funding of trades being run by the Muslims artisans.

(iv) The Small Industrial Development Bank of India (SIDB1) should set aside a dedicated fund for training for minorities under its Entrepreneurial Development Programme.

(v) Imparting skills both to those who have completed school education, and those who have dropped out of school but have completed middle education, needs to be reassessed. Most existing technical training programmes require higher secondary education. Given the school completion rates of Muslims and the significant need for skill upgradation. provision of certain types of skill training after middle education may be useful.

(vi) Given the precarious conditions of self-employed persons in the informal sector, especially the home-based workers, it is desirable to have a mandated social security system for such workers. Since the government is already in the process of drafting a scheme to cover the unorganised workers, an early implementation would benefit a large section of the Muslim population along with helping the larger segment of the informal sector workforce.

3. Access to Bank Credit

(a) Present Status

The access of Muslims to bank credit, including the Priority Sector Advance (PSA), is limited and this is well-documented. The average size of credit is also meagre compared with other groups both in public and private sector banks. The percentage of households availing banking facilities is much lower in villages where the share of Muslim population is high. While pan of this could be due to lower demand for credit owing to low income levels of the community, another reason for such an outcome could be non-availability of banking facilities in these villages.

This is a serious problem as a significantly larger proportion of Muslims are engaged in self-employment, especially home-based work. Non-availability of credit can have far-reaching implications for the socioeconomic and educational status of Muslims.

(b) Recommendations

(i) Non-availability of banking facilities should be addressed on a priority basis by providing incentives to banks to open more branches in backward districts.

(ii) To empower Muslims economically, it is necessary to ensure smooth flow of credit/micro-credit and Priority Sector Advances. Steps should be taken to specifically direct credit, create awareness of various credit schemes, organise entrepreneurial development programmes, and bring transparency in reporting of information about provision of banking services.

(iii) A policy to enhance the participation of minorities in the microcredit schemes of NABARD should be laid down. This should spell out the intervention required by NABARD and could be a mix of target and incentive schemes to enhance the participation of Muslims in micro-credit.

(iv) The practice of identifying 'negative geographical zones' where bank credit and other facilities are not easily provided needs to be reviewed to enable people to benefit fully from banking facilities in the light of government's socio-economic objectives of inclusion.

4. Access to Social and Physical Infrastructure and Government Programmes

(a) Present Status

Muslims are concentrated in locations with poor infrastructure] facilities. This affects their access to basic services like education, health facilities, transport etc.

Although there are many Centrally Sponsored Schemes and Central Plan Schemes available for the welfare of SCs, STs and OBCs, such schemes for the welfare of minorities are very few, arc inadequately funded and have not benefited many Muslims.

(b) Recommendations

(i) Public investment in infrastructure in Muslim concentration areas is urgently required to promote socio-economic development and access to public services.

(ii) A focus on backward districts and clusters where special artisanal groups exist will ensure a sharp reduction in disparities of access and attainment
(iii) Central Government should introduce a few schemes with large outlays for welfare of minorities with an equitable provision for Muslims.
(iv) A periodic monitoring and assessment of welfare and development programmes, and the extent to which the benefits accrue to Muslims, is imperative. The monitoring mechanism should be multi-level and should have a civil society component. This would enhance public confidence.

5. Public Employment and Recruitment Procedures

(a) Present Status

Analysis of data has shown very limited Muslim participation in government employment and other programmes. Lack of access to regular salaried jobs, especially in the public sector, has been a matter of major concern. The deficit in regular employment, especially in salaried jobs in the public sector or the much larger private sector, needs to be corrected.

(b) Recommendations

(i) It is imperative to increase the public employment share of Muslims particularly in areas requiring a good deal of public dealing. To achieve this, efforts should be made to increase the employment share of Muslims in the teaching community, health workers, police personnel, bank employees and oilier similar callings.
(ii) It would be desirable to have experts drawn from the Muslim community on relevant interview panels and Boards. This practice is already in vogue in the case of SCs/STs.
(iii) Measures like undertaking a visible recruitment process in areas and districts with high percentage of Muslims, job advertisements in Urdu and vernacular newspapers and other media, or simple messages like women, minority, and backward class candidates are encouraged to apply', should be undertaken to promote participation in public employment.

APPENDIX VII

Status of Implementation of the Follow-up Action on the Recommendations (Sachar Committee)

1. Special Development Initiatives

- Multi-sectoral Development Programme for minority concentration districts (MCDs)
  - Identified 90 minority concentration districts (MCDs) which are backward in basic amenities and socioeconomic parameters.
  - Baseline survey carried out to identify 'development deficits'. Thirteen reports already received.
  - Multi-sectoral development programme approved for addressing the 'development deficits' in areas of education, sanitation, pucca housing, drinking water and electricity supply etc.
- Special Development Initiatives in Urban Areas
  - Recommendations of an inter-ministerial task force set up to consider improvement in civic amenities and economic opportunities in 338 class I & II towns, with substantial minority population.

II. Measures to Improve Access to Credit

- All public sector banks directed to open more branches in identified minority concentration districts. 496 branches opened in 2007-08.
- Reserve Bank of India (RBI) revised the Master Circular on priority sector lending on 5.7.2007. Public sector banks were asked to step up lending to minorities from 9 per cent to 15 per cent over the next three years.

- Revised master circular provides for setting up of a special cell to ensure smooth flow of credit to minorities.

III. Measures to Improve Access to Education

- Under SSA, States advised to give primacy to opening Girls in only Upper Primary Schools in minority concentration areas. 270 KGBVs sanctioned in blocks having more than 20 per cent population of Muslims.
- Priority to be given to opening of secondary/senior secondary schools in areas of Muslim concentration. A scheme for universalising secondary education was being formulated.
- New Jan Shikshan Sansthans would be set up in all districts, with a substantial population of Muslims, not covered as yet with such Sansthans. Three JSSs sanctioned in minority concentration areas.
- Mid-day meal programme extended to upper primary level in all 3479 educationally backward blocks.
- Seventy seven blocks, with a high concentration of Muslims identified for establishment of BITEs for teacher education. Scheme for selling up of BITEs being modified.
- Provision of more girl's hostels in colleges and universities in minority concentration districts proposed under the existing University Grants Commission (UGC) scheme. Proposed also to open new polytechnics with hostel facilities in MCDs.
- The Madarssa modernisation programme being revised to make it more attractive by providing better salary to teachers, increased assistance for books, teaching aids, and computers, introduce vocational subjects, etc.
- UGC asked to work out modalities so that universities are encouraged to recognise Madarssa qualifications.
- NCERT has prepared text books for all classes in the light of the NCF 2005, except class V and VIII.
- Requirement of Urdu teachers from the states was

being ascertained and sanctioned for Andhra Pradesh and Himachal Pradesh.

VI. Plan for Skill Development

- Inter-ministerial group for skill and entrepreneurial development constituted for preparation of a comprehensive plan for development of artisanal clusters.

VII. Initiatives far Affirmative Action and Social Inclusion

- Affirmative Action
- Expert group constituted to study and recommend the structure and functions of an Equal Opportunity Commission.
- Expert group constituted for evolving an appropriate Diversity Index to measure diversity in the areas of education, housing, and employment.
- A National Data Bank, to compile data on the various socioe-conomic and basic amenities parameters for socio-economic religious communities, set up in the Ministry of Statistics and Programme Implementation.
- An autonomous Assessment & Monitoring Authority (AMA), to analyse data collected for taking appropriate and corrective policy decisions, set up in the Planning Commission.
- Unorganised Sector Social Security Bill, to provide safeguards to workers in the unorganised sector, a large proportion of them being from the minority communities, introduced in Rajya Sabha.
- Concerns raised by the Sachar Committee on the delimitation of constituencies considered by a High Level Committee.
- *Social Inclusion*
    - Thirteen Universities provided Rs. 40 lakhs each for starting centres for studying social exclusion and inclusive policy for minorities and SCs and STs.
    - Instructions issued to training institutes to include in their induction and in-training courses a module on social inclusion to sensitise government employees.

APPENDIX VIII

Plan of Action on Sachar Committee's Recommendations, 2008

1. The HLC-MHRD suggests a multi-pronged strategy in the XI Plan.
2. The Committee endorses the broad consensus emerging out of the meetings with the members of parliment and other stakeholders that no single strategy would work, in ensuring that the problem of educational backwardness of Muslims is addressed adequately and effectively.
3. The strategy must accommodate the aspirations of the different socio-economic groups within the Muslim community. It must also take in-to account the religious sensibilities and gender issues, while ensuring that out efforts lead to promotion of mainstreaming and inclusive education.

General Recommendations

4. There arc 724 CD B blocks with more than 20% Muslim population. 784 with more than 10% Muslims and 275 townships with more than 20% Muslim population. It is recommended that statistics in respect of villages and Panchyats as well as municipalities or urban local bodies with concentration of Muslim population. (graded on the basis of percentage of population) should be prepared for mapping educational institutions and meeting the institutional gaps. It is learnt that National Institute of Science, Technology and Development Studies has undertaken work of this nature and this must be explored.

5. For the purposes of educational programmes among Muslims, it is important that no distinction is made between under-developed and less developed areas (which is one of the criteria for identifying Minority Concentration Districts) (MCD).
6. Statistics on enrolment and other relevant indices should be maintained by the MHRD - under elementary and secondary schooling by the NUEPA and for Higher Education by the NUEPA/ UGC.
8. The Committee recommends that all educational institutions should have a uniform policy of observing the festivals of all faiths, with appropriate!) planned events.

Literacy and Adult Education

9. There arc 88 districts where the Muslim population is more than 20%. 57 of these have a female literacy rate lower than the national average (54.2%). All 88 districts should form the focus of attention under a special literacy campaign during the Xlth Plan. An estimated Rs. 750 crore would be the requirement under the Xlth Plan for organizing the various activities in mobilizing the Muslim masses for literacy and adult education. A special mobilization drive should be launched under the TLC linking vocational skills with literacy.
10. Jana Shikshan Sasthans have been sanctioned in 29 MCDs out of the 88 Districts with more than 20% population of Muslims. JSSs should be sanctioned in the remaining districts on condition that the MCBs with more than 20% Muslims are covered by the sub-cebters. Similarly, JSS already sanctioned should extend their sub-centers to such Blocks.

Primary Education

11. As on December, 2006 there were 388 Kasturba Gandhi Balika Vidyalayas (KGBVs) sanctioned in the MCBs. It is recommended that there snould be one

KGBV in each MCB and all MCBs covered in the Xlth Plan period. Each KGBV should have the option of opening an Urdu medium section with upto 40 girls per section. MHRD may consider setting up KGBV's in urban areas in which priority would be given to smaller towns with Muslim concentration.

12. Madrasas and aktabs which come forward for assistance under the Sarva Shiksha Ahiyan's guidelines, should be covered under the Xlth Plan period.
13. The guidelines of SSA would be amended in the Xlth Plan to enable additional "girls only" upper primary schools to be opened in village with a substantial Muslim population in blocks with more than 20% population of Muslims.
14. This Committee recommends that in the MCBs, in case there are students under the SSA who want to study in their mother tongue of Urdu, expenditure on additional teachers for teaching in Urdu medium should be permitted. The Central Government should launch a scheme for giving incentives to Stale governments for recruiting Urdu teachers.

Secondary Education

15. A scheme should be set in place by which financial grants arc provided to establish secondary/senior secondary schools (VIII to XII) exclusively for girls in 724 MCBs, where schools exclusively for girls, established, maintained or aided by the Government, do not exist with in a radius of 5 kms. Unless not fesible, such schools should be set up in such clusters where the concentration of Muslim population is the maximum. Apart from the above, efforts should be made to open combined co educational Secondary/ Senior Secondary schools in 275 towns having more than 20% Muslim population. Even in urban areas, as far as practicable, such schools should be set up in Mohallas and colonies which have the Maximum concentration of Muslims. Such schools

should be managed by the appropriate Panchayati Raj Institutions (PRIs) or Urban Local Bodies (ULBs), as the case may be. The schools will be open to all children. These schools should be affiliated to the Central Board of Secondary Education. It is expected that it would cost Rs. I crore to start each such school with classes 8th-12th and an annual recurring cost, with about 30 teachers, would be approximately Rs. 60 lakh.

16. The Jawahar Navedaya Vidyalayas (JNVs) situated in MCDs and having Urdu as mother tongue, should introduce a section in classes VI to VIII stage for students desirous of studying in Urdu medium. Correspondingly, the capacity of hostels in the JNVs would need to be expanded during the Xlth Plan period. A similar exercise should also be undertaken by the DIETs in the 88 MCDs.
17. There are 23 JNVs with Urdu being offered as a language upto the secondary level.
18. KVS may consider the feasibility of including a new category of socially and educationally backward classes including minoriiies to the existing priorities prescribed for admission to the Kendriya Vidyalayas.
19. The NCERT is being assisted to make available and design contents in the Urdu language. In the case of Urdu medium textbooks, the NCERT should liberally give its copyright to state governments and their bodies.
20. The Committee recommends that this awareness programme among Madrasas should be stepped up and the National Institute of Open Schooling (NIOS) should be appropriately strengthened for effective outreach.
21. The NIOS has also started translation of all vocational content in Urdu, which would be useful for the expansion of the vocational programme under the Jan Shikshan Sansthan (JSS) scheme in the relevant Blocks.
22. The scheme for introduction of modern subjects, in Madrasas volunteering to seek such help, should be revised to include vocational subjects. The scheme should also incorporate one-time assistance for non-

recurring expenditure and additional remuneration for engaging suitably qualified experts for imparting vocational education. The weakness of the present scheme, in which salary for only two teachers are provided, should be addressed. The one time grant for books and teaching aids at Rs. 7000 each per Madrasa is also inadequate. While retaining the scheme as voluntary, the proposed revisions may include vocational education and linking with the NIOS and the State Open Schools.

23. Block Institutes of Teacher Education should be established in MCBs, with an Urdu section where needed.

Higher Education

24. The University Grants Commission should provide special assistance to State and Central Universities, Deemed Universities and other institutions of higher learning with a high Diversity Index (DI) as reflected in high enrolment of students belonging to educationally backward minorities that cater to the Muslim population and are recognized under section 2(f) and 12B of the UGC Act, Hostel facilities for girl students in all identified MCDs could be assisted during the XIth Plan.
25. The University Grants Commission should address the issue of access to higher education for the Muslims as well as the issue of quality of higher education in institutions serving the Muslim population, It is recommended that the UGC should provide development grants to colleges located in MCBs in rural areas and smaller towns for building hostels, strengthening infrastructure and other facilities. The Muslim minority institutions of higher learning established in terms of Art 29 (1) of the Constitution should be taken up for priority recognition by the UGC under section 2(f) and 12B of the UGC Act, 1956.
26. Aligarh Muslim University (AMU) may examine the

feasibility of expanding its capacity without lowering its standards so as to increase access to good quality higher and professional education. The Committee recommends substantial assistance to the AMU by the Government of India to create adequate infrastructure and other facilities as may be proposed by the competent authority of the University.

27. Assistance should be provided to MANUU to address lack of quality school education, paucity of technical and vocational training. We recommend that MANUU should establish Polytechnics, Community Polytechnics, Vocational Training Institutes as also institutes such as colleges for teaching Unani Medicine, Pharmacy and Nursing. The Committee recommends substantial assistance should be provided to the University by the Government of India to enable them to take up the proposed expansion of their activities.
28. The Committee recommends that the UGC should also establish Centres for the Study of Minority-related issues in at least one University in every State and in the Central Universities.

Vocational Education

29. At least on Community Polytechnic could be established during the Xlth Five year Plan in each MCB.

Higher Education

30 The Committee feels that existing UGC scheme needs to be revamped. The Committee took note of the good work being done by the Jamia Hamdard through its Hamdard Study Circle and suggests that such study circles could be encouraged in other parts of the country.

31. The Committee suggests that the Ministry of Minority Affairs may consider introducing a suitable scholarship programme for the Muslim students for studying abroad on the lines of the Dr. Ambedkar Scholarship for the Scheduled Caste students.

Glossary

List of the Arabic, Persian & Urdu words used in this book with their literal meaning and in some cases with their special or wider connotations in the context of the subject matter of the subject.

Adhan/Azan : Call for Prayers.
Akhirat : The world here after, the Day of Judgment.
Alim : Learning man/scholar.
Amokhta : The previous lesson.
Aqlia : Rational
Ataleeq : Teachers.
Atiya : Donation for charitable purposes.
Ayat : Verses of Holy Qura'n.
Bismilah Khan : The ceremony when a child starts learning from the Holy Qura'n
Darul aman : Place or Country of peace.
Darul Islam : Islamic country.
Darul harab : The country of non believers or enemy country in Religious sense.
Darul uloom : University or seat of higher Learning.
Dargah : A shrine of Saint.
Darsgah : School or College.
Darse Nizamia : A system of Education started by Mullah Shirazi.
Faqir : A beggar, a man who leads a pious life/A person who abodes the house of worldly gains.
Fatwa : A judicial decree or judgment a sentence delivered by a Qazi.
Fitra : Special charity on the eve of Idul Fitr.
Fraid : Divine Commands/Divine duties.
Fraghat : Completion of a course, work/A degree Conferred after completion of a course.
Fiqah : Jurisprudence/The Islamic law.
Hadith : The Tradition/Sayings & practicing of Prophet

		Muhammad (P.B.U.H), which now bear the force of law.
Hifz	:	Memorization of the Holy Qura'n.
Ijtihad	:	Exertion with a view to form an independent Judgment on legal question.
Illahi ulloom	:	Divine Sciences.
Illmul Kalam	:	Scholastics.
Iman	:	A priest/A leader in religious matter/Person who Lead Namaz.
Jumah	:	Friday/ the special prayers offered every Friday by Muslims.
Jamia	:	Centre/Seat of higher learning, College/University.
Kafir	:	An infidel/non believer.
Kafeel	:	One who supports by all possible means.
Khanqah	:	Muslim Monastery where a Sufi or saint reside and Teaches.
Khutbah	:	A religious address/a sermon.
Khulfai Resheedin	:	The First Four caliphs who took reigns after prophet Muhammad (P.B.U.H).
Kitab Khana	:	Library.
Madarsa	:	A school or College for diffusing Islamic learning.
Maktab	:	A junior school.
Maktubat	:	A collection of letters addressed to the followers.
Malfuzat	:	A collection of conversations/sayings annals.
Mansab	:	Status/dignity/office ministry.
Maulvi	:	A learned man.
Moid Muawin	:	A senior student assigned to teach junior classes.
Muhaddis	:	Authority on Hadith.
Mufti	:	A judge.
Mujahid	:	A warrior, especially in the defense of the faith.
Mushrik	:	Idolaters.
Naqlia	:	Traditional.
Nezam-e-Jihalat	:	System of ignorance/evil System.
Pardah	:	A veil, especially the kind worn by Muslim lady for modesty.
Qadi	:	A muslim judge dispensing Justice according to Islamic Jurisprudence.
Qari	:	One who recites the Qura'n with correct pronunciation.
Qura'n	:	The Holy book of Muslim.
Reyazi	:	Mathematics.
Sanad	:	The seal of magistrate/degree/a sanad.
Shariah	:	The Islamic way of life.
Sawab Jaria	:	A work of continuous charity.

Sufi	:	A pious man/a holy man residing away from worldly Affairs.
Tabiyati uloom	:	Physical Sciences.
Takhti	:	A wooden tablet/slate.
Tafseer	:	Commentary on Holy Qura'n.
Talimi karvan	:	Educational caravan.
Ulema	:	The learned man of Islam/doctors of divinity in Islam.
Wasiyat	:	The last will.
Zakat	:	Charity/a compulsory tax to be paid by the rich Muslim to the Poor.

Bibliography

A. Official Documents

Census of India 1981 (religion) series No. 1 Paper 2 of 1982, Government of India Press, New Delhi 1983.

Census of India, 1991 (religion). series No. 1 Paper 2 of 1995. The Register General & Census Commissioner, Government of India Press, New Delhi 1995.

The Constituent Assembly Debate (official report) Vol. I to XII reprinted by Lok Sabha Secretariat, New Delhi, Manager, Government of India Press, New Delhi 1984.

The Constituent of India (text) as modified up to (the Constitution Seventy Fourth Amendment) Act 1993 Govt. of India Press, New Delhi 1948.

Draft Constitution of Indian, Prepared by the Drafting Committee, Constituent Assembly, Govt. of India Press, New Delhi 1984.

Govt. of Indian Resolution on establishment of minorities' commission 1978 and various annual reports of the Commission, Govt. of India, New Delhi.

India's Minorities—Publication Division Ministry of Education & Boardcasting, Government of India, New Delhi 1984.

Muslims in India—Publication Division, Ministry of Information & Broadcasting, Govt. of India Press, New Delhi 1967.

National Integration—Program of Union Ministry of Education and Youth Services, Govt. of India Press, New Delhi 1967.

National Policy of Education 1986 & Programme of Action 1986 & 1992 Govt. of India, New Delhi August 1986 and September 1992.

Prime Minister's letter to Home Ministry and Chief Minister on 15 points Programme for the Welfare of the Minorities 11th May 1983 & another letter on Programme 29th August 1985, Govt. of India, New Delhi.

Report of the Commissioner for Linguistic Minorities—Ministry of Home Affairs, Govt. of India, New Delhi 1962.

Report of the Committee on Educational Integration—Ministry of Education, Govt. of India, New Delhi 1962.

Report of Kothari Education Commission (1964-66), Government of India, New Delhi 1970.

Report of High Power (Gopal Singh) Panel on Minorities—Government of India 1983 and Government of India Statement on the report in Parliament 1990.

Report of the Committee for Promotion of Urdu (Gujral Committee) 1975 Government of India, New Delhi 1975.

Report of the Second Commission on Backward Classes (Mandal Commission), Government of India, New Delhi 1980.

B. Unofficial Documents

Educational survey report on Muslim managed schools and colleges in India 1982-83 conducted by Hamdard Education Society, Talimabad, New Delhi 1985.

Proceeding of the seminar on "Educational Rights of Minorities under the Indian Constitution, Parameters of Executive Action & Judicial Interpretation" organized by Institute of Objective Studies at Indian Law Institute, New Delhi 1994.

Proceeding of "Bihar state conference on Education, Employment and Economic status of Muslim Community of Bihar," sponsored by Muslim India Educational & Cultural Trust, Patna, 10-11 October 1992.

Proceeding of 7th conference of all India Muslim Educational Society, Talkatora Indoor Stadium, New Delhi, March 30 April 1 1984.

Proceeding of "the Seminar on Law and Minorities in India" organized by the Indian Law Institute, New Delhi (April 24-26 1971).

Proceeding of "the International Seminar on Islamic Economics and Economy of Indian Muslim" organized by Institute of Objective Studies, New Delhi (29-30 July 1991).

Proceeding of the National Seminar on "Constitutional Law and Minorities" organized by Institute of Objective Studies, New Delhi (January 13-14, 1990).

Proceeding of Seminar on "Problems of Employment & Education of Muslim" organized by Business & Employment Bureau, New Delhi at A.M.U., Aligarh (August 5 & 6 1983).

Proceeding of Milli Talimi Conference, New Delhi (April 6 to 8 1984).

Report of the Seminar on "Muslim Situation in India organized by Institute of Objective Studies, New Delhi (July 4-5 1987).

Report of Intellectual Meet on "Problem of Muslims Convened by Young Intellectuals Congress at Nehru Memorial Auditorium, Teem Murti House, New Delhi (June 5, 1983).

Report of the Seminar on "National Integration" (April 16-17 1958), University Grants Commission, New Delhi 1961.

Report of the Seminar "Mulk-o-Millat Ki Taameer Aur Deeni Madaris" by Jamiatul Falah Bilaria Gunj UP.

Report of the Seminar on "Distortion India History" (22-26 March 1988) Organised by Khuda Bakhsh Library, Patna 1995.

C. Miscellaneous

Concise English Dictionary, London, Blackie & Son, 1918.

Definition and Classification of Minorities, New York, United Nations 1949.

The Encyclopedia Americana Vol. XIX New York, Americana Corporation 1961.

The Encyclopedia Britannica Vol. XV U.S.A. Chicago, William Benton 1968.

The Encyclopedia of Religion Vol. II (ed.) James Hasting, Edinburgh, New York 1954.

International Encyclopedia of Social Sciences Vol. X (ed.), David I sills U.S.A. The Free Press 1968.

International Convention of Economic, Social & Cultural, Civil & Political Right adopted by the U.N. General assembly on 16 December 1966.

Protection of Linguistic, Racial & Religious Minorities, Geneva, League of Nations 1927.

Protection of Minorities, New York, United Nation 1967.

U.N. Declaration on Elimination of all Forms of Intolerance & Discrimination based on Belief or Religion 1981 adopted by U.N. General Assembly on November 15, 1981.

Study on the Right of Persons belonging to Ethnic, Religious and Linguistic Minorities by F. Capotorti—Special Rapportier U.N sub Commission on Minorities 1991.

Universal Declaration of Human Right (Text) adopted & proclaimed by U.N. General Assembly on 10 December 1948.

Webster New World Dictionary, Delhi, Pitamber Publication, 1981.

Year Book on Human Rights, U.N. Publication, 1950.

D. Contemporary Works

(a) English Book

Abidi, Ishtiaq (ed.)—*The Problem of Muslims* (New Delhi, Young Intellectual Congress, 1983).

Aggarwal, J.C.—*Development & Planning of Modern Education* (New Delhi, Vikas, 1982).

Aggarwal, R.N.—*Indian National Movement 1885-1947* (Delhi Metropolitan, 1971).

Ahmad, Akbar. S.—*Religion and politics in Muslim Society,* (Lahore, Cambridge, 1983).

Ahmad, Aziz—*Studies in Islamic Culture in Indian Environment* (London, Oxford, 1964).

Ahmad, Imtiaz (ed.)—*Caste and Social Stratification among the Muslims* (Delhi, Manohar, 1973).

——— (Ed.) *Modernisation and Social Change among Muslim in India* (New Delhi, Monohar, 1983).

Ahmad, Rafiuddin—*The Bengal Muslims 1871-1906* (London, Oxford University Press, 1981).

Akanda, latifa—*Social History of Muslim Bengal* (Dacca Islamic Culture Centre, 1988).

Akbar, M.J.—*India the Siege Within*—(England, Middle six, 1985).

Alattas, S.N.—*Aims and Objective of Islamic Education* (Jeddah, King Abdul Aziz University, 1979).

Ali, S. Amir—*Spirit of Islam* (London, 1896).

———, *Short History of Saracens* (London, 1899).

Ansari, Iqbal. A (ed.)—*The Muslim Situation in India* (Delhi, IOS, 1989).

Ashraf, Ali—*The Muslim Elite* (New Delhi, Atlantic, 1982).

Ashraf, Mujeab—*Muslim Attitudes towards British Rule and Western Culture in India* (Delhi, Adarah, 1982).

Askari, hasan—*Islam & Muslim in Medieval Bihar* (Patna, Khuda Bakhsh, 1989).

Baig, M.R.A—*The Muslim Dilemma in India* (Delhi, Vikas, 1974).

Baldev—*India Pakistan & Muslim Politics* (New Delhi, 1975).

Banerjee, D.N—*Our Fundamental Rights* (Calcutta, World Press, 1968).

Barier, N.G (Ed.)—*Roots of Communal Politics* (New Delhi, Arnold, 1976).

Barnier, Francious—*Travel in Mughal* Empire 1656-1668 (Calcutta).

Bombwal, K.R. & Chawdhry, L.P. (Ed) *Aspect of Democratic Government & Politics* (Delhi, Atma Ram, 1968).

Brass, Pual R.—*Language Religious Communities in India* (Delhi, Vikas, 1975).

Riots and Pogroms (New York, 1997).

Bruch, J.E.—*The Distribution of Religious Communities in India* (Washington, 1946).

Chander Shekhar, A.—*Incidence of polygamous Marriage In India* (Delhi, 1976).

Chaudhry, V.C.P.—*The Creation of Modern Bihar* (Patna, Motilal, 1980).

Chopra, P.—*Role Of Muslim In Struggle for Freedom* (New Delhi, 1979).

Choudhry, B.M.—*Muslim Polities in India* (Calcutta, Orient).

Choudhry, Nirad C.—*The Autobiography of an Unknown Indian* (Bombay, Jaico, 1951).

Chowdhry N.K.—Indian Constitution and Education (Delhi, Shipra, 2009)

Dalal, M.N.—*Whither Minorities* (Bombay, Taraporerla, 1940).

Dalwai, Hamid—*Muslim Politics in India* (Meerut, Nachiketa, 1970).
Desai, A.R.—*Social Background of India Nationalism* (Bombay, Popular, 1954).
Diwaker, R.R. (ed.) *Bihar Through the Ages* (Calcutta, 1959).
Duff, Alexander—*Missionary Address* (Edinburgh, 1882).
Dutta, K.K.—*History of Freedom Movement in Bihar,* Govt. of Bihar (Patna, 1957).
Dutta, K.K. and Jha J.S.—*Comprehensive History of Bihar* Vol. III (Patna, 1976).
Engineer, Asghar Ali—*Indian Muslim—A Study of the Minorities Problems in India* (Delhi, Ajanta, 1985).
Faridi, S.N.—*Economic Welfare of Indian Muslims* (Agra, Ram Prakash, 1965).
Faridi, F.R. & Siddiqi, M.N. (ed.)—*Social Structure of Indian Muslims* (New Delhi, Genuine, 1992).
Faridi, F.R.—*Islamic Economy & Economy of Indian Muslims* (New Delhi, Genuine, 1992).
Faruqi, Z.H.—*The Deoband School and Demand for Pakistan* (Bombay, Asia, 1963).
Farooqi, M.—*Indian Muslims Problem & Trends* (New Delhi, CPI, 1972).
Fazl, Abdul S.—*On the Mohammedans of India* (Calcutta, 1872).
Fyazee, A.A.A.—*The Reform of Muslim Personal Law* (Delhi, Nichiketa, 1972).
Gandhi, Raj, Mohan—*Understanding the Muslim Mind* (New Delhi, Penguin, 1987).
Glazer, Nathan & Moinihan—*Beyond the Melting Pot* (Cambridge, M.I.T. Press, 1963).
Gauba, K.L.—*Passive Voice* (Bombay, Thacker 1973).
Gopal, Ram—*Indian Muslims—A Political History 1858—1947* (New Delhi, Asia, 1949).
Hadson, M.V.—*The Great Divide—British, India & Pakistan* (London, Hutchinson, 1969).
Hardy, P.—*Partners in Freedom & True Muslims* (London, 1971).
Harmon, S.—*Plight of Muslims in India* (New Delhi, D.K., 1976).
Harison, S.S.—*India the Most Dangerous Decade* (Princeton, Oxford University Press, 1960).
Hartog, P.—*Some Aspects of Indian Education* (London, Oxford Univ. Press, 1939).
Haque, M.A.—*History of Muslim Education in Bengal* (Calcutta, 1917).
Haq, Mashirul—*Indian as a Secular State* (Shimla, IIAS, 1972).
Hayat, Abul—*Musalman of Bengal* (Calcutta, Rabi Art, 1966).
Henry, K.J.—*World Minorities* (Calcutta, Book Land, 1961).
Henry, H.T.—*Rebellion in India and our Future Policy* (Calcutta, 1858).
Hubaiti, A.K.—*Some Islamic Concept of Education* (Jeddah, 1981).

Hussain, S. Abid—*The Destiny of Indian Muslims* (Bombay, Asia, 1965).
Hussnain, S.E.—*The Indian Muslim Challenge & Opportunity* (Bombay, Lalvani, 1968).
Hussain, Zakir—*Educational Reconstruction in India* (Delhi, P.D., 1950).
Hutton, J.H.—*Caste in India* (Bombay, Oxford, 1951).
Hunter (sir) W.W.—*The Indian Musalman* (London, 1871).
Ikram, S.M.—*Muslim Civilization in India* (New York, 1964).
Iqbal, Jamil M.—*Muslim Population in India Patterns and Trends* (New Delhi, Institute of Objective Studies, 1989).
Iqbal, (sir) Mohamad—*The Reconstruction of Religious Thought in Islam* (Delhi, Kitab Publication, 1974).
Imam, Mohd (ed.)—*Minorities and the law* (Bombay, Tripati, 1972).
Imam, Muzaffer—*Role of Muslim in National Movement* (Delhi, Mittal, 1987).
Isaacs, H.R.—*India's Ex Untouchables* (New York, John Dey, 1965).
Jackson, Paul—Bihar—*Sharfuddin Yahya Maneri* (Patna, Navjyoti, 1980).
——, *Letter From Meneri* (New Delhi, Horizen, 1990).
Jaffar, S.M.—*Education In Muslim India* (Delhi, Adbiyat, 1939).
Jain, M.S.—*The Aligarh Movement its Origin & Development 1858-1906* (Agra, Sri Ram Mehra, 1965).
Jain, Shushila—*Muslim and Modernization* (Jaipur, Rawat, 1988).
Jata, J.S.—*Education in Bihar 1813-1859* (Patna, Jaiswal, 1979).
Java, S.P.—*The Social Structure of Hindu Muslims Community* (Delhi National, 1975).
Jenning, I.—*Some Characteristics of Indian Constitution* (London, Oxford Press, 1953).
Justice, Ministry, *Moslem Doctrine and Human Rights in Islam* (Riyadh, Govt. Publication, 1972).
Kabir, Hemayun—*Muslim Politics in India (1906-47) and other Essays* (Calcutta, Mukhopadhayaya, 1968).
———, *Minorities in a Democracy* (Calcutta, Mukhopadhayaya, 1968).
———, *Education in New India* (London, George Allen, 1959).
Karandikar, H.A.—*Islam in India Transition to Modernity* (Bombay, 1968).
Key, F.E. *Education in Ancient India* (London, Oxford, 1939).
Khaliquzzeman, Chaudhry—*Pathway to Pakistan* (Lahore, 1961).
Khanna, H.R.—*Constitution and Socio Economic Changes* (Delhi, Publication Division, 1979).
Khan, M.E.—*Family Playing Among Muslims in Indian* (New Delhi, Manohar, 1979).
Khan, Mazharul—*Social Pathology of Muslim Society* (Delhi, Amar Prakashan, 1978).
Khan, Mohd. Reza—*What Price Freedom* (Madras 1969).
Khan, M.S.—*Education & Religions in Politics—A Survey of Literature* (Delhi, 1971).

Krishna, K.B.—*The Problems of minorities or Communal Representation in India* (London, George, 1939).
Laponce, J.A.—*The Protection of Minorities* (California, Berkeley, 1960).
Law, N.N. *Promotion of Learning in India during Mohammedan Rules by Mohammedan* (Delhi, Adbiyat, 1973).
Leonard, Mosley—*The Last Days of British Raj* (London, 1961).
Lumby, E.W.R.—*The Transfer of Power in India* (London, George Allen, 1954).
Luthra, V.P.—*The Concept of Secular State in India* (Delhi, 1969).
Macartney, C.A.—*The National States & National Minorities* (London, Oxford, 1934).
Madhok, Balraj—*Indianisation* (New Delhi, Hind, 1965).
Majamdar, R.C.—*History of Freedom Movement* Vol. I (Calcutta, 1963).
Mahalanobis, P.C.—*Distribution of Muslim Population of India 1783-1893* (Aligarh, 1895).
Mohmood Tahir (ed.) *Minorities and state at the Indian Law* (New Delhi, Genuine, 1991).
Mallick A.R.—*British Policy and the Muslim in Bengal 1757-1856* (Dacca, Asiatic, 1961).
Menon, V.P.—*The Transfer of Power in India* (Delhi, Orient, 1957).
Miller, R.—*Education in Changing Society* (Ludhiana, Lyall, 1969).
Mirza, Baker Ali—*Islamic Influence on Indian Society* (Meerut, Meenakshi, 1971).
Misra, B.B.—*Indian Middle Classes, Their Growth in Modern Times* (London, Oxford, 1961).
Mohammad, Shan—*Writing and Speeches of Sir Syed* (Bombay, Nachiketa, 1972).
Moynihan, Daniel P., *The Negro Family—The Case of National Action* (Washigton 1965).
Mujeeb, M.—*The Indian Muslim* (London, George Allen, 1967).
———, *Islamic Influence upon India Society* (Meerut, Meenakshi, 1972).
———, *Education and Traditional Values* (Meerut, 1905).
Mukherjee, S.N.—*History of Education in India* (Baroda, Acharya, 1957).
Murty, B.S.—*Depressed and Oppressed—Forever in Agony* (New Delhi, S. Chand, 1972).
Muttalib, M.A.—*Voluntary Action in Education* (Delhi, Sterling, 1989).
Naik, J.P. & Nurullah—*A Student History of Education in India 1800-1973* (Delhi, Macmilen, 1969).
Nakosteen, N.—*History of Islamic Origin of Western Education—A.D. 800-1350* (Boulder, Colorado, 1964).
Nanvati, M.B. & Vakil (ed.)—*Group Prejudices in India* (Bombay, Vora, 1951).
Nehru, Jawaharlal—*Letters to Chief Ministers* Vol. IV (New Delhi, 1985).
Nizami, K.A.—*Politics and Society during Early Medieval Period* Vol. I (Delhi, 1974).

Ojha P.N—*Some Aspect of North Indian Social Life 1556-1707 A.D.* (Patna, Nagri Parkashan, 1961).

Pandey, B.N.—*Islam & Indian Culture* (Patna, Khuda Bakhsh, 1985).

Pandey, S.N.—*Education and Social Changes in Bihar 1900-1921* (Delhi, Motilal, 1975).

Peerzada, Shamsh—*Muslim Personal Law and Uniform Civil Code* (New Delhi, Markazi Maktaba, 1973).

Paylee, M.V.—*Constitutional Government in India* (New Delhi, Asia, 1960).

Qeymuddin, A. & Jha, J.S. — *Mazharul Haque Builders of Modern India* (Delhi, Publication Division, 1976).

Qurashi, M.A.—*Some Aspect of Muslim Education* (Baroda, M.S. University, 1970).

Qubain, F.I.—*Education and science in the Arab World* (Balti More, 1966).

Raj Gopal, P.R. — *Communal Violence in India* (New Delhi, Uppal P.H., 1987).

Rajni, Kotthari—*Politics in Indian* (New Delhi, Orient, 1970).

Ram Chandran, V.G.—*Fundamental Rights and Constitutional Remedies*. Vol. I & II (Lucknow, Eastern, 1970).

Rodenson, Maxime—*Islam & Capitalism* (London, 1970).

Ray, M.N.—*The Historical Role of Islam* (Bombay, Vora, 1937).

Ray, Sentimoy—*Role of Indian Muslims in Freedom Movement* (New Delhi, PPH, 1970).

Ray, Shibani—*Changing Status of Muslim Women in North India* (Delhi, D.K. Pub., 1979).

Sarkar, J.N.—*Glimpses of Medieval Bihar Economy* (Calcutta, Ratna Prakashan, 1978).

Saiyidain, K.G.—*Facets of Indian Education* (Delhi, NCERT, 1970).

———, *Education for international Understanding* (Bombay, Hind, 1948).

———, *Problem of Educational reconstruction* (Delhi, 1969).

Seal, Anil—*The Emergency of Indian Nationalism* (London, Cambridge, 1968).

Servai, H.M.—*Constitutional Law of India* (Bombay, Tripati, 1949).

———, *Partition of India, Legend & Reality* (Bombay, Emmenam Pub., 1989).

Servier, Andre—*Islam & Psychology of Musalman* (London, Capman, 1924).

Shah, A.B.—*Challenges to Secularism* (Bombay, Nicheketa Pub., 1969).

Shahay, Bhagwati—*History of Education in Bihar & Orissa Under British Rule* (Patna, 1969).

Shakir, Moin—*Khilafat to Partition* (Delhi, Kalanakar, 1972).

———, *Muslims in Free India* (New Delhi, California Uuniversity Press, 1966).

———, (ed.) *Religion, State & Politics in India* (Delhi, Ajanta, 1989).

———, *Islam in Indian Politics* (Delhi, Ajanta, 1983).

Sharp, H.—(ed.) *Selection From Education Records 1781-1893* (New Delhi, 1965).

Sharma, K.D. — *Education of a National Minority—A case study of Indian Muslim* (Delhi, Kalamkar 1978).

Shukla, V.N.—*Constitution of India* (Lucknow, Eastern, 1982).
Siddique, M.K.A.—*Educating a Backward Minority* (Calcutta, Abadi Pub., 1984).
———, *Hindu Muslim Relations* (Calcutta, Abadi, 1993).
Smart, Ninian—*The Religious Experience of Man Kind* (New York, Charles Scribner, 1969).
Smith, D.E.—*India as a Secular State* (London, Oxford, 1959).
———, *Social Change in Modern India* (California, Univ. Press, 1966).
Srivastav G.N.—*The Language Controversy and the Minorities* (Delhi, Atma Ram, 1970).
Tara Chand—*History of Freedom Movement* (Delhi, Publication Division, 1967).
———, *National Integration & Secularism* (Aligarh, AMU Press).
———, *Influence of Islam on Indian Culture* (Allahabad, 1939).
Thapar, Romilla—*Communalism and the Writings of Indian History* (Delhi, PPH, 1968).
Valentine, Charles—*The Culture of Poverty and Counter Proposals* (Chicago University, 1968).
Wadhwa, K.K.—*Minority Safeguards in India* (Faridabad, Thomson, 1975).
Wagley Charles (ed.)—*Minorities in the New World* (London, 1958).
Yasin, Mohammad—*Social History of Islamic India 1605-1748* (Lucknow, Upper India, 1958).
Zakaria, R.—*Rise of Muslims in India Politics* (Bombay, Semaniya, 1970).
Zaidi, Sabira K.—*Freedom and Responsibility* (Aligarh, AMU, 1964).

(b) Urdu Books

Abdullah, Sheikh Mohd—*Aatish Chinar* (Srinagar, Ali Mohd, 1988).
Ahmad, Khursheed—*Islam Ka Nazaria Taleem* (Delhi, Markazi, 1991).
Ahmad, Aziz—*HindoPak Mein Islami Culture* (Delhi, Educational, 1991).
Ahmad, M.N.—*Allama Iqbal ka Nazaria Talim* (Delhi, Markazi, 1991).
Ahmad, S.T.—*Musalmana Ka Roushan Mustaqbil* (Delhi, Kutub Khana Azizia, 1945).
Belkhi, Fasihuddin—*Tarikha Magadh* (Patna, 1953).
———, *Tazkira Niswan* (Patna, Iqbal, 1956).
Dasnavi, S.S.—*Technical Education Aur Musalman* (Delhi, Jamiatul Ulema, 1984).
Deeni Talimi Council—*Deeni Talimi Tahrik* (Lucknow, Council, 1959).
Farooqi, A.R.—*Abdul Kalam Azad Ka Talimi Tasawarat* (Gulburga, Anjuman, 1985).
Geelani, M.A.—*Hindustan Mein Musalmano ka Nizam Talim Wa Tarbiyat* (Delhi, Nadvatul Musannafeen 1966).
Hamind, Syed—*Nai Talimi Policy Aur Hindustani Musalman* (Patna, Khuda Bakhsh, 1988).
Hussain, Afzal—*Fun-e-Talim Wa Tarbiyat* (New Delhi, Markazi Maktaba, 1963).

Hussain, Zakir—*Talimi Khutbat* (New Delhi, Maktaba Jamia, 1982).
Ikram, S.M.—*Aab Kauser* (Delhi, Adibi Dunya, 1957).
———, *Roud Kausar* (Delhi, Abdi Dunya, 1986).
———, *Mauj Kausar* (Delhi, Abdi Dunya, 1962).
Iqbal, Muzafar—*Bihar Main Urdu Nasar Ka Irtiqa* (Patna, Kutub Khana, 1980).
Khan, M.H.—*Urdu Ka Almiya* (Aligarh, 1973).
Khan, M.G.H.—*Siyarul Mutakherin* (Patna, 1782).
Khan, (Sir) Syed—*Asbab Baghawat Hind* (Delhi, 1862).
Makki, M.A.—*Tehrik Azadi aur Hindustani Musalman* (New Delhi, Qazi Publisher, 2003).
Allama Iqbal Chand Jehtein (New Delhi, Qazi Publisher, 2004).
Tehrik azadi Kai Nomainda Mujahideen (Jamshedpur, Al Rehan Publishing House).
Mansoor Puri Q.S.—*Rahmatul Lil Aalameen* (Patiala, 1924).
Maudoodi, A.A.—*Naya Nizam-e-Talim* (Pathankot, Darus Salam, 1941).
Mehdi, Saughra—*Hindustan Mein Aurat Ka Hal Zar* (Delhi, Tarraqi Urdu, 1978).
Mohsani, S.R.—*Musalmano Ki Qaumi Talimi Tahreek* (New Delhi, Jamia, 1986).
Mohd, Mian Syed—*Ulma-e-Hind Ka Shandar Mazi* (Delhi, Aljamiat, 1961).
Mughni, Abdul—*Hindustan Mein Muslim Aqliyat Kay Masail* (Patna, 1972).
Nadvi, A.H.A.—*Islam Teghyur Pazeer Dunya Mein* (Lucknow, 1977).
———, *Insani Dunya Par Musalmano Ke Urooj wa Zawal Ka Asar* (Lucknow, Nadwa, 1974).
———, *Musalman Mamalik Mein Islamiyat Aur Maghrabiyat ki Kashmakash* (Lucknow, Tanveer Press, 1961).
Nadvi, Abul Hasnat—*Hindustan Ki Qadeem Islami Darsgahein*, (Azamgarh, Maarif, 1971).
Najeebadadi, A.S.—*Ain-e-Haqiqat Numa* (Bijnor, Madina Press, 1926).
———, *Tarikh Islam* (Saharanpur, Taj, 1925).
Rahmani, Akbar—*Aqliyatun Ka Talimi Haqooq Aur Masail* (Jalgaon, Educational Academy, 1990).
Rahman, S.S.A.—*Salateen Dehil Ke Ahad Mein Hindustan Sai Mohabat wa Shaftagi Kai Jazbat* (Lucknow, Urdu Academy, 1983).
———, *Mulim Hukumrano Ki Mazhabi Rawadari* (Azamgarh, Maarif, 1975).
Sajjad, Ahmad—*Hindustan Kai Musalmano Kai Bunyadi Masail Aur Unka Hal* (Ranchi, Islamic, 1973).
Saleem, S.M.—*Aghaz-e-Islam Mein Musalmano Ka Nizam Talim* (Delhi Markazi Maktaba, 1988).
Shahbuddin—*Shahabnamah* (Karachi, 1982).
Siddique, M.K.A.—*Faryad-e-Jaras* (Culcutta, Abadi, 1987).
Umar, Mohammad—*Hindustani Tahzeeb Ka Musalmano Per Asar* (Delhi, Publication Division, 1975).

Urdu Academy—(ed) *Nai Talimi Policy Aur Urdu Tadris* (Delhi, Urdu Academy, 1989).

Zaheer, Sajjad—*Urdu, Hindi Aur Hindustani* (Bombay, PBH, 1954).

(c) Articles

Ahmad, Akbar S.—Religion & Politics in Muslim Society, *The Times of India* (Bombay 4 September 1983).

Ahmad, Hasan—Starting Revelations, *The Nation and the World* (New Delhi, November 1993).

Ahmad, Imtiaz—The Problems of Muslim Educational Backwardness in Cotemporary India—An Inferential Analysis (*Journal, Institute of Muslim Minority Affairs*, Vol. 3 No. I Jeddah).

———, Plight of Urdu, *The Times of India*, 9 August 1994.

———, Indian Communal Problems—The Role of the Intellectual, *The Hindustan Times* (New Delhi 30 October 1969).

———, Pseudo Secularism, *The Sunday Statesman*, 11 August 1991.

Ahmad, Meraj—Communalism in Print Media—*Muslim India*, No 98 (New Delhi, February 1991).

Ahmad Siraj—Muslim Lost Millions (*Saudi Gazette*, Feb. 1, 1999).

Akbar, M.J.—Babri Masjid—Symbol of India's Struggle for Secular Order, *The Herald Annual*, January 1993.

Alam, Ansar—A Case Study of two Muslim Managed School of Delhi with reference to Academic, Administrative & Financial Affairs, *Journal of Objective Studies*, Vol. 6 (New Delhi July 1994).

Ali, Shahid—Problems of Education in Muslim world, *The Radiance*, XIX (New Delhi, 7 March 1982).

Ali, Shaukat—Muslim Zeer Intizam School Ki Halat, *The Tehzibul Akhlaq*, Vol. 3 No. 16 (Aligarh 1984).

Aiyar, Mani Shankar—Muslim Backwardness the Root Cause, *The Sunday*, Vol. 22 No. 44 (Calcutta, 5-11 Nov. 1995).

Ansari, Iqbal A.—*State Terrorism and Communal Violence, The Radiance* (Delhi, 5 April 1992).

Anand, Som—*Teaching of Urdu & its Future*, The Hindustan Times (New Delhi 2 July 1992).

Ashrafi, H.S.—Educational Problems of West Bengal Muslims, *The Radiance*, Vol. XIX No. 51 (Delhi, 29 April 1984).

Arif Mohd—Dilemma of India Muslims—*Journal of the Research Society of Pakistan* (University of Punjab Lahore, Vol. XXXV July 1998 No. 3 p. 48).

Ausaf, S.T.—Urdu Medium Education, *The Radiance*, Vol. XXXI No.13 (New Delhi 3 March 1996).

Azimabadi, Riaz—Bhagalpur Riots Commission Reports, *The Secular Democracy*, (July 1995).

Azmi, Z.R.—Hamari Taleem Aur Talimi Darsgahein, *Tehzibul Akhlaq*, Vol. 14 No. 13 (Aligarh, March 95).

Bakhat, Firoz—Plight of Urdu Schools, *The Hindustan Times* (Patna, July 27 1993).

Baig, M.R.A.—Thoughts on Secularism, *Secular Democracy* (August 1969).

Banatwala, G.M.—Minorities and the Constitution of India, *The Radiance*, Vol. XXVII No. 24 (New Delhi, 2 July 96).

Bhambhri, C.P.—Weak Secularism—No Antidote to Hindutva, *The Hindustan Times* (New Delhi, 2 July 96).

Bhandari, Namita—L. Fernandes & Minu Jain—*The Appeased Minority*, The Sunday (Calcutta, 13 February 1993).

Bhandari, & Others—Long Term Psychological Impact on Riot Victims, *The Mainstream*, 5 June 1993.

Bidwai, Praful—Communalism in Civil Services, *The Frontline* (Madras 12 August 1994).

———, Creating Evidence to prove Faith, *The Mid Day*, 8 September 1993.

Buch, M.N.—Muslim in India, *The Statesmen* (Calcutta 12 December 1990).

———, R.S.S Proposal to Convert, Kill or Push out Indian Muslims, *The Anti Corruption*, 22 December 1991.

———, Are Muslims Pampered, *Indian Express*, 13 December 1990.

Deshpande, Rajeev—The Hidden Hand of R.S.S. in V.H.P & B.J.P, *The Sunday Observer*, 6 October 1991.

Divaker, R.R.—Secularism only Way to Peace, *The Sunday Standard* (New Delhi, 23 August 1970).

Faridi, S.N.—Orthodox Muslim Out Look, *The Radiance*, XIX No. 45 (New Delhi 18 March 1984).

Faruqi, K.A.—Urdu Language without a Region, *The Hindustan Times* (New Delhi, 12 August 1969).

Gandhi, Raj Mohan—Secularism and the Secular Order, *The Hindustan Times* (New Delhi, 15 December 1991).

Gill, S.S.—R.S.S A Swadeshi Face of Fascism, *The Hindu* (Madurai, 30 June 1992).

Godboles, Madhav—Plea to Remedy—Neglect of Besieged Minorities, *The Times of India* (New Delhi, 23 February 1996).

Gopal, Krishna—The Politics of Partition, *The Times of India* (New Delhi, 10 February 1970).

Gould, Harnald. A—Fascism Wrapped in Saffron Robe, *The Times of India* (New Delhi, July 1993).

Gupta, O.P.—Why Muslim Community Shuns Government Schools in UP, *Education Review* (Madras, April 1983).

Hamid, Saiyid—Musalmanan Hind Ki Talimi Samji Aur Tehzibi Masail, *Tehzibul Akhlaq*, Vol. 3 No. 16 (Aligarh, 1984).

———, Murdum Shumari Ya Mardum Bizari, *Nadai Millat* (24 March 1991) p. 11-12.

———, Educational Status of Indian Muslim, *Muslim India,* Vol. 3 No. 36, (New Delhi, December 1985).

———, Reservation for Muslim, *The Nation and the World* (New Delhi, April 1996).

Hassan, Arif—Educational Backwardness of Muslims in India, *Journal of Objective Studies,* Vol. 5 No. 1 (New Delhi, January 1993).

Hubaiti, A.Q.—Some Islamic Concept of Education, *The Journal Al Alam Al Islami,* Vol. 8 No. 5 (Jeddah, March 1981).

Hussain, Afzal—Dichotomy of Religious and Secular Education, *The Radiance,* Vol. XX No. 23 (New Delhi, 14 October 1984).

Hussain, Mohammad—Urdu 1972, *The Hindustan Times* (New Delhi, 29 October 1972).

Iqbal, Masud—Nazism—Panslavism & Hindutva, *The Pioneer,* 4 January 1994.

Islahi, Sadruddin—Nizam-I Batil Ki Sath Taawun, *Monthly Zindagee,* Vol. VII No. 2 (Rampur July 1951).

Jyenger, Pushpa—Female Infanticide as a Cause of Lower Growth Rate, *The Times of India* (New Delhi, 6 May 1993).

Jamshedpuri, S.—Bihar Madarsa Education Board Patna, *Afkar Milli* (New Delhi, 15 April 1988).

Jain, Girilal—Indian Islam must be Rooted Nay Dissolved in Hindu Culture, *The Sunday Mail,* 5 May 1991.

Jain, Kalpana—Convergence of Muslim Growth Rate with Education and Economic Status, *The Times of India* (New Delhi, 25 October 1995).

Jha, A.K.—Myth of Minorities Vote Bank, *The Times of India* (New Delhi, 15 December 1995).

Kakar, Sudhir—High Caste Hindu Prejudice towards Islam and Muslims, *The Times of India* (New Delhi, 22 August 1993).

Kamonpuri, H.M.—Poverty & Planning in India, *The Radiance* (New Delhi, 3 July 1983).

Khan, Masood Ali—Reservation of Muslim, *The News From India* (New Delhi, July 1996).

Krishna, Murali—No Muslim in IB & RAW, *The Telegraph* (Calcutta, 18 March 1994).

Kulkarni V.B.—Threat to National Integrity, *Sunday Standard* (New Delhi, 4 February 1973).

Latifi Daniel—Redresal of Minority Grievances, *The Mainstream,* Vol. 3 No. 35, 2 May 1970.

Madan, T.N.—Religious Identity & Secularism, *The Times of India* (New Delhi, 23 April 1993).

Makki, M.A.—Muslim Mujahideen Azadi Aur Hamari Nisabi Kitabeen, *Tehzibul Akhlaq* (Aligarh, June 1995).

———, Hindustan Chhoro Tahreek Aur Bihar Ke Chand Muslim Shuhda, *The Azad Hind* (Calcutta 18, September 1994).

Malhotra, Inder—Minorities must be brought into National Mainstream, *The Statesmen* (New Delhi, 6 October 1969).

Maliakan, Joseph—Situation Report on Education for Minorities, *Muslim India* No. 154 (New Delhi, October 1995).

Malika B. Mistry—Women Education and Exposure to Mass Media—A Comparison of Muslim and Hindu Situations Religion and Law Review, *I.O.S.*, New Delhi, Summer 1997.

Masud, Iqbal—A Chadar will not buy Muslim Votes for Congress, *The Pioneer*, 11 December 1995.

Mathur, Grish—Majority, Minority Relation in India, *The Secular Democracy*, December 1973.

Mittal, Gopal—The Muslim Minorities Problems and Secularism, *The Swarajya*, Vol. 13 No. 20 (Delhi 10 November 1968).

Moracs, Frank—Exploiting the Minorities, *The Indian Express* (New Delhi, 18 May 1970).

Mughni, Abdul—Islamic Identity in Peril, *The Radiance*, Vol. XXVII No. 24 (New Delhi 5 April 1992).

———, Future Course of Action for Indian Muslims, *The Radiance*, op cit.

———, Problem of Muslims in India, *The Radiance* Vol. XXI No. VII (New Delhi, June 23 1985).

Narayan, J.P.—Muslim Minority in India, *The Swarajya*, Vol. III No. 44, May 2 1964.

Narayan, M.K.—Do not Appease but Heal their Wounds, *The Asian Age* (New Delhi, 11 March 1996).

Nigam—Laying Secular Foundation through Education, *The Secular Democracy* (Delhi, April 1960).

Noorani A.G.—Communalism is Still our major Problem, *Sunday Standerd* (New Delhi, 28 June 1970).

———, On Minorities, *The Statesman* (Calcutta, 14 June 1995).

———, R.S.S. Correspondence with the Govt. of India, February 1948 July 1949 & August 1975 July 1976—*The Muslim India*, No. 127 (New Delhi July 1993).

Prakesh, Sri—The Muslim Ghetto Psychology and its Consequences, *The Times of India* (New Delhi, 19 January 1991).

Pannen, P.C.—Shades of Animal Form—*The Hindustan Times* (New Delhi, November 6, 1998).

Rabbbani, Farqlit—Ehsas-e-Zeyan, *Tehzibul Akhlaq*, August 2001.

Rehman, A.—Historical and Social Background of Riots, *Azad Academy Journal* (Lucknow, March 1995).

Rajni, Kothari—Threats to National Integrity—Chauvinism, Elitism & Insecurity of Minority, *The Mainstream* (New Delhi, 19 January 1991).

Ram, N.—Appeasing Hindutwa—*The Frontline* (Madras, 29 January 1993).

Raza, Monis—Indian Muslim & India, *The AIM Journal* (New Delhi, October 1993).

Rao, Mohan—Muslim Population Growth Rate, *The Peoples Democracy* 24 December 1996.

Rao, P.V. Narsimha—Parliament Speech on 12 June 1996 How Many Crimes Shall B.J.P. Commit in the name of Uniformity and Hindu Nationalism, *The Muslims India,* No. 163 July 1996.

Rao, K. Ramchandran—Indian Muslims are Feeling Insecure, *Manjuwani* (Hyderabad, July 1983).

Reddy, H.R.—Muslim Response to Family Planning, *Muslim India,* No. 119 (New Delhi, November 1992).

Report on Minorities Educational Institutions, *The Times of India* (New Delhi, 19 October 1993).

Robinson, Rowena—A Sociological Analysis of Bhagalpur 1989 Riots, *The Social Action,* April-June 1996.

Salam, Abdus—Socio Economic Problems of Muslim of India *The Radiance,* XX No.1 (New Delhi 13 May 1996).

Samiuddin, Abida—Myth of the Muslim Growth Rate, *The Nation and the World* (New Delhi, May 1996).

Setalved, Atul—On Minorities, *The Times of India* (New Delhi, 6th February 1995).

Shahabuddin, Syed—Position of Muslim in UP Services Before Partition, *Muslim India,* No. 141 (New Delhi, September 1994).

———, Response to Mani Shankar Aiyar, *Muslim India,* No. 156 (New Delhi, December 1995).

Shamsuddin, Mufti—National Media and Muslim Passivity, *The Radiance* XXVII No. 24 (New Delhi, 5 April 1992).

Shah, K.A.K.—The Muslim Problem in India, *The Radiance* XIX No. 42 (New Delhi, 26 February 1984).

Shirwani A.R.—Assessing Educational Backwardness—A Right Approach, *The Radiance,* XX No. 32 (Delhi, 16 December 1984).

Singh, Khuswant—Problem of Indian Muslims—Anti Muslim Prejudice, *The Week,* 30 October 1994.

Sridhav, V.—Plight of the Minorities—Fiction or Fact, *Frontline* (Madras, June 1992).

Shukla, I.K.—Neo Hinduism—An Agenda for Political Disintegration and Social Conflict, *The Mainstream,* 18 November 1995.

Srivastav, N.M.P.—Minority Teachers Sores at Government Apathy, *The Hindustan Times* (Patna 19 September 1989).

Weeks Reports on Economics of Bombay Violence, *The Week,* 21 February 1993.

Wright, Theodore P.—Strategy for Protection of Minority Rights in India; *The Times of India* (New Delhi, 7 December 1989).

———, Identity Problems of Former Elite Minorities, *The Secular Democracy,* August 1972.

Yasin Mohammad—Problems of Minorities—A Historical Perspective, *The Hindustan Times* (New Delhi, 13 December 1970).

(d) Editorials

Beyond Reservation—*The Statesmen* (Calcutta, 2 December 1969).

Can Secularism be Restored for Lethal Dose of Authorianism—*Muslim India* (New Delhi, September 1993).

Census 1991 Muslim Indians and Sangh Parivar—*Muslim India* No. 153 September 1995.

Cost of Demolition—*The Illustrated Weekly of India* (Bombay, 14 May 1993).

Curbing Communalism—*The Hindustan Times* (New Delhi, 12 June 1995).

Educating the Muslim Community—*Muslim India,* No. 145 (New Delhi, January 1995).

Educating a Community—*Muslim India,* No. 91 (New Delhi, July, 1990).

Living in the Past—*The Times of India* (New Delhi, September 4, 1983).

Killers in Uniform—*The Asian Age* (New Delhi, November, 1994).

Muslim Indians—Terrorist & ISI Agents: Is India a Police State?—*Muslim India,* No. 141 (New Delhi, September 1994).

Playing the Communal Card—*The Telegraph* (Calcutta, 19 November 1989).

Reporting Communal Tension—*The Hindustan Times* (New Delhi, 24 May 1970).

Root of Backwardness—*The Indian Express* (New Delhi, 24 April 1984).

Shiv Senas True Face—*The Hindustan Times* (New Delhi, 18 January 1993).

Some Soul Searching—*The Hindustan Times* (Patna, August 9 1983).

Storm Signals—*The Hindustan Times* (New Delhi, 2 April 1970).

Times for Action—*The Hindustan Times* (New Delhi, 4 April 1970).

Towards New Action Plan For Minorities—*Muslim India* No. 93 (New Delhi, September 1990).

Why Debate on Uniform Civil Code on Eve of General Election—*Muslim India* No. 152 (New Delhi, August 1995).

Index

Academic aspirations, 57
Adult Education, 163, 180
Ahle Hadis, *see* Wahabis
Ahmad, Ahsanuddin, 22
Aiyar, Mani Shanker, 103, 143
Akhbaraul Akhiar, 21
Al Ameen Education Society, 151
Ali, Amjad, 21, 22
Aligarh Movement, 98, 102, 133, 140, 143, 151
Aligarh Muslim University, 151, 183
All India Muslim Education Society, 151
Ambedkar (Dr.) Scholarship, 184
Ameen Education Society Banglore, 151
Anganwadi Centres, 169
Anjuman Hayat-e-Islam, 22
Anjuman-i-Tehzeb (Cultural society), 22
Anjurman-e-Islam, 151
Antagonism, 93, 94
Anti Muslim
    forces, 129
    riots, 71, 76
    violence, 73

Bentinck, William, 19
Bhandare, Namita, 87
Bihar School Examination Board, 30
Bihar Scientific Society, 21
Bihar State Madarsa Education Act, 32
Bihar State Madrasa Education Board, 33
Bihar State Minorities Commission, 59, 120, 142, 145
Bihari Muslims, 7, 22, 140
British rule, 18, 19, 97, 100, 109

Central Board of Secondary Education, 182
Centrally Sponsored Schemes, 174
Charamposh, Ahmad, 14
Chaudhry, Nirad. C., 127
Christianity, 19, 94, 99
Collegiate schools, 21
Communal riots, 71, 73, 155
Community polytechnics, 124, 160, 161, 184
Computer literacy, 162
Contraceptives and oral pills, 87 *see also* Family planning
Curriculum and teaching methods, 107

Darse Nizamia, 33, 34
Darul Uloom Ahmadia Salfia, 22

Das, Govind, 82
Deoband school, 33
Deprivation, 3, 46, 122, 133, 167, 171
  minorities, 168
Discriminatory treatment, 2
Diversity Index (DI), 183
Divine commands Education, 25

Early childhood education centers, 161
East India Company, 18, 19, 94
Education Commission, 29
Education Policy and Programme of Action (1986), 6, 46
  extract from, 158
Educational advancement, 123, 144, 146
Educational alienation, 101
Educational Commission Report, 4
Educational deterioration, 140
Educational materials, 150
Educational regeneration, 21, 140
Educational rights, 29, 167-68
Educational societies, 21, 140
Employment opportunities, 61, 145, 172
Engineer, Asghar Ali, 28, 87
English Education, 8, 93
Equal Opportunity Commission, 178

Family planning, 86
Fardi, S.N., 123
Forced conversion to Islam, 128
Forum for Literacy Awareness and Muslim Education (FLAME), 145, 152

Girls schools, 162
Gokhale Institute of Politics and Economics, 86
Grant, Charles, 19, 20

Hadith, 32
Hamare Purvaj, 125
Hamdard Education Society, 10, 105, 115, 144, 151
Hameed, Hakeem Abdul, 104
Hasan, Samshul Ulema Md., 22
Hassan, Mohammad, 22
Hegemony, 70
Huda, S.N., 22
Hujjatul Islam Imam Al-Ghazali, 96
Hunter, W.W., 7, 94, 98
Hussain, Ahmad, 21, 22
Hussain, Qazi Riza, 22

Illustrated Weekly of India, 128
Indian Musalman (The), 7, 21, 133, 143
Institute of Arabic & Persian Research, 33
Institute of Objective Studies, 10, 144
Integrated Child Development Services (ICDS), 169
Intramural problems, 105, 133
Islah, Amjuman, 22
Islam, 1, 7, 13, 25, 69, 85-88, 94, 95, 97, 99, 108-10, 120, 127-28, 139-40, 142, 147
Islamic ethos, 59, 142
Islamic System of governance, 128
ITI courses, 172

Jamia Millia Islamia, 33, 160
Jan Shikshan Sansthan (JSS), 177, 182

Jawahar Navedaya Vidyalayas (JNVs), 182

Kabir, Hamayun, 65
Kasturba Gandhi Balika Vidyalaya Scheme, 169
Khalidoon, Ibn, 95
Khaliquzzama, Chaudhry, 77
Khan, Khuda Bakhsh, 22
Khan, Nawab Imdad Hussain, 22
Khan, Nawab Sarfraz Hussain, 22
Khan, Nawab Wilayat Ali, 22
Khan, Rasheeduddin, 9, 70, 81
Khan, Syed Ahmad, 21, 25, 93, 97, 102, 133, 140, 143, 151
Khan, Wilayat Ali, 21, 22
Khilafat Movement, 28
Khusro, A.M., 9, 78, 81, 103
Kothari Commission, 4
Krishna, Gopal, 6, 35, 103, 111, 141

Labour market segmentation, 60, 145
Lal Bahadur Shastri National Academy of Administration, 122
League of Nations, 66
Linguistic minorities, 30, 68, 69, 116, 141, 158-59, 161

Madarsa Education Board, 31, 32
Madarsa Islahul Muslimin, 22
Madarsa Modernisation Programme, 170
Madarsas, 14, 15, 22, 25, 31, 32, 33, 34, 64, 105, 139, 147
  modernisation programme, 177
Mahmood, Syed, 22, 29
Majoritarian chauvinism, 62
Marriage
  early, 107, 109
  polygamous, 86
Mass Media Campaign, 86
Maulana Azad Education Foundation, 170
Militant image Muslims masses, 87
Minorities welfare, 123, 155, 169, 174-75
Minority Educational Institutions, 150, 166-67
Mitchell, J. Muray, 99
Mohammadan Education Committee, 22
Mohammedan Anglo Oriental College, 98, 143
Momenin, Anjuman, 22
Moynihan, Daniel P., 3
Mughal rulers, 94
Multi-sectoral Development Programme, 176
Munshi, K.M., 82
Muslim Personal Law, 88
Muslims migrated to Pakistan, 28
Mutiny of 1857, 94
Muzakira Ilmiya of Arrah, 22

NABARD, 174
Nathan Glazer, 3
National Commission for Minorities Act, 1992, 167
National Commission for Minority Educational Institutions Act, 2004, 167
National Institute of Open Schooling (NIOS), 182, 183
National Sample Survey and Minority Commission, 144
National Sample Survey Organization (NSSO), 60

Navalakha, S., 111
NCERT, 30, 131, 160, 162, 177, 182
Negro-White situation, 3
Nehru, Pandit, 71
Nizamia, Darse, 33, 34
NUEPA, 180
Nursing, 184

Objectionable materials, 97, 125-26, 133
Orphanages, 22

Pakistan, creation of, 8, 28
Pant, Pandit Gobind Vallabh, 82, 102
Parental occupation, 48-50
Parsis, 68, 70
Passion politics, 81
Patel, Sardar, 77, 82
Personal laws, 14, 88, 89, 129, 142
Pharmacy, 184
Planning Commission, 4, 60, 178
Plato, 18, 96
15-Point Programme, 123, 155, 169
Poverty alleviation, 61, 62, 63, 142, 145
Prasad, Rajender, 82
Professional education, 154, 184
Programme of Action (POA), 123
Provincial Armed Constable (PAC), 72
Punnen, P.C., 88
Purdah system, 107, 109

Quality school education, 184
Quranic Shariat, 128

Racial and linguistic riots, 69
Racial minorities, 68, 69
Radiance, 9, 80, 152
Rao, K. Ram Chandra, 125
Registrar General of India, 10, 39
Religious beliefs, 101, 125-26
Religious decree, *see Fatwa*
Religious faith, 66, 68, 82, 124, 126, 152
Religious instructions, 97, 99, 101, 147
Remedial coaching, scheme for, 153
Research Analysis Wing (RAW), 81
Resource centers, 160-61
Riot Prone Area, 75, 76
Rituals, 72, 125-26
Rodinson, Maxime, 110
Royal Commission, 98, 99

Sachar Committee, 10, 46, 171, 176, 178, 179
Sarva Shiksha Abhiyan, 169
Saxena, N.C., 72, 109, 120, 122, 141
School of thought, 3, 4, 33, 34, 147
Secondary School Examination Board, 131
Secular education, 7, 8, 108, 124, 140, 148
Self-employment, 60, 172-73
Servier, Andre, 95
Shahabuddin, Syed, 9, 74, 113, 122, 124, 127, 129
Sharfuddin, Syed, 22, 24
Shia Waqf Board, 33
Shirwani, A.R., 9, 103, 116, 121
Singh, Langat, 21
Sir Syed's Scientific Society, 21
Skill development, 172, 178
Smith, D.E., 85
Social scientists, 3, 8, 9, 65, 113, 118, 128, 133
Social-economic backwardness, 4, 7, 46
Socio-economic status scale of Muslims, 48

Socio-religious Communities, 172
Special Development Initiatives, 176
Stagnation, intellectual, 114
Sunni Waqf Board, 33

Tandan, Puroshottandas, 82
Tashrihul Harrof (Explanation of words), 17
Tehzibul Akhlaq (The), 133, 143, 152
Three language formula, 150, 162
Treaty of Versailles, 66
Tughlaq, Firoz Shah, 14
Tughlaq, Sultan Mohammad, 14

Uniform civil code, 88, 89
University Grants Commission (UGC), 160, 177, 183
Urdu Education, 84, 131

Vocational education, 162, 183

Wakf properties, encroachment of, 157
Western civilization, 94, 95
Women literacy, 162

Zakat, 33, 147
Zamindars, 20